Urban Specters

Urban Specters

The Everyday Harms of Racial Capitalism

Sarah Mayorga

The University of North Carolina Press CHAPEL HILL

© 2023 The University of North Carolina Press
All rights reserved
Set in Merope Basic by Westchester Publishing Services
Manufactured in the United States of America

Library of Congress Cataloging-in-Publication Data
Names: Mayorga, Sarah, author.
Title: Urban specters : the everyday harms of racial capitalism /
    Sarah Mayorga.
Description: Chapel Hill : The University of North Carolina Press, [2023] |
    Includes bibliographical references and index.
Identifiers: LCCN 2023004235 | ISBN 9781469674926 (cloth ; alk. paper) |
    ISBN 9781469674933 (pbk. ; alk. paper) | ISBN 9781469674940 (ebook)
Subjects: LCSH: Working class African Americans—Ohio—Cincinnati—
    Economic conditions. | Working class white people—Ohio—Cincinnati—
    Economic conditions. | Working class Hispanic Americans—Ohio—
    Cincinnati—Economic conditions. | Capitalism—Social aspects—
    Ohio—Cincinnati. | Racism—Economic aspects—Ohio—Cincinnati. |
    Racism—Social aspects—Ohio—Cincinnati. | Cincinnati (Ohio)—
    Economic conditions. | Cincinnati (Ohio)—Social conditions.
Classification: LCC HD8085.C563 M39 2023 | DDC 305.5/620977178—
    dc23/eng/20230324
LC record available at https://lccn.loc.gov/2023004235

Cover illustrations: Silhouette on sidewalk by Kurt.SPK/shutterstock.com;
map of Cincinnati by netsign23/shutterstock.com.

For the "naïve" who dare to imagine a more just world

Contents

Illustrations

Author's Note

When I started my fieldwork in Cincinnati, I wanted to tell a story about the intersections of race and class in two working-class neighborhoods. I wasn't sure what I would find, which is the beauty of research. And for a while, it was hard to see how all the moving pieces—gentrification, immigration, the opioid crisis, poverty—all fit together. Through listening and reading, I have come to understand these outcomes as the effects of racial capitalism.

Having grown up in a place where nothing could be worse than communism, writing a book criticizing racial capitalism feels odd and fitting. As a kid, I didn't think about capitalism much. It was a taken-for-granted good. Certainly better than the communist alternative. And that's typically how people framed these conversations in Miami, where I was raised: *If you think capitalism or the United States is so bad, feel free to give communist Cuba a try.* Over the years, I've learned that this framing is not unique to South Florida but a national talking point.

Rather than argue that the US racial capitalist reality is better than some other, this book is an invitation to think about what we want—not just for ourselves, but also for our neighbors. I believe we deserve a world that fuels universal flourishing and relations of care. I am convinced that is not possible within racial capitalism.

I wrote this book for anyone looking to make sense of how our world continues to harm so many and how mundane, everyday acts are a part of that harm. I intend it to serve as a starting point for deeper engagement with these complex ideas.

In the end, whether you agree with my analysis or not, I invite you to reflect on where you live, too. Is it the best it can be? At the very least, I hope this book helps us better understand the assumptions and decisions creating inequality in our cities. It doesn't have to be this way, so how would you like it to be?

Urban Specters

INTRODUCTION

A Trick of the Light

Cincinnati, Ohio, is a place of duality.[1] It is midwestern but does not feel as traditionally "Rust Belt" as Cleveland. Cincinnati is home to a great university, although it is smaller than the one in Columbus (Ohio's capital). Cincinnati also lends its name to an airport, although it is technically located across state lines in Kentucky. The city's proximity to Kentucky and Indiana is something that, in my experience, often surprises nonlocals. The city features multiple corporate headquarters downtown and historic Tudor revival homes on tree-lined hills. Electorally, Cincinnati is a (somewhat recent) blue dot in a sea of red.[2] It has withstood its share of political scandals, corruption, and a Justice Department investigation of its police force.

Cincinnati is also gentrifying, with a downtown increasingly featured in national media outlets for its food scene, beer, and culture. However, not all of its food is celebrated, with chili on spaghetti regularly featured on "weirdest food" lists.[3] When you cross the Ohio River into the city, you are met with captivating views of downtown skyscrapers and a booming riverfront anchored by the Bengals' and Reds' home fields.[4] The National Underground Railroad Museum is located between these two stadiums, highlighting the city's history in a free state. Yet Cincinnati is one of the most racially segregated and economically unequal cities in the United States, with close to a quarter of all Cincinnatians living below the poverty line—double the national rate.[5]

How do residents experience Cincinnati's dual form? Do they report "a tale of two cities," a refrain commonly used to describe Cincinnati's racial and economic reality?[6] I spoke with poor and working-class residents living in two Cincinnati neighborhoods, Riverside and Carthage, to understand how these city-level processes and conversations mapped onto their own experiences. *Urban Specters* tells these residents' stories. There was, unsurprisingly, a lot of disagreement in how residents described their neighborhoods—sometimes even using opposing terms to describe the same space (e.g., convenient, inconvenient)—but I found that three major narratives still emerged across both neighborhoods. I present a dual account in this book that examines these patterns, one of racial capitalist harms and abolitionist possibilities.

1

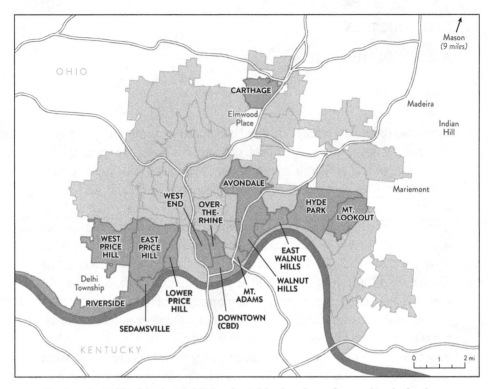

Cincinnati neighborhoods. Highlighted neighborhoods are featured in the book.
Map created by Erin Greb.

I identify racial capitalism as the "formation" that produces poverty in Cincinnati and the United States.[7] As sociologist Gargi Bhattacharyya argues, "Racial capitalism is a way of understanding the role of racism in enabling key moments of capitalist development."[8] Geographer Ruth Wilson Gilmore explains that the concept of racial capitalism describes the relations that produce exploitation, expropriation, dehumanization, and hierarchy.[9] Necessarily, much of the academic work on racial capitalism focuses on historical and macrolevel analyses and theorizations. In this book, I aim to bring this excellent and rich insight to a midwestern city in the United States to identify racial capitalism's everyday manifestations and relations. To do that, I describe and analyze how residents make sense of their lives and neighborhoods. I call these everyday descriptions *urban specters*, as they are often partial recognitions of the material realities of racial capitalism.[10]

Historically, both Riverside and Carthage are white, working-class neighborhoods. Now, Riverside is still a predominantly white neighborhood, while Carthage is multiracial. The residents I interviewed talked about neglect, trash, and security to interpret their neighborhood circumstances. They used these specters to explain the negative things happening in their neighborhoods, often obscuring the relations of racial capitalism that produced these conditions. I use the specter metaphor to help us understand what people see and what they do not. These specters, in sociological terms, are local ideologies that help explain and maintain racial capitalism as common sense and necessary.[11] Tracking how residents think about their neighborhoods is helpful in challenging racial capitalism in the here and now.

While racial capitalism, its harms, and its ideologies were ubiquitous in Riverside and Carthage, there were also challenges and moments of abolitionist possibility. When I use the word "abolition," I draw on the work of prison industrial complex (PIC) abolitionists who understand the need for broad-based strategies that reshape our society. For example, abolitionists Mariame Kaba and Andrea Ritchie argue in their book *No More Police: A Case for Abolition* that abolition "pushes us to break with the current order, to say, 'Not this,' while simultaneously forging new ground and building a different world. PIC abolition is a vision of a restructured society where we have everything we need to be safe, to not only survive but also thrive: food, shelter, education, health, art, beauty, clean water, and more. As trans abolitionist scholar Eric Stanley writes: 'Abolition is not simply a reaction to the [PIC] but a political commitment that makes the PIC impossible.'"[12] I take inspiration from this work to imagine abolition in broad terms as a restructuring of our society away from the harms of racial capitalism and toward a future where all residents thrive and their needs are met. As such, I discuss abolition when analyzing policing (chapter 4) and when discussing other racial capitalist relations that undermine resident safety and well-being. So while *Urban Specters* is centrally concerned with tracing how residents made sense of the harms they and their neighbors experienced, it also locates how residents enacted care and the undoing of racial capitalism's ravages in the everyday, paving the way for new ways of relating to one another. As Gilmore states, "Signs and traces of abolitionist geographies abound, even in their fragility." My intent in chronicling these moments of rupture is to show that what we need for abolition is already here; abolition is not just a vision for the future, but also a contemporary presence.[13]

To complete this project, I conducted in-depth interviews between 2014 and 2015 with 117 residents from Riverside, Carthage, and some surrounding communities (e.g., Sedamsville, Delhi, and Elmwood Place).[14] I chose Riverside and Carthage for their economic and demographic profiles, as well as their size. I wanted two working-class communities, home to both renters and owners, that differed in their racial demographics. I chose Carthage first because it is the neighborhood with the largest Latinx population in Cincinnati, and Riverside because it both fit the criteria and was comparable in size to Carthage.

What does it mean to say that a neighborhood is working class? Sociologists generally agree that class is a hard-to-define category, and we should use multiple indicators to capture its complexity, such as occupation, education, and authority at work. Across both neighborhoods, manufacturing was the most common employment industry, certainly fitting with traditional definitions of the working class. However, service and health care industries that reflect the changing face of the working class were also well represented. In 2010, the three most common industries in which Carthage residents worked were manufacturing (34 percent), health care and social assistance (22 percent), and retail (13 percent). In Riverside, the three most common industries were manufacturing (25 percent), administrative/support/waste management (23 percent), and transportation, warehousing, and utilities (10 percent). Control at work—or the lack thereof—is another important characteristic on which scholars define the working class. Only 13.5 percent of Carthage residents had occupations in management, business, science, or arts, while that number was less than 20 percent overall in Riverside (9.74 percent to 19.57 percent, respectively, across Riverside's two census blocks).[15] Not having a college degree is often another indicator used to differentiate the working class.[16] Among those twenty-five years of age or older in 2010, 11.5 percent had earned a bachelor's degree or higher in Carthage, and 3.6 percent and 12.4 percent, respectively, earned a bachelor's degree or higher in Riverside.

Working class is not just a definition I imposed, however; it was meaningful to most of the residents to whom I spoke. Just over half (52 percent) of the residents I interviewed identified as working class; 18 percent identified as middle class, 17 percent identified as lower class, and the remaining 10 percent identified as upper class or did not select a class identifier. Their occupations included mechanic, social worker, delivery driver, housekeeper, landscaper, paralegal, and nursing home worker. Some were not employed due to retirement, disability, or other circumstances. So while these neighborhoods are working class, not everyone within them is working class. Some, indeed, completed college and made much more than the median income in Cincinnati ($34,000 in 2014, when I was interviewing residents).[17] Likewise, others experienced poverty.[18] For a full summary of the class identities, income levels, educational attainment, and occupations of residents I interviewed, see table C.1 in appendix C.

Despite living in the same neighborhood, residents I interviewed differed in many ways. They were Cincinnati natives and more recent additions; homeowners and renters; the employed and those who could not find work; immigrants who were well-incorporated into city life and those who did not feel welcome. Their ages ranged from 19 to 92. Sixty-seven interviewees were white non-Hispanic, forty-one were Black non-Hispanic, and nine were Latinx.[19] For more on my recruitment strategy and experience in the field, see appendix A.

My focus on racial capitalism is in service of understanding the stories these residents shared. Despite their differences, I identified three urban specters that residents used to explain their lives, which were characterized by exploitation, dispossession, and dehumanization. When zooming out to capture the political-economic context in which residents were making sense of their lives, I pinpointed three racial capitalist relations producing the harms residents described. As such, the analysis in *Urban Specters* was produced iteratively; patterns first emerged from residents' stories, which were then contextualized within Cincinnati's history. I then put these findings into conversation with existing theoretical insights from scholars of racial capitalism to produce the analysis herein. As such, this book is not a history of racial capitalism in Cincinnati or about theories of racial capitalism. It is a book about two neighborhoods that illustrates how racial capitalism causes harm in urban spaces in the contemporary United States, how residents make sense of that harm, and moments of abolitionist possibility that are windows into a different world.

Chapter 1, "Ghost Stories," starts with what I mean by racial capitalism and why this theoretical conceptualization is useful for understanding Cincinnati's past and present. I proceed with a description of life in Riverside and Carthage to situate readers in the specifics of these two locations and their histories. In chapter 2, "Neglect and Underdevelopment," I identify the first of three urban specters that residents used to interpret and understand life in their neighborhoods. By investigating how residents discussed themes of neglect, I set the stage for an investigation of the racial capitalist relation it obscures—underdevelopment. In chapter 3, "Trash Talk and Private Property," I discuss how residents relied on trash talk to direct blame for their neighborhood ills outside the physical neighborhoods. This frame reinforced racial capitalist relations of private property that produced Carthage's and

Riverside's stigmatization. In chapter 4, "Security and Policing," I investigate how residents understood security and its absence. I also contrast these perspectives with abolitionist conceptualizations of safety. I specifically examine how policing is a relation that produces racial capitalist harm and dehumanization, and I present abolitionist possibilities that are challenging policing's logics and control in these two neighborhoods.

In chapter 5, "Respectability, Antiblackness, and Suspicion," I identify three norms of racial capitalism that are directly tied to the previously discussed specters. I trace how these norms produced exclusion and disconnection between residents. I conclude the book with an "Urban Exorcism" where I answer the question, Where can we go from here? I revisit the dreams held by residents of Carthage and Riverside and think through what it would take to make those dreams a reality. In short, I aim to make the complex macrosystem of racial capitalism legible in the everyday with an eye toward how we may work collectively to undo its relations of harm.

CHAPTER ONE

Ghost Stories

My goal in this book is to take seriously what residents said and how they made sense of their neighborhoods. I overlay their interpretations with an analysis of how the racial capitalist exploitation, dispossession, and dehumanization they identified happens in Cincinnati. As such, racial capitalism is the backdrop for the stories of and challenges to the everyday harm that residents reported. In the next two sections, I give brief overviews of racial capitalism and ideology so that readers will know what I mean when I use these terms and why I focus on them. While it can sometimes feel disconnected, theory is a powerful tool to help us understand our lives and work toward a better world.[1]

Capitalism, Racism, and Racial Capitalism

Capitalism is a system organized around accumulation, which is chiefly facilitated by exploitation and dispossession. "Exploitation" refers to how classes (crudely defined, capitalists and workers) relate to one another. To borrow from sociologist Erik Olin Wright, it is not just that workers experience oppression at the hands of capitalists, but also that capitalists would not exist as such without workers.[2] That interdependence is the core trait of exploitation. To a lesser extent, I discuss dispossession, whose definition I borrow from political theorist Rob Nichols. He argues that dispossession "transforms nonproprietary relations into proprietary ones."[3] In other words, dispossession is "not (only) about the transfer of property but the transformation into property." Importantly, Nichols argues that property is not about "things" that are owned as much as it is about a type of relationship, "namely, a relation of exclusion."[4] As such, I investigate how dispossession marks not only the historical (and continuing) transformation of land into property in settler colonial Cincinnati but also the relations between residents (e.g., renter and owner).

Dehumanization is a critical part of the racialization process under racial capitalism. By dehumanization, I mean the process by which some individuals are deemed less than others. As geographer Laura Pulido argues, theories of racial capitalism allow us to capture "the racialized production of differential value."[5] In other words, racial differentiation depends on not just difference but also hierarchy and dehumanization. The racial hierarchy, which in the United States is historically white supremacist and antiblack, is explained and justified via racist dehumanization of Black, Indigenous, and other people of color. Similarly, poor people in the United States are also dehumanized via both policy and ideology. In short, while capitalism produces differential valuation (across race and class categories), dehumanization normalizes it.

Racial capitalism describes the current formation of our economic, political, and social systems.[6] The term identifies the interconnectedness of racism — particularly racial hierarchy and dehumanization — and capitalism, which relies on dispossession and exploitation. In my analysis of Riverside and Carthage, I cite examples of exploitation, dispossession, and dehumanization to illustrate racial capitalism at work. But racial capitalism is not just a story about how racism and capitalism both matter. Racial capitalism points to how capitalism and racism work in tandem and interdependently.

A grounding in racial capitalism helps us understand issues that a singular focus on racism or capitalism misinterprets or only partially explains. For example, much has been written about the white working class's false consciousness or misaligned class interests in the United States. However, a racial capitalist lens helps us recognize that class interests are not the only ones people consider when they make decisions. Race as an ideology (as conceptualized by sociologist Karen Fields and historian Barbara Fields in their book *Racecraft*) helps create these misalignments of white working-class economic interests and behaviors. In short, white workers aligning with white capitalists is not purely false class consciousness. Racism provides rewards that are not always economic, such as social support.

The structure of our racialized social system — white supremacy — produces power and status that is often tied to economic rewards but occasionally independent of them. However, the independence of racism and economic inequality is more theoretical than actual. While racial structures produce statuses, these statuses are also grounded in class relations, even if we experience them as solely "racial." Urban centers — places of profound inequality — are excellent sites in which to study contemporary racial capitalist relations. Cities continue to be places where exploitation, dispossession, and dehumanization occur. In cities, "race" is continually remade into a significant category of exclusion and exploitation and used to justify capitalist accumulation. Racial capitalism shapes not just how cities develop but also how residents make sense of that development.

I use "white supremacy" to name Cincinnati's hierarchical and categorical reality. Naming white supremacy, however, does not mean that white people do not experience exploitation or even dehumanization. I share examples of both throughout this book. Some groups of white people experience dehumanization and exploitation because their marginalization serves capitalists' interests (exploitation). Generally, these groups are also blamed and pathologized for their poverty (dehumanization). Appalachians and poor whites ("white trash") are two examples of this.[7] The term "white supremacy" identifies a relationship between categories (e.g., white/nonwhite), not an absolute truth for all individuals within those categories. As such, white individuals may also experience dehumanization and exploitation, and people of color may also enact exploitative dynamics as capitalists.

Take the case of white Appalachians. Appalachian migration is a notable part of Cincinnati's past and present. According to the Urban Appalachian Community Coalition (UACC), over 35,000 Cincinnati residents identified as Appalachian between 2005 and 2009. Their website explains, "[Appalachian] migration had been occurring slowly from the mountains of Kentucky and Tennessee into Cincinnati since the beginning of the nineteenth century, but Appalachia suffered the greatest population decline during the Great Migration of the 1940s to 1960s, when it experienced a net loss of four million residents to Eastern and Midwestern industrial cities like Cincinnati to live in neighborhoods such as Over-the-Rhine, Camp Washington, East End, South Fairmount and Carthage." As sociologist Phillip J. Obermiller described, "Most of the migrants did well economically, but often at great cost socially. Their labor was welcome, but their 'ways' were not."[8]

The UACC identifies anti-Appalachian sentiment and discrimination as a continuing problem for urban Appalachians in Cincinnati. In my interviews, descriptions of Appalachians in negative terms were not uncommon and were generally stated in a playful manner (I mean this merely as a description of tone rather than a negation of its harm). Working-class whites, in particular, referenced Appalachians as if they were kin, much the way one might refer to a loveable but wayward cousin. As historian Elizabeth Catte addresses in her book *What You Are Getting Wrong about Appalachia*, associations of Appalachians with poverty, drug addiction, and pathology are not new tropes.

At the same time, even those whites who experience exploitation and dehumanization have a set of resources that others may not, because of their access (however tenuous) to the "white" category. Sometimes these resources are psychological and can lead to "political acts of self-sabotage," as argued by Jonathan Metzl in *Dying of Whiteness*.[9] Still other times they are material and lead to economic protections. In Cincinnati, that looked like access to property and union jobs. For example, in the first half of the twentieth century, working-class whites had access to property ownership at a broader scale than their Black counterparts or middle-class Black people. Where Black residents were allowed access to housing was often limited to less valued locations due to restrictive covenants and other forms of exclusion.[10] For instance, in 1921, the Cincinnati Real Estate Board created a new policy whereby "no agent shall rent or sell property to colored [*sic*] in an established white section or neighborhood and this inhibition shall be particularly applicable to the hilltops and suburban property."[11] These policies confined Black renters and homeowners alike to "over-crowded and declining neighborhoods" such as the West End.[12]

It was not just these explicitly racist policies that created segregated neighborhoods. Historian Henry Louis Taylor Jr. argues that "the rise of the industrial city, the emergence of mass homeownership, zoning laws, building codes, city planning, and subdivision regulations led to the formation of a black ghetto-slum in Cincinnati. . . . The location of African Americans at the bottom of the economic ladder placed them at a disadvantage in the quest for good housing and neighborhood conditions. . . . These forces, operating within the context of racial hostility, gave rise to the twentieth-century ghetto."[13] These racist and classist historical housing policies and patterns also have long arcs, shaping contemporary neighborhood experiences. For example, the West End neighborhood, where over 90 percent of Cincinnati's Black residents resided in 1940, remains predominantly Black, with 83 percent of its residents identifying as such in 2020.

Similarly, white residents' historical access to homeownership continues to shape the present. Especially in Riverside, many white residents passed down properties or the wealth accumulated via previous property ownership to future generations. While exploitation and dehumanization shape the lives of all working-class and poor Cincinnatians, so does white supremacy. That leads to different outcomes for poor and working-class Black and white people on the whole.

Notably, identifying white supremacy does not need to lead to "who has it worse?" contests. The power of a critical racial capitalist lens is that it invites a deeper understanding of the contours and nuances of modern exploitation and dehumanization. In fact, by recognizing these differences in outcomes between groups, we are better equipped to identify the processes or relations that produce them, and to ultimately organize against the underlying common systems of harm. This clear-eyed insight facilitates a reimagining of our world that does not rely on *anyone's* exploitation or dehumanization. That is my goal.

More than an interesting theoretical concept, racial capitalism captures the social, political, and economic reality of the United States. In *Urban Specters*, I identify how racial capitalism functions within a single city. Rather than a general theory, I present a specific case to illustrate precisely what racial capitalism looks like in Cincinnati and its neighborhoods, relying on the specifics of two neighborhoods to illuminate processes of exploitation and dehumanization that are foundational to racial capitalism at large. In short, *Urban Specters* seeks to contribute to our understanding of how racial capitalism manifests and reproduces in urban spaces. As such, I analyze relations of racial capitalism at the city and neighborhood level, and residents' stories, logics, and subsequent practices.

Ideologies and Specters

Studying ideologies is vital to understanding how structures are maintained, because ideologies "stabilize a particular form of power and domination."[14] By interviewing Riverside and Carthage residents about how they made sense of their own lives and the state of their neighborhoods, we see the connections between what people say and do—between ideologies and practices. Most importantly, using residents' experiences and understandings as the starting point helps us see where challenges to racial capitalism may form and potentially lead to greater equity in our cities.

I am interested in not just the details of what people said, however, but also the underlying assumptions of those statements and rationalizations. What matters to me is how people talked about neighborhood changes and how they made sense of them, specifically the logics they used to describe and understand their lives. The difference may seem subtle, but it is an important one. Studying logics helps us see connections between ideas we may not have thought of as related.

While ideologies are about ideas and ways of thinking, they are also material. By material, I mean both that they reflect a social, political, and economic reality, and that ideologies have real-world stakes. Ideologies are part of how we become social actors or subjects in a particular social formation. According to social theorist Louis Althusser, "All ideology hails or interpellates concrete individuals as concrete subjects"[15] and, as such, "'transforms' the individuals into subjects."[16] This means the reality of our situation precedes us, so we—as subjects in a particular relation—always already exist. Through ideology (or "common sense"), we are drawn into a specific social arrangement and reproduce the social order.

In other words, ideologies are partially how social structures, such as white supremacy and capitalism, entangle everyday people like us in their functioning. While dominant ideologies represent the interests of those in power and are normalized and transmitted via social institutions such as mass media and education, *Urban Specters* focuses on how everyday people interact with ideologies. So, although working-class and poor people did not create these dominant ideologies, they are still subject to them.

I investigate which local ideologies residents used to explain their circumstances. When we understand the logics that residents function under, we can see the points of tension where alternative, liberatory ideologies could challenge the stories of racial capitalism. So while ideology may seem like high theory, it is a valuable language for understanding how inequality continues in the abstract and on the ground; how all of us are subjects of our social conditions. And denaturalizing these ideologies, as I do in chapters 2–4, facilitates further interrogation and understanding of the material realities they partially explain or outright obscure. By studying and understanding these ideologies, we are better equipped to challenge the rules of the game so they benefit more than just the dominant group.

Finally, what is the relationship between specters and ideologies? Specters are local ideologies—the people, places, and things that loom large in residents' imaginations. These specters have explanatory power for residents' circumstances and give us insight into how racial capitalism has shaped Cincinnati. By studying ideologies in this historical context, we can better understand how people "acquire consciousness of their position," and specifically what stories and logics are obscuring consciousness of racial capitalism's relations of exploitation and dehumanization.[17]

So, how did residents talk about Riverside and Carthage? These are the stories I turn to next, beginning with an individual from each neighborhood who encompasses some key themes I want to highlight. Meghan's view of Riverside illustrates how intergenerational wealth transfers (an important mechanism for embedding historical inequality into contemporary home-ownership) are understood by white residents and how the racial capitalist relation of property leads not only to wealth accumulation but also to social support. Sue's discussion of Carthage and how it has changed since her youth presents a picture of a decaying neighborhood whose social problems were brought on by racialized and classed others. Despite their contrary feelings toward their neighborhoods (Meghan's positive and Sue's negative), both stories normalize or ignore the workings of racial capitalist relations. After each story, I zoom out for a broader tour of Riverside and Carthage, contextualizing the neighborhood snapshots Meghan and Sue presented.[18]

Meghan's Riverside

Meghan is a Cincinnati-area native in her mid-fifties who moved to Riverside in the early 1990s. Her mom had purchased multiple Riverside properties and helped Meghan find her current home. Meghan had been living in Kentucky with her then-boyfriend, but her mom convinced her to move back to Ohio after they broke up. Meghan explained, "That was her plan to get me back over here, buy me — help me buy a house over this way." She described herself as happy with the neighborhood and had no interest in moving. She had the chance in 2008 and did not leave.

Meghan explained that the "price was right" on her house, for which she paid just under $24,000. "So I'm sitting on my retirement [*laughs*]." Meghan's income as an assistant manager was between $25,000 and $29,999, making her initial home price just under a current year's salary. Riverside's two census tracts had median household incomes of $17,316 and $44,205 in 2014, the year I interviewed Meghan. She explained that her ability to buy a home depended on her mother's help. This financial support both helped her become a homeowner and opened the door for additional social support from her neighbors.

Riverside, a white, working-class community on the West Side of Cincinnati, is a long strip of a neighborhood. Once railroads were built in the mid-1800s, Riverside and the other towns along the river, including neighboring Sedamsville, became commuter suburbs for those working downtown. Given Riverside and Sedamsville's size and proximity to one another, historians often combined them in reports on demographics and local history. While Sedamsville held smaller lots for "worker housing," Riverside included a broader mix of homes for working-, middle-, and upper-class families. The rise of railroads also created new industry opportunities in Riverside and Sedamsville. For example, the Fleischmann's yeast factory and distillery were built during the 1870s in Riverside and stayed open until the 1960s.

When I asked Meghan to describe the people in Riverside, she said they were kind and generous, although not outgoing. "You know, they come up to you, and they'll talk to you, and they'll be nice to you, even when they have to initiate the first 'hi, you know, I'm —' that kind of thing. But other than

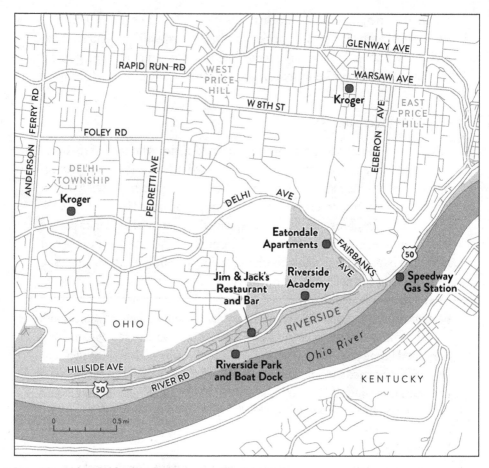

Riverside neighborhood. Map created by Erin Greb.

that, everybody's pretty friendly. I never really have a problem with anybody."
Her street only had three occupied homes besides hers; two households were
white, and a "Black gentleman" rented another. Later in the interview she
explained, "I don't have any interaction with him whatsoever really."

Connie, whom Meghan said "[is] like my best friend right now," lived on
the other side of Meghan. "Her husband lived there almost the whole time I
lived there, and he just died last year of a heart attack. Her and I, we talk every
day. I actually help her out, take her to the store, take her to work because
she don't drive." Meghan described how she and her neighbors "have little
parties and have the family down and we'll do cornholing, grilling out, and
that kind of thing. We were all together last Saturday as a matter of fact, and
grilled out." When I asked her how these events were coordinated, she ex-

plained, "We just—I look at her, she looks at me and say, 'Are you inviting your family?' I say, 'Yeah, are you inviting yours?' I say, 'Yeah.' We all bring food together and that's about it." It seemed that while "all" her neighbors got together, the core of the social activities involved her and Connie.

Having a close tie with a next-door neighbor brought Meghan a lot of satisfaction. So did having her family in neighboring Delhi Township, where her mom and most of her siblings lived.[19] Meghan also had other ties in the neighborhood. In fact, she got a phone call during our interview from another neighbor with whom she socialized regularly. "I keep in touch with her, 'How you doing? Are you okay? Come on down, and we'll have dinner,' and that kind of thing." She said part of the reason she stayed in Riverside was that she had no problems there. She said other than the occasional conflicts between families, which she knew well enough to keep out of, "we never have any really big issues down here. It's always been pretty well quiet. That's why I've stayed here as long as I have. If there's been any issues, I wouldn't be here." Meghan appreciated the care her neighbors gave her; "the neighbors look after each other down through here." In Meghan's story, we see the role of intergenerational wealth transfers in facilitating housing security and community connections.

Riverside: Isolated, but Home

Riverside feels far away even though it is only about a ten-minute drive from downtown. Indeed, it is easy to fly through Riverside and cruise down the main thoroughfare, River Road/US 50. If you are heading west toward neighboring Anderson Ferry, the Ohio River is to your left, as is Kentucky. Driving down River Road now, one sees a six-acre campus for Peter Cremer North America, an "oleochemical products and services" company purchased in 2015. However, in comparison to "The Banks," a new riverside development with restaurants and retail near downtown, Riverside's riverfront remains underdeveloped. River Road itself features very little commercial business for residents, highlights of which were the Speedway gas station and Jim and Jack's bar and restaurant. There is also a small park on the riverfront, which residents called Riverside Park and Gilday Park (with a recreation center named after Daniel J. Gilday, a member of the local powerhouse family "the Gildays"). The park is next to a boat launch ramp, which residents said was a neighborhood highlight.

While a handful of residents described the neighborhood's location as convenient (given its proximity to downtown and access to I-75 and I-71),

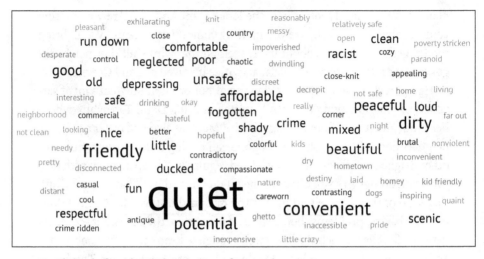

Word cloud of residents' descriptions of Riverside.

many others described it as far off, "ducked off," or isolated. One of the most formative events on this side of Cincinnati was the widening of River Road in the 1950s. The city expanded the central thoroughfare to create better land access for the river terminals. The city demolished many stores and homes to make room for the road development, leading to population shifts in the area. The changes to River Road had devastating effects on Sedamsville, which lost its central business district, including a post office, theater, funeral home, and over thirty stores. Sedamsville's public school closed in 1963 and was remodeled into apartments. Sedamsville and Riverside experienced population loss starting in the 1960s and continuing through 2020 (see graph 1.1).

Everyone who described Riverside's seclusion in a negative light was a Black renter. Black renters said that it was difficult to get family and friends to come out to this part of the West Side, especially with the poor bus service in the area. Cherise (Black renter, thirties) stated that people often missed Riverside as they drove by because it's "ducked off." "A lot [of] people [ask] 'where you stay at?' I'm like, 'I stay right here; you rolled passed it.' If you don't know exactly where it's at, and it's your first time being down here, you would drive past it, I think." While Cherise liked how quiet it was and her "good neighbors," without a car it was inconvenient to live there.

Cathy (Black renter, forties) and her daughter Anita (Black renter, twenties) lived in Eatondale Apartments, a predominantly Black, low-income housing complex on the Riverside-Sedamsville border.[20] Cathy and Anita

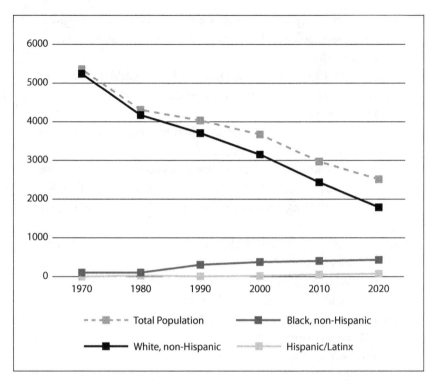

GRAPH 1.1 Riverside population change, 1970–2020. Data source: US Census. Note: These data include parts of Sedamsville and Sayler Park due to census block configurations.

talked about how different Riverside was from other neighborhoods they'd lived in.

CATHY: It's way different. People even smell different.

SARAH: People even smell different?

ANITA: Yes, because when you come in here—like if you've been in here for so long, you be sneezing and everything. It's like a different community—

CATHY: It's like you're in a whole different—you know how you go to different states, and their environment is different from ours, and you come back, and you might have a cold or something? Like that. [*laughs*] When we first moved here, oh my god.

ANITA: And you will see like stores. Like we ain't got nothing but Speedway, and Speedway is too far—

CATHY: It's woods. We just got woods and people.

ANITA: —as far as trying to get there and back. Well, I was pregnant, and it at least took me like twenty minutes to get there and back. So [*laughs*]

CATHY: Right. I wouldn't do it for nothing in the world. [*laughs*] And then we only have—The two buses we do have, one come here every two hours, come past here.

ANITA: And that's only two hours. It only runs like three times a day.

CATHY: It only runs like three times a day.

SARAH: Wow. Okay. So the bus service is not good.

CATHY: Not really, but look how far we is. So, really, don't nobody really catch the bus. That's why a lot of people got cars on this side of town.

ANITA: And the 50 [bus route], that runs you can say like two hours, three hours a day.

CATHY: Two hours, almost three hours. Two and a half.

ANITA: You will be down there for like two hours. You gotta be—

CATHY: If you don't know the schedule.

ANITA: You got to time it. Yes.

CATHY: I don't even try to be bothered with it at all.

Riverside's isolation made it a difficult place to live if you did not own a car due to the poor bus service and lack of walkable options. There was also no grocery store in Riverside. The closest thing was the market inside of the Speedway gas station. However, getting to the grocery store was not the only consideration residents had to weigh. In addition to the logistical barriers, poor Black residents discussed how they were targeted en route to and within the grocery store, including getting pulled over by Delhi police, leading some to choose a grocery store in lower-income Price Hill despite there being no direct bus route to its Warsaw Avenue Kroger. (For more on how grocery stores can also be sites of racial capitalist exploitation and dehumanization, see my research with Megan Underhill and Lauren Crosser.[21])

Erika (white homeowner, forties) said the neighborhood felt like a hometown, describing it as a "cozy, corner, nook." While these descriptions certainly capture the social element of the community, they also capture its infrastructural isolation. For Meghan, being isolated was what she loved about Riverside. "I like living here just because [of] the way it is. It's quiet; it's peaceful. And where I'm at, it's awful quiet. There's only the three or four of us that live on that little road right there. And we're left pretty much alone. Nobody really bothers us. Not bad for almost twenty-five years." Many Riverside residents relished the neighborhood's natural landscape, which framed its "far off" feel in a positive light. Craig (Black renter, twenties) said, "I love the view of the river; you can't beat it." Agnes (white homeowner, nineties) had lived in Riverside since childhood and described Riverside as "homey, and you have a feel of country driving over Hillside [Avenue]. . . . Homes are not close together." Riverside did feel surprisingly outdoorsy for an urban neighborhood, with Hillside Avenue lush with trees.

As I learned from life-long resident Cait (white homeowner, sixties), the city tried to build a bridge to Kentucky in Riverside, near Anderson Ferry Road in 1991. Kevin (white homeowner, sixties), Cait's husband, explained, "The bridge was being put in for land developers to put more subdivisions in Kentucky and stuff. So it wouldn't have benefited the community." Residents feared the increased traffic, pollution, and decreased revenue for their area. As Cait clarified, "Nobody's gonna come over here to nothing. Everybody is going to go to Kentucky and get all their stuff, you know?" So Riverside residents and their Delhi neighbors got organized. The city eventually abandoned the Riverside bridge proposal. "I think the last proposal [was for the] Queensgate area," Kevin added, between Lower Price Hill and the central business district.

Rich (white renter, fifties) commented on Riverside's lack of commercialization when describing the neighborhood, "On the river, there's been not a lot of effort to try and commercialize or do anything in there. [. . .] We always joke about it being like Appalachia or something, you know? It's very—a lot of just working-class people just trying to make ends meet and not a lot of money there, so it's a good place if you want to deal drugs and do sketchy things, old houses, people are scrapping the houses, and there's that kind of thing that goes on."

For Rich, the lack of riverfront businesses for the public to patronize and the working-class character of the neighborhood created opportunities for criminal behavior. This included scrapping old houses for copper, which was indeed a problem in vacant homes across Cincinnati. Rich's reference to Appalachia is also noteworthy. While seemingly meant in a light-hearted manner, Rich's comments exemplify how many referenced Appalachians in conversations with me: as a vaguely criminal, poor population that did not live in the best conditions. Their insularity—presumably to protect their shady dealings—was also embedded in these stereotypes.[22]

Federico (white renter, forties) was a fast talker and a cutup who toggled back and forth on the pros and cons of living in Riverside. When I asked for his description of the neighborhood, he responded:

Man, don't do this to me. Affordable. I'm trying to be nice here. Affordable. Actually, relatively safe. As far as I can see—see, what's weird is my delusions have been crushed by other people occasionally where they'll go, "Oh my God, it's crazy back there." Are you sure? Because I live right here, and there's never anything going on. "There are cops back there." But I think it's relatively safe. It's definitely affordable. [. . .] And you know what? When you do run into some-body, they're nice. So, pleasant, I guess. Surprisingly pleasant. It's actually a pretty good value now that I'm thinking about it. Yeah, to be that safe for that amount of money, you need to get in there. So, I believe—it's all my perceptions. I haven't looked any of this up. I believe there is a higher percentage of ownership than most of the downtrodden neighborhoods in Cincinnati, the West Side, anyway.

Federico explained that because families tend to pass down house deeds to their children, homeownership rates in Riverside are pretty high despite the modest income levels of the residents. According to the 2010 Census, 61.1 percent of housing units in Cincinnati were renter-occupied, so it is in-deed a city of renters. The rentership rate in Riverside was below that, at 54.9 percent, while the Carthage rate was lower still, at 48 percent. The nearby East Price Hill rentership rate was 64.5 percent; Federico was right that River-side's homeownership rate is higher than other West Side neighborhoods.

Federico continued, "These guys came up probably to work at automotive plants maybe in the fifties kind of deal. And they're all Appalachians, right? And then they've handed these houses down, shitty as they are. Obviously, you look at the deed and, yeah, they just hand them down, hand them down, hand them down." Federico's discussion references the history of Appala-chians who came to the Cincinnati area looking for manufacturing work. Those who acquired well-paying union jobs could afford modest homes on the West Side, which they have since passed down to younger generations. As the UACC explains, "Some [Appalachian migrants] still work in good pay-ing union scale manufacturing jobs. Most of those retired from such jobs are homeowners living well into their later years."[23]

Loss of these jobs via deindustrialization made economic insecurity a shared experience of the urban Appalachian community in Cincinnati by the 1970s.[24] The UACC also describes how "Appalachians in Cincinnati were the victims of 'active discrimination' that negatively affected their job opportu-nities, education, health care, living conditions, and sense of identity and community."[25] Interestingly, "the City of Cincinnati passed a Human Rights

Ordinance in 1992 that remains the only known U.S. law to proscribe Appalachian discrimination."[26] In a *Washington Post* article published a year after it passed, "Maureen Sullivan, director of Cincinnati's Urban Appalachian Council, [said she] knows of no documented cases where someone was denied housing or a job because he or she was Appalachian. And no complaints have been filed under that provision since the ordinance was passed."[27] Nevertheless, advocates chronicle a stigma attached to Appalachian heritage that many say shaped job opportunities in particular.[28]

Through the lens of racial capitalism, we can see how the fiction of Appalachian pathology serves capitalist ends. Transforming white Appalachians into "hillbillies" helps justify their economic marginalization as a product of inferior culture and poor decision-making rather than the reality—one of economic shifts and shrinking living wage jobs in Appalachia and Cincinnati. As historian Elizabeth Catte explains, "Many Appalachians are poor, but their poverty has a deep and coherent history rooted in economic exploitation."[29] In turn, the economic insecurity of Appalachian migrants in Riverside and Carthage left them with fewer economic resources than their non-Appalachian white counterparts, including for housing maintenance. So while Federico associates "shitty" houses with Appalachians, we need to identify the political economic conditions that produced these relationships and counter long-standing stereotypes about Appalachian deficiency.

At the same time, Federico's description of homeownership in Riverside is an excellent illustration of how intergenerational wealth transfers happen. Even if the houses are not worth as much as in white middle-class neighborhoods on the East Side or if residents have fewer resources to invest in their houses, these homes are still an asset that white residents inherited from their families. These intergenerational wealth transfers were possible because the white working class was not subject to racist housing policies such as redlining or racial covenants. The transfers facilitated wealth accumulation and helped explain how even white people in the lowest income brackets— such as residents of Riverside—had higher wealth than higher-income Black people.[30] This is why it is imperative to name white supremacy alongside capitalist exploitation to understand urban inequality. As opposed to an "either/or" frame, the lens of racial capitalism allows us to understand the "both/and" of Appalachians' economic marginalization and stigmatization alongside their (tenuous) access to whiteness in Cincinnati. Interestingly, most of the white residents I spoke with did not identify as Appalachian. A few did, such as Helen (white homeowner, sixties), who said she was "German Appalachian Caucasian." No residents of color identified as Appalachian.

References to previous neighborhoods were also a part of residents' place-making descriptions. Evelyn (white renter, twenties) and Victor (Black renter, twenties) were one of a handful of Black and white interracial couples who lived in Eatondale Apartments. They characterized the area as kid-friendly and less violent. As Victor said, "This is just totally a better atmosphere for us to start over." For him and Evelyn, the opportunity of a fresh start for themselves and their two young kids was key to how they framed living in Eatondale. They focused on safer parks and better schools compared to their previous home downtown. When I asked Ivory (Black renter, twenties) to describe the neighborhood to someone unfamiliar with the area, she said it's respectful, quiet, and nonviolent. For Ivory, the threat of violence in her previous living situation in Lower Price Hill accentuated the quiet of Riverside, in terms of literal noise and a sense of calm.

Barb (Black renter, fifties) agreed that Riverside was nice and quiet. "It's small, and people mind their own business. I mind my own business and, therefore, nobody has their business up in my business. So that's what I like about it." Barb mentioned people keeping to themselves as a positive, which ran counter to the stories that longtime white residents told about Riverside. They framed it as a place where everyone knew everyone, and that's what kept them safe. For example, Tina (white homeowner, fifties) and Cait painted a picture of Riverside residents as friendly and pleasant.

Tina, who had also lived nearby in Sayler Park and Delhi Township, said that Riverside was the friendliest of the three: "I think Riverside is much more family-friendly oriented, because the neighbors talk to one another around here. When we moved to Delhi, we were told, you know, 'We don't talk to people. We're your neighbors, but we keep to ourselves.' And I wasn't the only one told that when—A friend of mine moved from Sayler Park to Delhi, and Delhi just doesn't seem as friendly." Cait, who identified as a fifth-generation Riverside resident, said that the neighborhood was old, friendly, and beautiful. She said that most people don't know anything about Riverside. "They don't know anything about the community or the people or what's there. But they automatic—like my son. He was born and raised down there, and he lives in Delhi. And it's like, 'Mom, when are you gonna move? You need to move. You don't need to be down there.' But it's the safest place. We have the lowest crime rate down there. Everybody knows each other." In her defense of Riverside, she commented, "We're not doing all that stuff" and that it was non-Riverside residents who committed crimes.

Like Cait, some residents focused on positive attributes to combat territorial stigmatization.[31] Emily (white homeowner, forties) lived in Sedamsville and was a paralegal whose earnings were just under $40,000. She described the area as "antique. Interesting. Trying to stay positive [*laughs*] . . . and colorful [*laughs*]." Her house had been in her family for sixty years, originally purchased by her grandfather. She bought the house from her brother once his family outgrew it. Life-long Riverside resident Brandon (white resident, nineteen) stated, "I don't wanna talk bad about where I live because I'm proud of it."[32] Scott (white homeowner, thirties) did not have much positive to say, although he lamented that fact: "It's a sad neighborhood. I hate saying that, but it's true. I'm trying to think of a good description. It's like there's no—there's nothing drawing people there. It's depressing, and West Side, typical. [*laughs*] I don't know, sorry."

I view Scott's comments as closer to those who described Riverside positively because they did not want to malign where they lived. Scott wanted to be positive but just did not see how. His reference to West Side as a description is also noteworthy. The stereotypes most commonly associated with the West Side—as insular, white, working-class, and conservative—largely echo the stereotypes about Appalachians. One critical exception is Catholicism, which is tied to the West Side but not Appalachia. With these descriptions, we see how residents not only define their sense of place but also agree with and reject negative characterizations from outsiders.

In contrast, Aisha (Black renter, thirties) did not have a kind word to spare for her neighborhood: "To me, and no offense, to me, this is a white world. If I had to use three words to describe this area, I would say racist, hateful, [*pause*] and selfish. Very selfish." Aisha spent much of the interview sharing her experiences in the area marked by institutional and interpersonal racism. We will hear more from her—as well as other Riverside residents—in subsequent chapters.

In short, some residents saw Riverside as a respite from the hustle and bustle of the city. Others felt isolated from their loved ones. But most agreed it was not a place that was thriving. It had been forgotten, and, as a result, residents had to travel to meet their needs. I investigate what happened to Riverside in more detail in chapter 2. But I now turn to an overview of Carthage, once again starting with a resident's view and then zooming out for a broader perspective.

Sue's Carthage

Sue (white renter, sixties) was a retired seamstress with generational ties to Carthage. Her family moved to the neighborhood before her second birthday.

As an adult, she moved away to nearby Finneytown, but her family still centered their life in Carthage: "We went to church here. My kids went to school here. My mother lived here. We were always part of Carthage. Everything we did was down here, not in Finneytown. So I've always been associated with it. My grandparents lived here. My dad grew up here. It's home." Those deep roots shaped how Sue assessed the neighborhood. Carthage had undeniably changed since her childhood, and this was a significant thread she developed during her interview. "We used to be able to shop for anything in the neighborhood. There were three drugstores. There were grocery stores, anything but shoes. We had to go to Elmwood [Place] for shoes. But anything else you could get right here, and you can't do that anymore. You have to go far to get what you want now."

Sue explained that Carthage "should be a nice place; those are nice houses." She lamented her neighbors moving away but also sympathized, "If I wasn't up here [on a hill], I'd be gone, too. And I hate [to say that] 'cause it's home. And I wish I knew why. The people have definitely changed. It used to be a family community. I don't see the families that I used to see." She described the people who lived in Carthage now as a mixture:

> Used to be a lot of blue-collar workers. Now it's—it seems to be a lot of people that are on welfare. A lot of us in this building are low income. Well, we have to be to [live] here. I see a lot of Hispanic people. I see a lot of Black people. Not a lot. Looks like it'd be about half white and half Hispanic. I think more Black people in [this building] here than out in Carthage. Not so many white-collared people. Used to be, let's say, fifteen, twenty years ago, mostly old people, but they've died off. The houses were inexpensive, and it seems to be a lower place, the people who moved in now. The houses, a lot of 'em got run-down, a lot of the people don't care about 'em. And the ones that do are fighting like heck to get it back up again.

Carthage is located in north-central Cincinnati, in the Mill Creek Valley. Captain John White founded a settlement there in the 1790s in lands occupied by the Miami and Shawnee people. Settlers and Indigenous peoples fought several battles, in which allied Indigenous tribes were originally victorious. After multiple settler victories, however, tribal leaders signed treaties that stripped the Miami and Shawnee of most of their land and they relocated to reservations within Ohio. Both the Shawnee and Miami tribes were eventually forced to move west, prior to and after the Indian Removal Act of 1830.

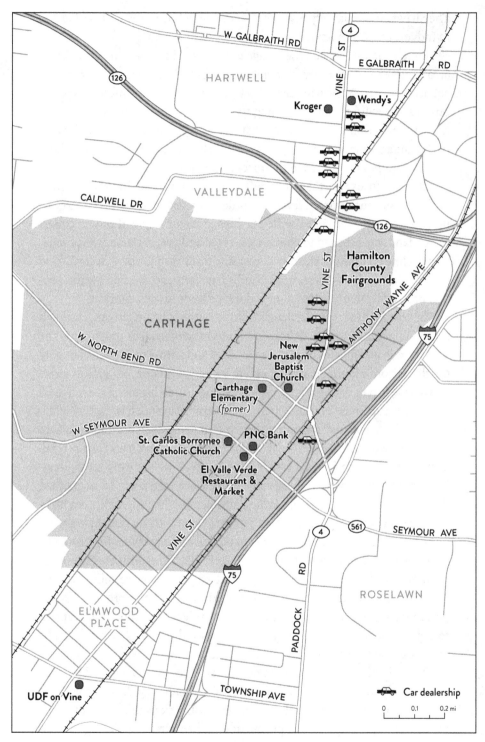

Carthage neighborhood. Map created by Erin Greb.

The Shawnee now largely reside in Oklahoma, while the Miami are located in Indiana and Oklahoma.[33]

White's son established the village of Carthage in 1815 as an agricultural area. As in Riverside, railroads helped transform Carthage into a commuter suburb in the 1870s. During the following decades, many different types of businesses would appear, changing the shape of this farming village. Carthage's population slowly grew as industries continued to expand. The City of Cincinnati annexed Carthage in 1911, and home construction for middle-income families continued in the 1920s and 1930s.

After the 1930s, Carthage's population growth slowed and then slightly declined. As housing aged, few new residents moved in, and those who grew up in the area moved out. Car dealerships, a major staple of the neighborhood's landscape, began to open in the 1950s and 1960s. Carthage's population decline continued, steadily decreasing from 1970 to 2000. According to 1970 Census data, 7.3 percent of families in Carthage lived below the poverty line, while that number almost doubled by 2010 (13.2 percent).

The year 2010 brought Carthage's first overall population growth, although the white population of Carthage continued to decline (see graph 1.2). The 2010 growth was due to the increase in Black and Latinx residents, changing Carthage from a white neighborhood to a multiracial one. Now if you drive down Vine Street, you see car dealerships and Latinx businesses, such as El Valle Verde supermarket and Taqueria Valle Verde. Cincinnati is a new destination city for Latinx immigration. Over the past three decades, immigrants to the United States have increasingly settled in nontraditional sites such as small and midsize cities in the Midwest and the South. Since the early 2000s, thousands of Latinx immigrants have come to the Cincinnati area and established thriving communities. Carthage is the Cincinnati neighborhood with the highest percentage of Latinx residents, 18 percent in 2010 and 29.7 percent in 2019.[34]

Sue described the change in types of business as a problem for Carthage: "The businesses are different. It's—they don't look like legitimate businesses anymore. And the last few have gone out 'cause they were selling drugs. They're not—they don't appeal to, I don't know what the word is. They appeal more to drug type people now, not to family type people." Sue went on to explain that one of her family members used drugs, and he could tell by looking at the storefronts that these businesses would cater to his interests. As she put it, "He went right in to see if he could get some drugs and he did." Interestingly, while Sue distinguished between family and "drug people," one of her family members was a drug user. The distinctions that residents drew were often exclusively for people outside of their circles, pointing to sym-

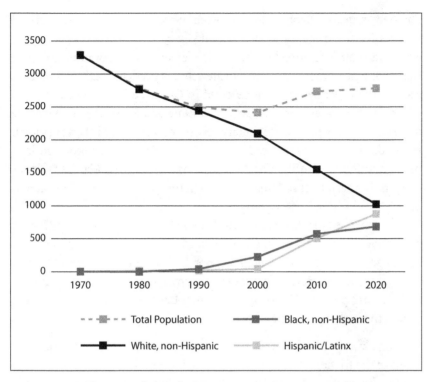

GRAPH 1.2 Carthage population change, 1970–2020. Data source: US Census.

bolic boundaries that had less to do with capturing a firm category and more with constructing the self as valuable in some way. In this instance, Sue's value came from being a legitimate claims-maker about Carthage's decline by referencing Carthage's past. After crafting her legitimacy, she marked herself and Carthage as deserving of better circumstances.

When describing the changes in Carthage, Sue also highlighted the loss of community and social support. She explained, "Your friends were here before. You went to school, either to St. Charles or you went to Carthage School, so the kids you went to school with were your playmates, and now the kids you go to school with live so far away from you that you don't know the kids that are in your neighborhood." According to census data, the percentage of children in Carthage under age eighteen decreased between 1970 and 2010 by 19 percent. However, the decrease in Carthage was less stark than the city's 29 percent reduction. Nonetheless, Carthage Paideia Academy Elementary School closed in 2009. It has since reopened under a new name, Rising Stars at Carthage, and only offers prekindergarten and kindergarten. While I was in the field, no public school was open in Carthage.

The New Jerusalem Baptist Church owned the school property and provided services for the neighborhood, including exercise classes. Parents I spoke with said their kids attended the public elementary school in neighboring Hartwell, while others attended private schools. Marcos (Latino, nineteen) was the youngest person I interviewed in Carthage, and he had recently graduated from a private high school in Elmwood Place. He said when he first started at his private elementary school, he was the only Latinx student enrolled. Due to a voucher program run by EdChoice that provided low-income students with funding to attend private schools, Marcos's friends and family began to enroll their children in this private school.[35] As Marcos put it, "I had a little society going on."

Sue continued her description of what had been lost in Carthage, "People don't know their neighbors anymore. It used to be if you got a phone call and had to go someplace, you call a neighbor and had a babysitter right away, and that's changed a lot. People aren't as open as they were to making friends and trusting people. It's just gone." When I asked Sue what she thought caused these changes, she responded:

> I don't know. I think people are working more; they're not home to make the friends. People used to be outside with their kids and talk over the fence, and when they're home during the day, they would meet people. Now, they're only home in the evening, and there's so much to do that they don't meet anybody. It's so different. And I think people—they're not as open to meeting other people. There's such a mixture of people now that used to be all—no culture mixes back then. And there's so many preconceived notions now about what people are like without waiting to find out what they're like.

Sue said she had experienced exclusion as a white woman for the first time in her building. As she put it, "I didn't realize what it was like to be in the minority until I moved in here, which I've learned from." She then explained that things were looking up for her. "In the building, after you're here a while, it breaks down. They invite me to bingo now. The ladies, the white ladies that are here, are included, but you have to work up to it. I've been here four years now, so now they [are] starting to bring me in, but it took a while."

Carthage: Changing and Needy

Carthage, unlike Riverside, is filled with businesses on its main thorough-fare. That is the first thing I noticed when coming down Vine Street after ex-

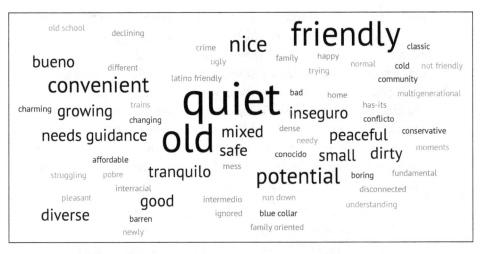

Word cloud of residents' descriptions of Carthage.

iting I-75. Car lots, repair shops, and tire vendors stood out in particular. Like Riverside, Carthage is small, and before you know it, you find yourself at the United Dairy Farmers (UDF) in neighboring Elmwood Place, about a mile and a half from where Carthage starts on Vine. But unlike Riverside, there is much to see as you make your way down the central boulevard. There are multiple churches—small storefronts and larger parishes alike—with English- and Spanish-language services. Bus stops, banks, fast-food places, and mom-and-pop hardware stores are interspersed with apartment buildings. Most single-family homes are located in Carthage's interior, on numbered streets west of Vine Street. In short, Carthage is very much bustling with activity and people. A comparison to sparse Riverside undoubtedly shaped my impression. In contrast, residents' most common descriptor of the area was "quiet," likely shaped by their experiences living in the interior of Carthage.

References to quiet often coincided with mentions of its size (small) and the age of the housing stock (old). Skylar and Timmy, white renters in their twenties who were originally from the suburbs of Cincinnati, used all of the most common descriptors for Carthage. They called it quiet, small, classic, old-school, and friendly. Residents also described Carthage as centrally located, dense, and convenient. Being close to I-75 provided residents with easy access to the north and south of the city. But there was no consensus on the positives and negatives of the neighborhood. For example, more people described Carthage as friendly than not, but some specifically described people as *not* friendly. For instance, Gwen (white homeowner, sixties) said,

"People here will help you with anything. You can have a big beautiful home, but you can't always have great neighbors. We have great neighbors."

In contrast, Hugh (white homeowner, fifties) described the neighborhood as cold, which he clarified as a reference to the people that lived there. Margaret (Black homeowner, twenties) agreed with Hugh that Carthage was not friendly: "It seems like it's going on the decline, and like I said, people don't speak, and it's dirty." Elisabeth (white renter, thirties) said that she didn't find Carthage as friendly as West Chester Township, where she grew up. She liked that Carthage was more densely populated than West Chester. Still, she described living in Carthage as a challenge:

> It just feels depressed. It feels like there's a lot of people that are miserable. It just seems like there's a lot of conflict that I see on a day-to-day basis that I didn't necessarily see in other places that I've lived. I have solid neighbors — the neighbors that I talk to — but just in general, it feels like it's a little bit isolated. I don't really enjoy walking up to Vine Street. I don't feel safe walking my dog. Like, if you go a few streets over, the feeling is very different. Some streets feel very safe, some streets feel happy, family-oriented, and some, it just feels like you're sort of unwelcome.

As with Riverside, mixed potential and experiences were common descriptors of Carthage, and residents intertwined them with ambivalence and affection. As Pam (white homeowner, sixties) detailed, "I think potential, and pleasant, in general, I would say pleasant, which is funny because I've also said I don't wanna walk the streets alone by myself. I don't know if that even makes sense. [. . .] I mean for a single woman, it's not — it doesn't feel safe and comfortable all times. But other times, it's like this is my home, and I really like my house, so I'm conflicted [laughs]." Pam explained that the potential of Carthage was because of homeowners; she associated renters with "disconnection" and a lack of neighborhood investment. (I discuss these criticisms of renters further in chapters 3 and 5.) Interestingly, Carthage has long been home to renters. According to census data, 46 percent of occupied housing units were renter-occupied in 1970, compared to 48 percent in 2010.

However, some descriptions of potential were much less fraught and just an account of a promising place. Pam said the neighborhood was "pleasant" and has potential. Felipe (Latino homeowner, fifties) said Carthage was "simpatico" and a "buen lugar" (charming, good place). He also said that Carthage "tiene futuro" and "tiene potencial" — it had a future and potential. Ben (white renter, fifties) recalled a film title to describe Carthage, calling it "The

Good, the Bad, and the Ugly." Earlier in our conversation, he said, "I think the community, the working people, the kids in school—the majority of people in Carthage do want a good community." Angelina (Black homeowner, forties) also described the residents as hardworking: "It's a lot of people that's getting up and going to work. I see a lot of families, a few generations on my street . . . they all just kind of keep to themselves, keep their yards nice, and just hardworking people." Many Carthage residents referred to their neighbors as hardworking people, using it as their first description when I asked them to characterize the people in the neighborhood. These descriptions matter because they tell us about Carthage and how residents seem themselves. While it may seem like a banal characterization, there is research that shows how people in the United States allude to hard work and education to reference race and class tropes without saying "poor" or "Black."[36] In these descriptions, residents characterize the neighborhood as one that is under-resourced but where people work—a clear distinction from poor neighborhoods where people rely on social safety nets.

Deacon (white male, thirties) lived with his grandmother after temporarily leaving Carthage. Compared to the neighborhood of his youth, he said now in Carthage it "seems like people move more fast, there's a lot more happening, a lot more of like your hustle-type thing going on, a lot of wheeling and dealing going on. That sales of drugs and whatnot. And when I was a child growing up everything seemed to be fine. There was more businesses around. Things seemed to be more happy. Whereas it seems kind of gloomy, and it just really depresses me to be honest." Nonetheless when I asked Deacon if he could describe Carthage later in the interview, he settled on "it's just a happy place." Deacon and other Carthage and Riverside natives framed their hometown neighborhoods in favorable terms, even when they readily identified some of the issues that plagued them.

Carthage's designation as the Cincinnati neighborhood with the largest Latinx population was important for how residents talked about the area. Residents used words such as "growing," "diverse," and "changing" to reference the demographics of Carthage over the last few decades. Latinx residents' generally characterized Carthage as welcoming to Latinxs, devoid of conflict, and "conocido" (familiar). Carmen (Latina homeowner, forties) praised how she felt residents welcomed the Latinx community. At the same time, she also thought Carthage was unsafe because the police ignored it. (I discuss these feelings of insecurity and safety in more detail in chapter 4.)

Adolfo (Latino homeowner, forties) said he chose Carthage because he wanted to be part of a Latinx community, "Sí, quería estar en un área donde hubiera Latinos y una de las razones por las que compre la casa donde estoy es porque está una iglesia que da servicios en español y está cerca." ("Yes, I wanted to be in an area where there were Latinos, and one of the reasons that I bought the house where I am is because there's a church that holds services in Spanish and is close by.") While Adolfo did not have many Latinxs on his street, St. Charles Borromeo served as a Latinx community space that helped him feel at home in Carthage. The Archdiocese of Cincinnati founded St. Charles Borromeo Parish in 1869. The parish closed in 1998, but the Latinx community—meeting elsewhere—started using the building to hold Spanish-language mass and as a gathering space. In 2018, the Latinx community relocated services to St. Boniface Church in Northside despite pleas from many parishioners to remain in Carthage. The Archdiocese of Cincinnati demolished the historic parish building in early 2021.

However, not everyone was pleased about Latinxs having spaces in Carthage. Dick (white homeowner, fifties) lived in Carthage "off and on all my life" and lamented what he saw as a Latinx takeover:

> I believe here pretty soon that the white people are going to be the minority. For the simple fact that you've got so many Mexicans crossing the border now. You know, they're pretty well taking over. Like you go down to Carthage, I don't know how many people you've interviewed, but down around 69th street where the little Mexican restaurant and stores and stuff—they call that Little Mexico. Which you go down there, that's all that's down there. But if the whites go down there, they get harassed. If the Blacks go down there, they get harassed. There's fights that break out. It's almost like a stupid turf thing. But—and I hate the world is like that. Why can't we all be united—unity. You know what I'm saying? I don't mock you if you want to come here and work but do it legally. I can't sneak into your country; what would happen to me if I sneak into your country? And don't do it legally? You've got rules and regulations.

While Carthage's Latinx and Black populations have increased in recent decades, the neighborhood is still majority white.

The association of Carthage with Latinxs was something many people mentioned. Erik (white renter, late sixties) said that his loved ones warned him off from moving to Carthage. "Some people said don't move to Carthage, there's trouble and all that, but I never had a problem, knock wood wherever there is. This block is safe. I mean, going towards Vine [Street], there's incidents, but that can happen in the best neighborhoods." When I asked what people warned him about specifically, Erik said, "Well, I have nothing against anybody. They said too many Mexicans, and they cause trouble. I learned a long time ago that there's good and bad in everybody. Most people just want to get along, do their business, so I never had any problem." Erik reiterated this point as we wrapped up our interview, "I think in various areas, even when they're bad or have had problems, there are turnarounds. Basically, people don't want to—unless they really don't care, people don't want to live in squalor or let a neighborhood go to pot. They want to be proud. People here cut their lawns; they do take care of their property. Yes, there's some older buildings, but they take care of it. I've also had to sideline home improvements, so anything—almost anything could be refurbished, so basically there is neighborhood pride to some degree." Erik wanted me to understand that this was a neighborhood of proud people doing their best and taking care of what they could.

More so than Riverside, Carthage's story is one of change, with residents seeing that negatively. However, that did not cause them to see Carthage as totally negative. There was plenty to celebrate and look forward to while also mourning how Carthage felt "ignored," "declining," and "needy." Despite the differential demographic realities of these two neighborhoods, there were also eerie similarities in how residents talked about the neighborhoods.

To understand these similarities and points of convergence, I turn to the broader picture of racial capitalism in Cincinnati. By investigating how racial capitalism has manifested in Cincinnati, we can begin to unwind the microlevel dynamics of Riverside and Carthage. In the following chapters, I focus on a relation of racial capitalism and a specter that helped justify and obscure its workings. I conclude each chapter with a discussion of other possibilities that already existed in Riverside and Carthage that challenged the mechanisms of racial capitalism on the ground. We start with underdevelopment and neglect, the themes of chapter 2.

CHAPTER TWO

Neglect and Underdevelopment

We get nothing. We need some help, but how are we gonna get it?
—CAIT, sixties, Riverside homeowner

As we saw in chapter 1, how Riverside and Carthage residents described and experienced their neighborhoods often differed. While they sometimes agreed on the details (e.g., quiet, far away), they did not necessarily agree on their evaluation (e.g., good, bad). But they also did not necessarily agree on the details, as contrasting terms were used for the same neighborhood (e.g., convenient and inconvenient). Despite these descriptive differences, I found that residents shared three common stories about living in Riverside and Carthage regardless of whether they loved it or hated it. These stories, or specters, centered on neglect, trash, and security. In this chapter, I explore how residents used the specter of neglect to interpret the exploitative and dehumanizing conditions of underdevelopment (a relation of racial capitalism). Neglect, however, provides an incomplete picture of underdevelopment. Therefore, I also describe underdevelopment in Cincinnati, giving us a fuller account of racial capitalism's shape and harms.

We begin with Julius, who takes us not to Riverside or Carthage, but to Over-the-Rhine (OTR). I start with OTR because it—alongside Price Hill—played a vital role in the stories that residents told about Riverside, Carthage, and their place within Cincinnati. This relational understanding sets the scene for the larger story about underdevelopment that I elucidate in this chapter. In contrast to most of the individuals I spoke with, Julius had a keen understanding of how racial capitalism was shaping development decisions in Cincinnati.

"What Rich People Have Always Done"

Meeting Julius was a happy accident. I wrote down his phone number from a voice mail I received while recruiting participants from Riverside. Unlike the other residents I spoke with, who chose neighborhood locales, he preferred to meet close to the University of Cincinnati campus where I worked. Once we started talking, it became clear that he did not live in Riverside. That explained his preference to meet near campus, which was closer to his home. We never quite figured out what happened; I must have written down the wrong phone number. Rather than tell me so, Julius scheduled an interview anyway. He shared about his life in Cincinnati and how the city is changing, and like a good social scientist, I listened. I was grateful for his time, candidness, and insight.

Julius, a Black renter in his mid-thirties, used to live downtown but has since moved to East Walnut Hills. Like Riverside, East Walnut Hills is near the southern border of Cincinnati and the Ohio River, which separates Cincinnati from Covington, Kentucky. And like residents from Riverside whom I spoke with, Julius's attention eventually turned to the gentrification of downtown neighborhood Over-the-Rhine.

A neighborhood adjacent to the city's central business district, OTR has experienced many transformations since the mid-1800s. In 1875, it was seen as a vibrant jewel of Cincinnati: "London has its Greenwich, Paris its Bois, Vienna its Prater, Brussels its Arcade, and Cincinnati its 'Over-the-Rhine.'"[1] It changed from an economically diverse neighborhood of immigrants to a working-class neighborhood of Appalachian migrants to a low-income, predominantly Black neighborhood post-urban renewal. Discussions of revitalizing OTR began in the 1970s and 1980s, but no city or private efforts ever materialized. As such, OTR remained a highly segregated and impoverished neighborhood. But that is no longer the case. According to the 2020 Census, OTR's population is now majority white, with 50 percent identifying as white alone and 43 percent identifying as Black alone. The neighborhood's median household income in 2020 was $64,695, much higher than the city-wide median of $42,663. How did this change happen?

In 2001, Cincinnati and OTR made national headlines: the residents of OTR were rioting. The impetus for these uprisings was the killing of Timothy Thomas, a Black teenager, by Stephen Roach, a white police officer. Thomas was the fifteenth unarmed Black man killed by a Cincinnati police officer in six years, and the fourth in the previous six months. Roach, along with several other officers, was pursuing Thomas because, as police audio indicates, Roach identified him as having outstanding warrants. These warrants were for misdemeanors, including a dozen traffic violations.[2] As Roach approached, Thomas ran away, turning into an alley. Roach shot Thomas in the chest at close range in the alley. Roach was eventually tried for negligent homicide and acquitted.

The day after Thomas's murder, Black Cincinnati residents demanded answers and transparency from police and city council members. They were met with silence. Three days of resistance followed in Over-the-Rhine. The City of Cincinnati implemented a city-wide curfew, which was inequitably applied as police arrested Black residents in Over-the-Rhine. In contrast, white residents moved about other parts of the city without penalty. A state of emergency came next, and police arrested hundreds by the end of the three days. The riots are said to have cost the city just over $3.5 million due to property damage and the cost of emergency responders. Soon after, the US Justice Department opened an investigation into the Cincinnati Police Department. This investigation, alongside the advocacy of local organizers, eventually produced a community–police agreement that established a new set of police practices, including citizen oversight and increased documentation of police stops to identify patterns of racial profiling.[3]

Since 2001 the city has been trying to rebrand, and OTR has been at the center of these efforts. In 2003, the Cincinnati Center City Development Corporation (3CDC) was established to "increase the effectiveness and efficiency of development activities in the City of Cincinnati." This public-private venture staked the future of Cincinnati's economic growth on establishing a "strong, vibrant downtown business and entertainment district." These revitalization plans also included OTR, for multiple reasons: its proximity to downtown, its cultural history, and the city's desire to remarket the neighborhood after the 2001 uprisings.

The result? Over-the-Rhine gentrified. As Julius described it, "They're forcing everyone out, and then they're rebuilding. So instead of rebuilding with the people who are already there, they're putting those people out and basically saying this is someone else's problem. . . . The city is doing this— they're doing this so slow, this has been a twenty-year process. . . . they're not giving all these low-income areas—there is no opportunity for anyone to be positive." Julius pointed out that the gentrification of OTR depended on pushing low-income people out of their neighborhood. While the city and businesses invested in OTR, they excluded poor Black residents from the same opportunities for economic advancement.

Julius also explained how, in addition to physical displacement, residents of downtown neighborhoods were experiencing social displacement:

> Low-income people and people who have money have different interests as far as how to relax. Most low-income people are not going to go to a art museum.[4] So if you put a art museum in a low-income area, no one is really going to take advantage of that opportunity. So you're not really making that for that person. . . . When I was living

in downtown, there were no restaurants, there were no shops, there were no places where—the people who lived down there didn't have jobs—where they could actually say, "Hey, can I come here and work?" There were none of these things there.

In concert with the city, developers constructed breweries and upscale restaurants targeting middle-class professionals and displacing the businesses in OTR that once served lower-income residents. For example, in the 2016 short documentary *Good White People*, the audience follows the owner of a penny candy store and community dojo as he is pushed out of OTR. The building owner decided to sell the building, and the new owners were building luxury condos. Longtime residents, who were subject to over-policing and city disinvestment for decades, could not afford to partake in OTR's improvements, a warning given by community organizers when discussions of historic preservation and redevelopment first happened in the 1980s. This kind of social displacement, where new businesses cater to a different clientele than longtime residents, is central to designating a neighborhood "revitalized" and no longer belonging to those who allegedly stripped it of its vitality.

The irony, of course, is that the city and its corporate partners are responsible for OTR's underdevelopment and its revitalization. The story of OTR provides a textbook example of gentrification and how racism and capitalism intersect in the uneven development of cities. Julius later described how gentrification was also coming to Walnut Hills, evidenced by new restaurants not catering to current residents. As he put it, "If you're poor, you're not going to be eating artichoke hearts and lamb."

When I asked Julius why this was happening, particularly downtown, he directly connected gentrification and the city's desire for social control after the 2001 uprisings: "Because of what happened with the riots, they don't want that to ever happen again. . . . 'cause basically, when the riots happened, no one could come to work. They basically shut down the city financially. They don't ever want that to happen again, so they're basically moving all the low-income people into what we consider the suburbs. . . . Why did they do this? They doing it because that's what rich people have always done." Julius identified the interdependent nature of racism and capitalism, and used those lenses to interpret the particular trajectory of OTR and poor Black people in Cincinnati. He saw capitalist interests ("no one could come to work") and connected them to present day actions ("they don't ever want that to happen again"). He also saw the interconnectedness of urban living, where what happened in one space shaped the outcomes in other places.[5]

As Julius recognized, development and neighborhood investment under racial capitalism are relational processes. What happens to one neighborhood matters for what happens in another. As historian Walter Rodney has argued, underdeveloped is not just a relative definition of a place (e.g., Riverside is underdeveloped compared to OTR) but also a definition of a relationship between places (e.g., OTR is developed at the expense of Riverside).[6] In this chapter, I explore the specter of neglect to understand the racial capitalist process of underdevelopment in Riverside, Carthage, and Cincinnati.

Neglected by the City

As I approached Riverside homeowners Carl and Maggie's front door for their interview, I noticed a sign that said I was being recorded. Carl soon appeared and greeted me with a handshake, letting me inside. I walked toward the kitchen table and took in the vintage advertisements that adorned their home. As I took my seat, Maggie, Carl's wife, said hello. She explained that she would leave me and Carl to talk, since the two of them together got too riled up. About five minutes into our conversation, after chiming in a few times, Maggie came and stood in the kitchen where Carl and I were seated. She stood there for the rest of the over two-hour interview, jumping in throughout.

Carl and Maggie had a lot to say about life in Riverside. In their early fifties, they moved into their home five years ago. While they identified as currently lower class, their stated income was between $60,000 and $64,000, which put them above the median income for the neighborhood and the city. Their income was among the highest of those I interviewed in Riverside. They viewed their home as their place of retirement. Unfortunately, life in Riverside had not gone quite as they imagined. "If we could pick this house up and move it somewhere else, it would be perfect," Carl said.

Carl and Maggie felt like they were dealing with neglect and mismanagement from the city. As Carl explained, "Things that were done on handshakes years ago are disappearing. And now you're getting a bunch of houses that are just getting boarded up and torn down, which could be a good thing. But some of these houses down here are nice." Carl and Maggie said that the older homes in Riverside, including theirs, were well built and in good shape but needed some work. The couple wanted more support for homeowners like themselves who were trying to do right by the neighborhood and take care of these older homes. However, they were finding it an uphill battle. Maggie bragged that they saved a home in Cincinnati—one that the city would have torn down, Carl added. The city tended to approach neglected property in Riverside and neighboring Sedamsville with removal rather than rehabilitation. Preservation was something reserved for revitalizing neighborhoods. So while the city and its partners were investing in OTR and rebranding it, Riverside remained untouched and forgotten.

Neglect by the city government was mentioned by residents of both Riverside and Carthage. However, it was generally white residents that used this frame. Neglect-related terms, such as "needs attention," "forgotten," "ignored," and "needy," were popular in resident descriptions across neighborhoods. Carl and Maggie made it clear that multiple entities were neglecting Riverside: the police, the City of Cincinnati, the Water Works, and the Metropolitan Sewer District of Greater Cincinnati. "They all need to pay attention to what's going on down here because none of them are," Carl chided. Many residents of Riverside and Carthage had a clear sense that they were being left behind. Craig (Black renter, twenties) said that Riverside "feels like a forgotten part of the city to me" because it is so quiet and there is not much to do in the area. Tom (white homeowner, seventies) agreed, describing Riverside as run-down and forgotten. Erin and Dean (white homeowners, fifties and sixties, respectively) identified neglect as a street-by-street issue. Dean described how "you can go from one street that looks really nice to the next street that's like—if I say war zone, I know that's a hyperbole." Erin then jumped in, "It's run-down." Some residents, however, viewed these long-forgotten pieces of Cincinnati history with affection and attention. For instance, Rich (white renter, fifties) called the area careworn, "It's run-down, but there's just a heart underneath it." The older homes help ground the neighborhood as perhaps forgotten by the city but well loved by its residents.

Carthage residents also saw their neighborhood as low on the city's priority list, drawing on themes of deservingness and victimization reminiscent of a politics of resentment.[7] For example, residents interpreted the lack of prompt snow removal as city neglect. Lilian (white homeowner, forties) explained they plowed the main streets, however "we got snowed-in here, but they don't come and plow the side street. Which is kind of weird because I don't know if there's just not enough money to where they're not investing in it [plowing side streets]." In Riverside, Elsie (white homeowner, sixties) similarly complained about how the city did not do enough when it snowed. She said Delhi Township, rather than the City of Cincinnati, usually treated their streets. Elsie's sister Cait (white homeowner, sixties) then explained how residents had to salt their roads to make them walkable, which her neighbors did. Tom said about potholes in Riverside: "There never seems to be any big hurry to do anything about it. But you go to Hyde Park [on the East Side] or someplace like that, all you gotta do is read the newspaper, and you'd see who does what for who." When I asked if he feels that the city ignores Riverside, he replied, "For a lot, for somewhat." Tom constructed Riverside's powerlessness as a result of the attention paid to more affluent East Side neighborhoods, such as Hyde Park. Hugh (white homeowner, mid-fifties) also complained that the city did not seem to care about a foreclosed property next door to his Carthage home. "It really angers me enough to the point that okay I'm done with the city." He dreamed of moving "somewhere north," perhaps Butler or Warren County.[8]

Cincinnati residents generally understood the city's West Side as a white working-class stronghold. It is known for its German Catholic residents and its insularity. This is in contrast to the city's East Side, which is more affluent yet still white. Black, and now Latinx, residents are concentrated in the center of the city, in places like Carthage and Avondale, a longtime Black residential hub. Of course, this segregation by race and class is not an accident. While many residents take this segregation for granted as a natural occurrence, Cincinnati's history points to how policies constructed segregated spaces. For example, Avondale was a predominantly white neighborhood before the 1940s. "Slum clearance," as well as highway construction, led to the bulldozing of predominantly Black communities in the 1940s and 1950s. As the housing in segregated Black neighborhoods decreased and the Black population grew due to increased migration to Cincinnati from the South, Black people began to move into once-restricted neighborhoods. As happened in many other cities, "As whites vacated their used central city housing for new suburban housing and neighborhoods, Blacks moved in."[9] Avondale and Walnut Hills became new destinations for poor and working-class Black people within Cincinnati; in my research, both were also frequently cited by Black residents as neighborhoods in which they previously lived.

Many residents from Riverside and Carthage referenced East Side neighborhoods, such as Hyde Park and Mt. Adams, alongside suburbs, such as Mason, as places where elites lived and where the city and county funneled resources first. In this way, working-class Cincinnati residents had a pretty strong sense of where they stood regarding city priorities. Claudia (white homeowner, sixties), who lived in Carthage, explained what she saw taking place in Cincinnati politics:

CLAUDIA: I wish the city would spend some more money on neighborhoods and maybe a little less on The Banks and Over-the-Rhine and that crazy streetcar, which I think is a good idea, but it has gotten out of hand with the costs. . . . I do wish the city would spend more on neighborhoods—well, they spend money on certain neighborhoods where white upper-class people live because we lived in Mt. Washington for twenty years, so we were right next to Hyde Park and Mt. Lookout. Always money spent there.

SARAH: And so you feel like the same attention isn't paid to Carthage?

CLAUDIA: Absolutely, and I think it's to the city's disadvantage. . . . the suburbs don't survive unless the urban area lives. I don't care how fancy Mason is. I don't know; maybe it could exist on its own 'cause it's got enough money, maybe the money would hold it together. [*laughs*]

Claudia's comments point to the relationality of place and underdevelopment. While she laughed about suburban Mason's viability, she is right. Scholars of suburbs have documented the intentional boundaries drawn between suburbs and their urban counterparts in the United States to facilitate resource-hoarding in segregated suburban communities.[10] This relational development and dependency, or creative extraction, as Danielle Purifoy and Louise Seamster call it, is a foundational characteristic of racial capitalism in cities.[11]

Quinn (white renter, twenties), who grew up in Riverside and now lives in Carthage, shared that she believed the city did not respond quickly enough to issues in Carthage. She connected this to the privileging of wealthy, white suburbs: "They go to the ones that has money like Madeira, Mariemont, places like that. They go there first and fix those places up first because that's where the money went. Then when everything else is all said and done, they come see us, the lower-class people, throw some blacktop on there and call it good. . . . I figure that they choose. They go with the places that have money, and then they come see us. Then they do a half-assed job at that. It's all about money." Like Claudia, Quinn thinks about the city of Cincinnati in relation to its surrounding suburbs, which are considerably whiter and wealthier than most Cincinnati neighborhoods. As of 2017, Madeira was 92 percent white non-Hispanic, while Mariemont was 95 percent white non-Hispanic. While the city of Cincinnati is technically an independent financial entity from Madeira and Mariemont, Quinn's thinking reflects a key argument of suburban studies, namely that "the histories of cities and sub-urbs are fundamentally intertwined, even as municipal boundaries kept them politically separate."[12] The ability of wealthier residents to move to class- and race-segregated suburbs and hoard resources has shaped the economic tra-jectory of cities, Cincinnati included.

Residents also framed the development of Over-the-Rhine as a city fail-ure that put other neighborhoods ahead of both Carthage and Riverside. Elsie specifically connected Riverside's neglect to the attention paid down-town, "Help is offered everywhere else—if you're downtown, you've got it made in the shade. If you're down past that one point, you're on your own, sucker. Forget it." Patty (white homeowner, seventies) had lived in Carthage for twenty-five years. Her late husband was from Carthage, born there in the 1940s. When they married in the 1990s, she moved in with him. She argued, "They're more interested in downtown now than in us. That really makes me mad because when I was a little girl and I was raised down there, nobody cared about it. Now that everybody wants to go downtown to The Banks and all that stuff. Now it's important. They seem to do everything backwards." Patty's comments denaturalize the investment in OTR. It was formerly neglected—just like Riverside and Carthage felt now. Yet what changed was not OTR but the financial interests at play. While Patty said, "Everybody wants to go downtown," the truth is that OTR and the city cater to a young, professional middle-class.

Riverside resident Tom also bemoaned the focus on OTR. "Let's do some-thing for somebody besides Over-the-Rhine. I'm tired of all the damn money they spend on Over-the-Rhine. Like I say, everything seems to be parks and bike trails. [*laughs*] That's—I don't give a damn about a bike trail anymore; my bike days are long gone." The coalition of actors at the center of OTR's gentrification includes the city and the nonprofit development cor-poration 3CDC. While it is a nonprofit, over thirty corporate partners pri-vately fund 3CDC, including PNC Bank, Procter & Gamble, and Kroger—all three of which have headquarters in Cincinnati. The nonprofit was estab-lished in 2003, two years after the uprisings in Over-the-Rhine. Its stated focus is revitalizing and connecting the central business district and OTR through real estate redevelopment. Some of the projects that 3CDC has un-dertaken include the renovations of Fountain Square, Washington Park, and Music Hall. These renovations have transformed downtown into a space that caters to middle-class tastes and elite economic interests of profit making. As Julius explained, and *Good White People* chronicled, these renovations have led to the physical displacement of poor residents and working-class business owners, and the cultural displacement of poor and working-class people. What Riverside and Carthage residents point to with the language of neglect is how OTR's development shaped their neighborhood's underdevelopment.

Take the case of the Cincinnati Bell Connector, otherwise known as the streetcar.[13] The streetcar navigates around a 3.6-mile loop and connects the riverfront ("The Banks"), downtown, and OTR. On the official website of the Cincinnati Bell Connector, the City of Cincinnati laid out its purpose by identifying the problems the streetcar addressed, in a section titled "Background & Benefits." The website pointed to population decline and declining businesses, as well as urban flight and "lagging competitively": "The problem is keeping young, smart talent who want to be in active, walkable cities like Chicago, San Francisco and New York. Because Cincinnati's urban core hasn't been as vibrant as it should have been for the past 50 years, there's a problem in keeping smart, young people around. How Do We Fix It? Cincinnati needs more jobs, more development and more people. A streetcar is a way to do that."

Echoing arguments made by urban studies scholar Richard Florida and others about the importance of attracting the "creative class" for urban sustainability, the City of Cincinnati invested in the streetcar to attract young professionals back downtown, as well as businesses. The city directly stated that it wanted to continue the gentrification of OTR and downtown; that was the goal of the streetcar: "In Over-the-Rhine specifically, there is still a long way to go in turning around that neighborhood (particularly when you look north of Liberty Street). The buildings there are likely to be occupied by people who don't want a place to keep their car—they want to be connected through a useful transit system. So for all this development to be sustainable and cost-effective, a streetcar system is necessary to keep going."[14] The city clearly stated that it needed the streetcar to continue the redevelopment of downtown for the professional class. The total cost of the streetcar was over $148 million, with both federal and city money committed.

While Over-the-Rhine is the site of investment in public transportation, what does public transit look like in Riverside and Carthage? Looking at public transportation helps illustrate how underdevelopment is a relation. Many residents of Riverside complained about the terrible bus service in their neighborhood. The 50 bus had a two- to three-hour loop due to its route from the East Side to the city's West Side. Only one local bus route, the 77, went north to neighboring Delhi Township, where local grocery stores were located. The schedule, however, was sparse: it ran Monday through Friday 6:00–8:00 A.M. and 3:40–6:00 P.M. The bus routes were much more regular in Carthage, with the 78 and others connecting Carthaginians to other parts of the city.

Kalisha (Black renter, twenties) said the only thing she did not like about the Riverside area was that the buses took a long time to come. Stefanie (white renter, thirties) said that the bus issues had existed for years. In describing where she went grocery shopping, she explained how she got to Delhi Township:

> If you take a bus — fifty percent of these people don't have vehicles — they take the bus everywhere like I do. And if you take the bus, [it] doesn't come all the way down to River Road, which always upset me because so many people could take that bus right up into Delhi, go to Kroger, and come back. It's been like that for years, so there's nothin' gonna change anytime soon, but you gotta take the bus all the way to downtown, and then to Delhi, and then Delhi to back [downtown], it takes you two hours there and takes you two hours back. It's insane.

A two-hour one-way trip to the grocery store is a significant hardship, especially when it is under three miles from River Road. With a car, it is a seven-minute drive, according to Google Maps.

Douglas (white homeowner, seventies) lamented the reduction in bus service since he moved to the neighborhood almost thirty years ago.

> When [my partner and I] moved here twenty-nine years ago, [bus fare] was thirty-five cents, and there was a bus like every twenty minutes. And now, it's $1.75; only I'm getting a senior — eighty-five cents with my senior card. But the bus costs a lot more, and it's down to thirteen buses a day, and it was something like thirty-nine buses a day. And I think in America, this country is very badly organized. When the economy is tanking is exactly the time that the government should be able to spend more on things like public transportation. And instead, the bus service declined most of all in the 2008 recession. Because the city income was down, so they cut back on the bus service. But that's exactly when people needed the bus service more. And by reducing the service so badly, they've made people find other ways to get around because it's so hard. I mean, I cannot take a bus to church on Sunday morning, for example. There's just no bus within hours of the Sunday morning service. I can take a bus home. So, if someone gives me a ride. I mean, if [my partner] Tim has a gallery show or something, he gives me a ride to church, and then I take a bus home. But

that's the way it is. And on Saturdays, I can't take a bus to swim because the amount of time it takes for me to swim and change and shower and all that and get back, the next bus has gone and it's an hour and a half to wait for the next one. So, the weekend service is really bad, and even during the week, it's not at all what it used to be, and I feel very sorry about that.

Besides complaining about the lack of bus transportation in the neighborhood, like many other residents, Douglas also provided a critique of austerity, whereby governments reduce services when people are struggling economically and need them most. In turn, he presents us with an alternative to capitalist logics, whereby the needs of residents dictate service schedules.

The justification for Riverside's reduced bus service is likely its steady population loss over the years. That has undoubtedly resulted in decreased ridership in the area. However, Craig, who had recently moved from Clifton, a middle-class neighborhood on the edge of the University of Cincinnati campus, explained that he "never encountered that many bus riders that actually use the city bus system" until he moved to Riverside. "Out of my thirty-two unit complex, I'd say twenty-four of thirty-two are active bus riders that don't even have cars."

Juxtaposing Riverside (see graph 1.1 in chapter 1) with Over-the-Rhine's trajectory shows that city officials do not necessarily meet depopulation with decreased services. In fact, the entire justification for the streetcar was that investment *leads* to population growth. So what drives the difference in policies? One key factor seems to be for whom the city is making the investment. There is nothing wrong with creating spaces with upper-class tastes in mind, but those seem to be the only tastes about which cities care. Is a streetcar running on a 3.6-mile loop for revelers to navigate between different business and restaurant districts the best use of city money? Why aren't the residents in Riverside attempting to go food shopping at the top of the priority list? While the answer may seem obvious—they are poor, so they do not bring in revenue for the city—a critical framework of underdevelopment forces us to contend with how developers, planners, and politicians design cities to maximize revenue, even if it means catering to a hoped-for professional class over addressing the needs of the already-present poor and working classes.

It is not just the loss of bus services that residents mourned. It was the loss of businesses. Bernice (Black renter, seventies) criticized the city's focus: "I just feel that the government, as they go about and you see them all breaking ground and doing this over in Clifton and over here at Mason and this one and that one, what did you do? Forget about Carthage?" Tom agreed, "It's not just the city itself; it's groceries and stuff like that." He complained that there were no businesses in Riverside, "You've got all the pizza places you want, but decent restaurants and stuff like that you don't see; you're gonna go out to Glenway Avenue out there."

Residents characterized these local stores as providing amenities alongside a sense of community and ties to place. As Helen (white homeowner, sixties) described, "In the twelve years that we've lived here, I have seen Sedamsville just empty out completely. People will talk a lot about the idea of having, of being bought out by the big box stores. Or they say that there's one or two maybe developers who have got interest there. And it just, even at that, there were still pockets of it that you could identify as a community. And I would say in the last two years . . . maybe two and a half years, even that has disappeared. It's gone." When I asked her how that happened, she responded, "Well, nobody owned." Helen blamed the shift on the lack of homeownership in the community. Her comment transformed the problem of structural disinvestment into a process of resident disinvestment. Residents regularly assumed renters cared less about their neighborhoods than homeowners. (I discuss this pattern in more detail in chapter 3.) Agnes (white homeowner, nineties) described a similar loss of business and, as Helen alluded, she blamed "the larger stores in Delhi," with which Riverside businesses could not compete.

Patty, who used to live in OTR, also complained about the difficulty of opening businesses in Carthage in comparison to other areas:

> It's hard to even have a restaurant down here. They all want to build in Mason and over in Hyde Park and down in Over-the-Rhine. I thought they were gonna close up this Kroger's across the street for a while. I don't know where you'd go to the grocery store. So it's like they're gonna ignore us now and redo downtown so they can get what they want downtown. I guess that's the way politics is, but I don't get it. I'm just not that bright. I think everybody should be treated fairly. They're renting, selling condos down there for half a million dollars, and we're up here fighting people that are not being educated to speak English and helping us learn Spanish so that we can live out here together without it being a dump.

Patty's comments point to an important caveat of the neglect specter. While residents used it to explain their position vis-à-vis more affluent middle-class spaces, this relational understanding was often intertwined with racism, as white residents resented that their lower-class position meant they could not buffer themselves from interacting with Black and Latinx residents in their neighborhoods. As Stuart Hall famously argued, race is the prism through which we experience class.[15] White residents' class status is simultaneously shaped by racist understandings of themselves (and nonwhites). (I discuss this in more detail in chapter 3.)

Schools also prompted white residents to engage in conversations of neglect by the city and even accusations of "reverse racism." Due to budget constraints on the school system and low enrollments after years of population decline and white flight, some Cincinnati neighborhood schools were closed during the 1970s and 1980s. Riverside-Harrison School was one of those closed in 1982.[16] Longtime residents said there was a mass exodus from Riverside after the school closed and its students were bused to other neighborhoods. At the time, the Cincinnati Public Schools (CPS) district was majority Black, with Black students comprising 58 percent of those enrolled in 1984 — a far cry from Riverside-Harrison's 6.64 percent Black student population in 1982.[17] White population declines across the city, starting in the 1950s, in addition to white parents taking their children out of the public school system and putting them in private schools or homeschooling them, led to the underutilization of CPS and the closing of many neighborhood schools. Interestingly, contrary to Riverside's claims of "reverse racism," most of the shuttered schools were predominantly Black, prompting the *Bronson v. Board of Education of City School District* lawsuit in 1974. After this lawsuit, Cincinnati instituted its voluntary school integration program by creating magnet schools. There was no forced busing in Cincinnati to promote integration, but students from areas with no schools, including Riverside, were bused to other neighborhoods.

Riverside-Harrison School was a big topic of conversation when I interviewed longtime residents Elsie, Cait, and Kevin (white homeowner, sixties) at Wendy's in neighboring Delhi. Elsie described Riverside as having lost its identity when the school closed: "Riverside had lost out a long time ago. When they closed the school, everybody wanted better education for the kids, and they kept saying no, you're gonna have to go downtown." Kevin saw busing as a form of reverse discrimination. Segregated white schools were framed as the "healthy and productive settings for teaching and learning" in contrast to the stressful environments of integrated schools.[18] To frame themselves as the victims of these policies, white residents avoided discussing how Black children experienced school closings and segregation.

To wit, Kevin explained, "When they threaten the school in any community, people leave the community and there was reverse discrimination done. School board officials sent Riverside children downtown, which no one wanted. So there was picketing across from the school." Cait echoed her dissatisfaction with the school situation in Riverside. Her son was sent to Hays-Porter for elementary school and Taft for high school, both located in the predominantly Black West End neighborhood adjacent to Over-the-Rhine. She said her son "was like the only white child in his class. So they were supposed to have swimming and gym, but they couldn't do it because he was the only white kid and you'd have to change. And they couldn't give him a private place, so they had to just go in study halls then." Cait could not imagine her son as a white child incorporating into a Black space. As she later put it, "Our kids—their culture and our culture did not match. It was not good and the schools—like I said, the schools were inferior." The school allowed Cait's son to skip gym for study hall.[19] Whites portrayed the closing of Riverside-Harrison as a "racialized hardship" despite evidence that Black residents were most likely to be affected by school closings. Cait's stories about her son helped her, Kevin, and Elsie construct a parallel narrative of neglect and victimization.[20]

Erin also blamed busing for neighborhood change. She explained, "A big thing that hurt our neighborhood was when they started busing, and so everybody started moving out because they didn't want to go to the other—to the schools that they were being forced to go to. Businesses just started closing, and they took our school away. This is a charter school now. So the neighborhood's completely different than when I was a kid. Completely different." She went on to say that most parents put their kids in Catholic schools or homeschooled their children, which was what she initially did. Since she was working part-time, Erin could no longer homeschool her children, which she bemoaned. She later brought up busing again as the turning point for her neighborhood's decline: "When you take away people's neighborhood schools and their neighborhood stores. I tell ya—" her husband Dean then finished her sentence, "It's no longer a neighborhood then." White residents framed the school closing as a result of busing. Yet busing did not start until Riverside-Harrison closed due to low enrollment. This neglect narrative flips the order of white families deciding to move away from Riverside and removing their children from the public school system with city-level decision-making. While Riverside families were framed as reacting to structure, the ways they shaped the structure themselves via white flight were obscured.[21]

Like Cait and Kevin, Erin used race to explain why Riverside was not a city-wide priority: "A poorer white neighborhood doesn't really get much attention. I know if you live in [wealthy] Indian Hill you do get a lot of attention. You get things taken care of quickly because tax dollars go to support politicians. In an African American neighborhood you'll even get more attention because you're a minority neighborhood than in a white—." Her husband Dean jumped in to add, "Working poor, in other words. It's easy to ignore." Erin continued, "Yeah, Appalachian area. And this is Appalachian, considered an Appalachian area through here. I think this has a major impact on it. And there's a reason why when they started busing they didn't bus the kids in Indian Hill. They didn't touch those neighborhoods. It was the poor white neighborhoods and the African American neighborhoods that got bused. So, that's the way it goes unfortunately." Erin and Dean pointed to racism and classism, perceiving city officials as caring more about wealthy whites and Black residents' complaints than poor whites.

While the urban specter of neglect helps residents understand the relational aspects of underdevelopment, it is only a partial recognition of the structural reality of Cincinnati. White residents also painted over the fact of white flight with the specter of neglect. Talk of neglect obscured how antiblackness and racial residential segregation were drivers of underdevelopment in the city. In the following section, I use the case of Price Hill to address how incorporating an analysis of racial segregation alongside neglect gives us a fuller understanding of underdevelopment as a process of racial capitalism.

Cautionary Tale: Price Hill

For many white Riverside residents I spoke with, fellow West Side neighborhood Price Hill was a white, working-class neighborhood that had been "destroyed" by an influx of less upstanding Black residents from downtown and OTR. Price Hill was particularly potent as a reference, not just because of its proximity to Riverside but also because of its history as a white working-class area. Interestingly, despite how white Riverside residents talked about it, Price Hill was still a predominantly white area. It includes three neighborhoods—East Price Hill, West Price Hill, and Lower Price Hill. In 2010, East Price Hill, which abuts Riverside and Sedamsville, was 52 percent white non-Hispanic, 39 percent Black non-Hispanic, and 7 percent Latinx.[22] Between 1990 and 2000, East Price Hill experienced a 24 percent loss of its white population, with 4,200 white residents leaving and 2,139 Black residents moving in—a 124 percent increase in its Black population. In 2010, Lower Price Hill, which is east of East Price Hill, was 65 percent white, 25 percent Black, and 13 percent Latinx, while West Price Hill was 70 percent white, 24 percent Black, and 4 percent Latinx. Given the city demographics, whites were overrepresented in all three neighborhoods.

White Riverside residents traced the decline of Price Hill to the arrival of new residents who had been pushed out of predominantly Black downtown neighborhoods. These narratives drew on ideas of city neglect and elite powerbrokers. Federico (white renter, forties), a longtime West Side Cincinnati resident, saw changes across the West Side as explicitly connected to downtown developments, saying, "The yuppies would rather have downtown. So, they shove them out here." He elaborated:

> My understanding is in lieu of civic improvements that there was kind of a deal cut when they displaced a lot of the people downtown to inject them en masse into, not here, but really more like Price Hill basically. And you noticed it when it happened. And I'm trying to be delicate because I'm not really judging anybody here. I'm not pointing the finger at any one particular group outside of the fact that they're downtrodden drug addicts, I guess, for lack of a better term. But right after they did that, the change was immediate and everlasting, apparently. So, it went from middle-class to lower-middle-class people that worked to middle-class, lower-class people that don't. Not all the way around, but there was a huge injection of them. And it just changes things when you rent instead of own.

While Federico characterized his reference to "downtrodden drug addicts" as "delicate," it is hard not to interpret this as code for newer Black residents, given what we know about Price Hill's demographic changes. Eatondale resident John (white renter, thirties) made his reference explicit. He explained how the Price Hill of his youth is no more: "Price Hill . . . quite a few years ago . . . the place wasn't nothing like it is now, you know what I mean. It's like I said, I'm not a prejudiced, you know what I mean, but [*quietly*] once all these Black people start moving in up in Price Hill, it just started becoming worse and worse and worse, and it's did nothing but get worse, you know what I mean." While some may take John's antiblack racism for granted, we must not naturalize it. There is nothing natural about a poor white person disidentifying from Black people. Our racial capitalist system produces these habituated responses from nonblack people (and sometimes Black people, too). To wit, political scientist Charisse Burden-Stelly argues that antiblackness is a core tenet of modern racial capitalism in the United States.[23] (I discuss antiblackness as a neighborhood norm in chapter 5.)

Identifying the humanity of Black residents pushed out of downtown and OTR could have led Federico to a different set of analyses, whereby his assessment of the deal struck between the "yuppies" and powers that be to displace residents would not be framed as the catalyst for Price Hill decline, but instead could have prompted further questions about the flow of resources and city priorities. Rather than engage in "trash talk" about drug users and renters (see chapter 3), Federico could have gotten curious about the economic conditions at large. The decline that he felt could be related to the recession of 2008, which even the City of Cincinnati blamed for the loss of revenue.[24] In addition, Federico used the word "injection" to describe the movement of new residents into Price Hill, denoting a forced process to which Price Hill residents were subject. Federico's comments also marked a social actor: elite decision-makers. Federico intertwined his critique of elite interests with racist and classist assessments of poor and Black residents. This partial understanding did not challenge racial capitalist thinking but reinforced it. At its core, it was also a misunderstanding. Federico and John's comments illustrate how racism does the dirty work of capitalism; people do not need to ask more questions about how things work when racist ideas "make sense" (as they did for Federico and John).

When we denaturalize these "commonsense" ideas, we can better identify what underlying relations they obscure. For example, in 2014 (the year I spoke with Federico), the 2014–2015 city approved budget reduced funding for "community councils, neighborhood business districts, and outside social service agencies" yet continued to fund "long-term strategic initiatives," including the streetcar. This distinction shows that while Carthage and Riverside funds were grouped under neighborhood interests, downtown initiatives were "strategic" and were funded at the expense of narrower neighborhood interests. This process relied on framing downtown initiatives as beneficial for all, despite benefiting primarily the middle class and elites. In short, elite interests were misrepresented as universal.

Neglected by Civic Organizations

To address this city-level neglect, many residents approached neighborhood-specific power brokers, such as civic and neighborhood organizations, for help with their concerns.[25] In what is often called a city of neighborhoods,

Cincinnati neighborhood associations had the power to apply for resources from the city to address issues. While it might seem like civic clubs are inconsequential beyond litigating interneighbor squabbles or planning social events, these clubs often play a crucial role in neighborhood strategic planning. They are the public-facing entity of a community. For example, in Carthage, the city council approved a Neighborhood Business Strategy Plan in March 2019. According to the publicly available plan document, "The planning process was lead [sic] by the Carthage Civic League—a group of Carthage community leaders, residents, property owners and business owners with help from the Department of City Planning." The planning document was based on a neighborhood survey conducted at a 2013 "strategy meeting" with "about 30 stakeholders" from the neighborhood. With the city council's approval, this plan will serve as the basis for future funding requests to the city and other entities. In other words, the civic league was intimately involved in deciding the future of Carthage and would receive funds to enact these visions.

As Morgan (white resident, sixties) explained, the civic league also had control over city funds dispensed to the neighborhood to address local issues. Morgan grew up in Elmwood Place, an unincorporated village that borders Carthage. When she got married, she moved to the West Side of Cincinnati, but she returned home after her divorce. Morgan lived with her mother in Elmwood Place until she passed, and then Morgan moved in with her son, who owned a home in Carthage. She clarified that "we live in the same house but not the same space." Morgan was actively involved in the civic league and said it was the only thing keeping Carthage going. She described Carthage as having "really gone downhill, but we have a strong, strong community council." She pointed to the civic league's activities as part of its strength, including a "real active senior group which I belong to, but I haven't been going." She explained that "our civic league just donated $10,000 to help improve" the then-closed Carthage school, which New Jerusalem Baptist Church occupied. She then remembered that another neighborhood project cost about $30,000, illustrating the league's active status. Morgan explained that the civic league received funds from the city to improve its neighborhood business district, from which most of that donation came. She described the funding process:

> Sometimes there are things through the city they apply for. I don't
> know the names of the groups, but we get so much city money, and we
> have fundraisers, which I don't imagine raise a whole lot, like we had a

yard sale. There's an annual yard sale in Carthage that's still going on in the first weekend of June, maybe? The group donates funds to there and some of the businesses; we have quite a few businesses, and they donate money. I don't know how the balance got so large, honestly, because we have to use—if we get say $5,000 from the city for the business district, it has to be used, I guess, in that fiscal year, or, otherwise, I guess, we lose it.

Lourdes (Latina homeowner, forties), who owned a business in Carthage, confirmed local businesses' involvement in the civic league. She said the civic league supported her and her business by mentioning them during meetings. Lourdes, in turn, attended league meetings, though it conducted them in English. She said she mostly followed along, though otherwise she was not very involved.

In Riverside, Shauna (white homeowner, fifties) was intimately involved and proud of the work of the civic club. Shauna was a West Side Cincinnati native who moved to Riverside after marrying her husband, a native Riverside resident. She explained that while Riverside had changed since she hung out in the neighborhood as a teenager, "The people are the same. The people that have been here for a long time have been here a long time, and they're very, very territorial." When I asked her what she meant by territorial, she explained that they've been here a long time and do not like change. She said this goes for riding a bike in the middle of the road like longtime residents did when they were kids or fishing in the renovated waterfront park. With the renovation came new rules that people could not fish off the docks. "They can't go out on the dock because it's really not safe, and it's against the law to be there because that's for the—we have a boat ramp." She said she saw complaints about this new policy from longtime residents on Facebook. Given that she is a part of the civic club leadership, I asked her if she felt obligated to respond. She said she types responses but deletes them "because that's where I'm not a longtime resident, so I can't say anything. And I've seen people who have said things that are longtime residents get ridiculed for not taking the side of the longtime residents." She said that the civic club invited someone from the parks department to speak to residents about the changes, and nobody with a complaint came to the meeting.

Shauna explained that the civic club was a mix of newer and longtime residents. She originally joined to learn more about the neighborhood and eventually got involved because she was concerned with her property and stormwater damage, "They mentioned doing something about stormwater.

And somebody made the comment, 'If you want us to fight stormwater, you fight them.' And that's when I was still kinda new, and I said, 'Okay, I will.' And I did, and I got heard. And then all of the sudden, it's like, 'Oh, she puts her money where her mouth is.' So it wasn't my money. It was more my connections." Shauna worked for a general contractor, so she used her insider knowledge to get her complaint letter to the right people. While the City of Cincinnati did not initially reply, it directed Cincinnati Stormwater Management to respond when she complained to Hamilton County. "And they come down, and they did a whole tour of Riverside. And they didn't only make me happy. They made Riverside happy." Shauna's ability to use her workplace networks to get the city's stormwater management team down to Riverside, and to fix the issues not only with her property but across the neighborhood, helped her make inroads with her new neighbors, who first approached her with skepticism.

While Shauna said it was hard to get to know your neighbors in some parts of Riverside due to the distance between houses, she knew people because she went to civic club meetings. At one point during our interview, when she described what happened with stormwater management, she corrected herself when characterizing the relationship between the city and the neighborhood civic club, worried that it could be interpreted that she was badmouthing the club's executive council. "It wasn't the council's fault now," she explained. She then asked if we could stop the interview tape, and I assured her we could move on to the next question. She relaxed. During our conversation, Shauna seemed hesitant, as if she did not want to step a toe out of line in describing her neighborhood. She seemed to feel a hefty responsibility to represent Riverside well.

While some residents found community in the civic organizations, others found more neglect, which made them feel truly isolated. Maggie and Carl were such an example.

> MAGGIE: I've never ever, in all the places we've lived, have I ever felt so unsafe and so lost because there's nobody you can trust or turn to.
> CARL: Yeah, there's just nothing here. There really isn't. There's no guidance down here. The civic club is just a joke. They just collect the money is all they do. They don't care about nobody or anything but themselves.
> MAGGIE: Only if it suits the president. There's an apartment building at the corner here, Anderson Ferry and Hillside. And he had a buddy that lived there, and he wanted everybody to fight because they were

gonna make it Section 8. The only reason he was fighting for that was because he knew somebody that lived there. That's the only reason. Otherwise, it wouldn't have been an issue. Who cares?

This view of civic associations as insular and focused on the needs of insiders was repeated—and contested—in Riverside and Carthage. The prickliness of the Riverside civic club was even mentioned by those who were intimately involved in it, like Shauna. These repeated instances of abandonment from those they turned to for help led Carl and Maggie to retreat. As Carl put it, "We want to be left alone like everybody else. Let's live our life in peace. Leave us alone, and we'll leave you alone."

In Carthage, Gwen (white homeowner, sixties) also felt unwelcome by the inner circle of the civic league. She had her ideas repeatedly rejected or ignored, despite going to great lengths to research her proposals. One idea she had was to build shelters next to the bus stops so people would not have to stand in the rain:

I researched about putting over the benches near the Metro Station pickups along Vine Street. We even had somebody that would have paid for all the materials to put up the covers, so people didn't have to sit in the rain, or stand in the rain. I researched it. I found out who you had to go to have it approved. I took pictures of different places, Wyoming, Springdale, all different kinds of shelters, and put it in a folder and gave it to somebody in the civic league. And they were afraid that there would be homeless people sleeping in them. But there's lots of people that ride the bus that were standing in the pouring rain. [laughs]

Due to antihomeless fears, Gwen's proposal to benefit bus riders was deemed impractical. The existence of unhoused people is a product of a society that values housing not as a human right but as a mode of wealth accumulation. This accumulation and housing's value depends on differentiation (homeowner/renter) and false scarcity (If everyone has a home, how can it be an investment?). To normalize housing as a commodity, we frame homelessness as a personal failure rather than a societal one. Cities use hostility and relocation as guiding principles when dealing with the unhoused.[26] These punitive responses to social problems create worse conditions overall. For example, making it harder to ride public transportation also has environmental impacts. Who wants to wait for the bus in the rain when you can drive your car and stay dry? Here we see that neglect can also be an active practice that neighborhood associations engage in—neglect not only of resident ideas but also of the needs of those deemed outside the ideal community (e.g., the unhoused).

But Gwen did not allow this response to deter her enthusiasm, at least not immediately. She also attended a civic league meeting to suggest using the then-shuttered school as a community center. "I had gone to the civic meeting, and offered to—why don't we turn that into a recreation center, police substation, council on aging office, community theater—all kinds of things, and they weren't open to that." After being rejected twice, Gwen decided to disengage from the civic league, saying, "Now I just focus on what's going on around me and my people, and my street."

For example, Gwen formed a garden club that produced deep connections with her neighbors:

> I started a garden club about six years ago, seven years ago. And Eve joined the garden club, but—and it's still in existence, although we aren't involved in it anymore. But I just thought that a garden club could be something that people could share, share ideas, share—have a perennial swap every year, and things like that, just community-based. And when we were doing the garden club, I had proposed that we take a bouquet of flowers to shut-ins, or people recovering from surgery, or someone had lost a husband or a wife. So I would cut flowers out of my own yard and take them to these people. And I served as president for two years, and then I decided to step out of it. I had some health issues, I suffered from cancer, so I decided to step out of it, but it's still going strong, so hooray for that.

Eve (white homeowner, eighties) and Gwen had a strong relationship and spoke daily—either over the phone or from their porches. If Eve needed something from the grocery store, Gwen would run out and get it, or she might drive Eve to Whole Foods to shop. As Eve put it, "We're close." They provided each other with companionship and support with small favors, such as errand running and ride-sharing. So while neglected by the civic association, Gwen found her community next door.

Underdevelopment in Cincinnati

Understanding underdevelopment as a relation of racial capitalism means identifying how it facilitates exploitation and dehumanization. From their descriptions, it was clear that Riverside and Carthage residents had a sense of their subordinate status in the Cincinnati neighborhood hierarchy. Many connected this to government officials valuing upper-class residents more than working-class people. At the same time, some intertwined their class analysis with antiblack racism, a theme I expand on in the following chapter. Residents often framed this neighborhood hierarchy in terms of neglect or exclusion from capitalist investment. In other words, Riverside and Carthage were losing at the expense of places like Over-the-Rhine. But underdevelopment is not really about exclusion. It facilitates exploitative inclusion or, as sociologists Louise Seamster and Raphaël Charron-Chénier have called it, predatory inclusion.[27] Historian Keeanga-Yamahtta Taylor also uses the term "predatory inclusion" to describe "how African American homebuyers were granted access to conventional real estate practices and mortgage financing, but on more expensive and comparatively unequal terms."[28] As historian Manning Marable argued in his classic text *How Capitalism Underdeveloped Black America*, "Capitalist development has occurred not in spite of the exclusion of Blacks, but because of the brutal exploitation of Blacks as workers and consumers. Blacks have never been equal partners in the American Social Contract, because the system exists not to develop, but to *underdevelop Black people.*"[29] While neighborhood residents understood Riverside and Carthage's status through neglect, a frame of underdevelopment helps us identify how cities and developers successfully incorporate poor and Black people into capitalist exploitation.

Black homeowners Harry and Miriam's experience exemplified underdevelopment and predatory inclusion. Miriam and Harry (both in their late sixties) were Cincinnati natives who lived in the Mills of Carthage, a new development with its own homeowners' association. Their yellow home with its contrasting cream door immediately charmed me. Inside, their space was pristine, sun-soaked, and smelled of citrus. They explained that most Mills of Carthage residents were transplants to the area. As Harry said, "Just about everybody in these houses come from outside of Carthage. It's not someone in Carthage that's buying the house that's moving in. Part of the thing was the tax abatement to get you in. A lot of people came in. And then they got disappointed. They tried to move. And they couldn't sell the house. That's when the renters came in. The first wave was, I guess, about two or three years. Then a lot of houses started to foreclose. People just didn't meet their obligations. I don't know."

Property tax abatements in the city of Cincinnati are temporary reductions in property tax for new or renovated property for ten to fifteen years. Miriam explained, "You got a fifteen-year tax abatement on the house. And then you got a ten-year tax abatement on the land." These initial tax abatements appealed to the original wave of homebuyers in the Mills; as Harry put it, "That was a nice attraction." While tax reductions helped Harry and Miriam buy their home, it did not protect them from the volatility of the 2008–2010 housing market or their neighbors' mass exodus from the area. After the original homeowners moved into the neighborhood, many of them did not want to stay.

Harry and Miriam did not specify what caused their neighbors to feel disappointed in the area and leave. It is possible that because it was a new subdivision, residents assumed they were buying into a suburban oasis in Cincinnati. Suburban dreams and investments, however, are upheld by policing and exclusion.[30] As discussed in chapter 4, policing in Carthage and Riverside did not function the way that many homeowners desired or expected. To wit, Harry and Miriam said they chose Carthage because of its low crime rate but were disappointed with neighborhood crime. Harry mentioned that air conditioning units were vandalized for copper wiring the previous summer but said it was a citywide problem.[31]

While Miriam and Harry wanted to move, they felt they did not have that option.

MIRIAM: We would like to move. Or I would like to move.
HARRY: We would like to move. We're trapped basically because of the way the price fell in the recession. And we're under that mortgage where you owe more than your house is worth or whatever.
MIRIAM: And then the question would be where could we move that we could live and afford it? But if we could, we would leave.
HARRY: We'd almost have to walk away from this. We wouldn't get any money.

Due to the 2008 recession and its effect on property values, the couple now owed more money on their home than it was worth. Having negative equity in their home certainly weighed on Miriam and Harry. It explained their feelings of resignation when describing the neighborhood and their situation. As Harry put it, they were trapped in their Mills of Carthage house unless they wanted to lose their investment completely. The great recession, which plummeted home values across the country, led to many foreclosures and increased negative home equity. In 2008, according to a report by First American CoreLogic, 22 percent of all mortgages in Ohio were underwater, while in Nevada, which was heavily hit by dropping home values, 48 percent of homeowners were underwater.[32] When large swaths of the population experience these events, we have to evaluate the circumstances that produce them. It cannot be that almost a quarter of Ohioans were personally irresponsible.

When we view the recession through the lens of predatory inclusion and underdevelopment, we can see that Harry and Miriam's story is part of a larger pattern of exploitation at the hands of banks and the financial industry. As Zainab Mehkeri described the recession, "Financial institutions purposefully issued mortgages that were made to default in order to ensure profitability for their collateralized debt obligations (CDOs). By using this fraudulent tactic, financial institutions were able to obtain big, short-term gain at the expense of American homeowners. This was an exploitation of the most disempowered communities of the United States by the most powerful companies in American finance. Despite the financial collapse of 2008, minority communities can still feel the expense of such exploitation today."[33] Even if Harry and Miriam were not subject to predatory loans, they were collateral damage in a broader scheme that led home values to plummet.

Neglected by Landlords

While the previous sections have dealt with the specter of neglect and underdevelopment as a racial capitalist relation, here I focus on the third type of neglect that residents highlighted: neglect by landlords. Unsurprisingly, those who identified neglect by landlords were renters. This narrative of neglect partially recognized a distinct relation of racial capitalism: private property. While property relations are further detailed in chapter 3, I introduce the topic here because renters used the specter of neglect to understand their experiences as tenants. In contrast, in chapter 3 I focus on how residents talked about renters via the specter of "trash talk." Both specters normalize private property, but each approaches it from a different vantage point.

Aisha (Black renter, thirties) talked about living in Eatondale Apartments and the antiblack racism that permeated life in Cincinnati. She told me:

> Black people that are here are strong. We take a lot of stuff every day, even from the building. From the people that own the building—even the fucking people that own the building are semi-racist. They'll rent to you, but they won't respect you, you see what I'm saying. They don't care. They figure we ain't gotta live like this, and I understand that. People have company that come over here and trash the building, but

that still has nothing to do with y'all main wear and tear. What is y'all doing to help this? Y'all don't care that our kids are coming in here without asthma but leaving with asthma, you know what I'm saying. Allergies that they never had—Y'all don't care nothing about none of that.

Aisha perceived the property management company as not caring about its residents because of the (literal) trash around the building. In effect, because the residents did not keep the complex clean, the management company did not either. From Aisha's view, the management company was negligent of its responsibility as landlords, and she and other tenants had to endure a lot of mistreatment. She did not believe a tenant deservingness threshold should exist for landlords to complete their duties.

Aisha's concerns about the health and safety of children in her building were well founded. The US Department of Housing and Urban Development (HUD) reported that current HUD-assisted adults, like Aisha, were almost two times as likely as the general adult population to report currently experiencing asthma.[34] Poorly maintained housing units can trigger asthma in a variety of ways, including "pest infestations, deteriorated asbestos, lead hazards, dampness and mold that trigger asthma, inadequate ventilation and temperature control, and crowded conditions that spread infectious disease." Mold was an issue in Eatondale. When a new owner bought the building in 2018, one resident reported to the local ABC News affiliate that the previous owners, The Community Builders, had come and inspected his unit and determined it was unlivable due to the mold. Six months had passed, and no one had cleaned his unit or relocated him.[35] Rachel (Black renter, twenties) also said that mold was an issue in her bathroom at Eatondale, in addition to a cracked foundation and heat that would not work during the winter.

Camille (Black renter, twenties) and Lindsey (Black renter, thirties) learned similar lessons at Eatondale about property management. While management listened to what residents said, Camille believed the company had no intention of changing its policies and practices to serve tenants better. Lindsey agreed, "I've spoken to the landlord before. And this was a couple of years ago, but it gets tiresome when you keep complaining. All you learn to do is stick to yourself and stay by yourself. And you'll stay safest that way around this area. . . . I guess since we don't pay rent, it gets kind of nonchalant about our feelings. [You don't seem to matter] as much as people that are paying $600. It seems that sometimes those voices tend to be heard a little earlier than others do." Lindsey was one of the only residents to observe a difference in the treatment of those who paid no rent and those that paid a portion of their income for rent; $600 was the upper limit. One area landlord, Nick (white homeowner, thirties), also distinguished between "types" of Section 8 voucher holders by the amount they paid. (We will hear more from Nick in chapter 3.)

Though they lived in separate apartments, Donald (Black renter, mid-forties) and Tasha (Black renter, mid-twenties) spent much of their time together and preferred I interview them as a pair. When I arrived at Tasha's apartment, Donald jump-started our conversation, immediately sharing his experience with public transportation and the difficulties of getting to any job with the poor bus service in Riverside. One theme that came across clearly during our interview was that Donald was working hard to get a foot in the door and build a better life.

After speaking for a few minutes unprompted, Tasha cut in—"Okay, sweetie. Let's see what she has to say. Does she have any questions or—," creating space for me to ask my prepared questions. The exchange was warm and a small window into their dynamic as a couple. Donald acquiesced, adding self-deprecatingly, "'cause she knows I'll just talk." I reassured them that I was interested in whatever they wanted to share and that Donald's comments were great. We then transitioned to my interview guide, but our conversation was sprawling, covering their various experiences at Eatondale Apartments—over the past six years for Tasha and four years for Donald.

Both Cincinnati natives and high school graduates, Tasha lived in Lincoln Heights and Colerain Township before moving to Eatondale; Donald lived all over Cincinnati—most recently in South Cumminsville and the downtown area. His apartment downtown was "one of the rattiest buildings you could find," so he was grateful for the transfer to Eatondale that coincided with his friend vacating the apartment Donald would then move into. Donald and Tasha met at the Eatondale complex.

They had a lot of positive things to say about the apartments at the start of our interview. Eatondale gave them independence and a safer place to live than their previous homes. Donald detailed, "I can say this situation as far as the drugs and the guys it's worse, but the apartment is 100 percent better because of where I came from. . . . I had to call the health department in order to be transferred here. So as far as the apartment, great. It's 100 percent great, and it's a better change because there was never a door locked down there. There was always some violence. The violence here—I just—'okay, that's what's going on.' But as far as the apartment, it's like [*sighs in relief*]." While there were social components of Eatondale that made life difficult, such as the neighbors and interpersonal violence, the infrastructure was better—perhaps because Donald was able to physically separate himself from trouble with locked doors. Tasha, however, said it was the "horriblest place I ever lived. . . . I'm not saying that it's not going on elsewhere also, but definitely, in my experience, this is the worst ever." Donald agreed that there were parts of Eatondale life that were the worst he had seen, but he also grounded his comparison in the dangerous conditions he experienced downtown.

Despite his favorable assessment of his living space, one thing did bother Donald: property management's approach to Eatondale. He explained, "the only time the property management shows up is if there's a murder, if there's a beating where there's news or something like that shows up, then they come. But other than that, it takes two weeks for them to put in a work order. So I do most of the work around my own house." Donald explained that the property management company seemed more interested in collecting rent checks than providing a positive experience for tenants. As he put it, "I think they're more in tune with just the money, and I think more than anything we're just numbers. We are not people." Donald's comment that they are "just numbers" aligns with definitions of tenant and landlord relationships as exploitative. The entire premise of making profits on housing relies on landlords keeping their costs down. While it might seem that poor renters would not be a source of high profits, sociologists Matthew Desmond and Nathan Wilmers found the opposite is true.[36] In their study, landlords in poor neighborhoods made higher profits due to overcharging rent relative to the property's market value. Poor tenants were exploitable because they had nowhere else to turn for housing. They needed somewhere to live and, for various factors (e.g., income, race, eviction records), were excluded from nonpoor neighborhoods.

In the case of Eatondale, Section 8 housing costs cannot exceed "Fair Market Rent." The private management company that ran Eatondale contracted with the Cincinnati Metropolitan Housing Authority to provide subsidized low-income housing to eligible residents with housing vouchers. Eatondale property management did not incur the same risks of nonpayment as other landlords because payment was guaranteed through the Section 8 program via direct subsidy payment.[37] Donald described how he thought the management company seemed to purposefully keep tenants uninformed about opportunities to transfer to other low-income units.[38] Donald and Tasha also described how the management office rushed them to recertify their leases:

TASHA: Knocking on our doors, making us hurry up and sign papers where we can't even read over it real quick or—just hurry up and sign.

DONALD: Yeah, they just tell you where to sign. And when you question it, it's like they'll tell you, "well, you can be evicted if you don't sign this." Yeah, and this is going on with the realty company. They changed names three or four times. They do an assessment of these apartments every single year and not one time have they fixed the windows. Not one time have they changed out the air conditioner—

TASHA: Or turned our heat on because my apartment is really cold in the wintertime.

DONALD: Yeah. The carpets—they never change the carpets. . . . I have cleaned this carpet seven or eight times, rented my own [carpet cleaner], and they asked me where did I get that income. So I had to go and get my mom and fill out a paper stating that she rented me a Rug Doctor and I had to get it certified and take it to the rent office because they called that an income. They make everything you do and every one of your attempts [at improving your situation] an income to where you have to have certification. Or you have to have someone sign for this or sign for that or they ask you "how do you get your hair cut, how do you get your supplies for your personal items." You have to say free store. You have to say churches. You can't say your family's helping you because that's counted as an income and it hurts you because they want rent for it. . . . It's almost like they're digging deep into your skin to find out things that really shouldn't matter. "Do you have a bank account?" If I have a bank account then that means I need to pay more rent. So now you can't get a bank account.

Residents perceived that property management controlled information, both in withholding options for residents and in demanding justifications of expenses from residents. Donald explained how the policies he felt subjected to, such as certifying all payments for services rendered as additional income, limited the agency of beneficiaries of subsidized housing. At the same time, he saw very little recourse for the company's negligence in properly maintaining the apartments.

Donald wanted to work with the property management company to improve Eatondale. He even lobbied the front office for a position to do maintenance work, and they eventually agreed. The terms, however, were not workable for Donald:

> I cleaned the whole property in the summertime by myself because they promised me that they would hire me to do landscaping and cleaning the hallways. Never happened. Never happened. She told me, "well, you're a tenant, and they're gonna charge you rent." I said I don't have a problem if you want to pay me on the regular. They wanted me to get it under the table. And they wanted to pay me $150 a month, which is like, slavery pay. Because I'm not going to clean up over there and do all of those buildings, clean the lots, clean these buildings for $100 under the table. That means you've created a job, but you wanna take your cut out of it and pay me some of it. I've been around the road too many times to know better.

While Donald took the initiative to contact the property management company to see if they could create a mutually beneficial arrangement, he felt the management company proposed exploitative conditions.

This focus on profits over empowering individuals ran deep. As Donald explained, "It's like they're trying to keep you from working. Stay in this one setting and just rot. And if you try and go out and get an education, they want to know how you're getting the money." He continued:

> You can't go to work anywhere more than two days because you can't exceed $200 in [income to maintain your subsidized rent]. If I exceed $200 [in income], they're going to send me a notice for a third of $200 in one month [as a rent payment]. So it's so hard to dig out of a hole because at the moment you exceed $200, your [food] stamps are gone, your rent's going up, you got to pay gas and electric now because you're not going to be on their programs or anything. So you totally get dropped. So it's like the bottom falling out. And it's so hard to climb back out.

In addition to the mental gymnastics of making sure that they did not lose their benefits, residents had to manage the stress of navigating harsh bureaucratic systems. As scholars of poverty governance have illustrated, programs for the poor "support the impoverished in ways designed to make poor communities more manageable and to shepherd the poor into the lower reaches of societal institutions."[39] In other words, these systems are punitive, limiting, and dehumanizing by design.

While in theory it may seem like a reasonable rule to document all services that residents receive, in reality a haircut is not going to make the difference between affording market rent or not. That some view this surveillance practice as logical (rather than ridiculous) helps us see that poverty governance is not just a disciplining arm of the state but an ideological one.[40] Documenting all services as income reinforces an individualist understanding of poverty, whereby consumption patterns or a person's employment status can explain a person's poverty status. The reality is that poverty exists because of policy decisions, not because an individual pays for a haircut or, as I discuss in chapter 4, a smartphone.

Donald said that navigating this bureaucracy created the most stress he had experienced in his whole life, saying, "It makes you gray because you're constantly worrying about if I don't sign my lease, they're going to put me out. You're worried about if I leave is somebody going to mess with me. If I buy too much, if I feel like putting a couch set and a flat-screen TV in my apartment, is somebody going to walk by and see it in the parking lot, and before you know it, everybody knows who went in your house, but nobody's telling." Tasha sought mental health support to deal with the stress of living at Eatondale: "It's been so bad since I've been living down here we probably ain't even giving you to the fullest extent of what's been happening over the years down here. I've been—went to go seek counseling and mental health. I'm on depression medicine." She went on to describe how living at Eatondale affects her mental health, "I'm okay as long as I'm [away] from down here. Then it seems like as soon as I get off the bus and I come right back down here, and then it's like I get depressed all over again." While walking me out of the apartment, Donald concluded, "This place is supposed to be a step up, and it's actually more like a graveyard."

Nevertheless, he envisioned a better way. Donald reimagined subsidized housing as an actual stepping stone to paying market rent, rather than the restrictive model currently in place:

I would be more than happy to sign a paper or a waiver stating that if you give me X amount of years to get my stuff together rent-free and I can get a job and hold a job, it will be easier because there's not that big strain on you that as soon as you get a paycheck, they're contacting you saying you owe X amount of dollars for rent and stuff like that. It's like they don't want to help you. . . . There's no program that says "well, okay, you can live here for a year or two, and you get a job and save your money and then at the end of that, we'll take a look at all of what you've done and see are you still working, are you still— full-time, now you can move or now you can stay if you don't have anything," but we need some choices out here because we don't have any really. It's like nobody has a say-so, and I don't feel like I have a voice.

As sociologist Gargi Bhattacharyya notes, "When people are marginalized or excluded from the workings of capitalist production, they express a desire to leap into, not out of, capitalist relations."[41] More than anyone I spoke with, Donald embodied this desire. He wanted to experience the promises of capitalist living (a life filled with hard work and autonomy). Instead, he experienced the realities of capitalist living (exploitation and dehumanization).

Donald was frustrated by his experience with poverty governance, but he also absorbed its logics. He just wanted a fair shot at a piece of the pie, not to upend the system. In this way, while Donald's social position gives him insight into how exploitation happens, he is still subject to the same capitalist ideologies as everyone else. Our society reinforces these common ways of thinking at every turn. These ideas, like meritocracy and the American Dream, are particularly effective because they connect to our lived reality while obscuring a complete view of how society works. As the saying goes, "It is easier to imagine an end to the world than an end to capitalism." That is not by accident but the work of ideology. In challenging structures of oppression, an essential task is extending the realm of the possible or, as Noam Chomsky put it, "the bounds of thinkable thought."

Capitalist relations of production cannot absorb all populations.[42] Donald is an example of what it is like to be deemed extraneous by an economic system—dispensable and dehumanized. While racial capitalism does not incorporate everyone as a worker, it does imbue all of us with a desire to be one. Within racial capitalism, our status as a worker, as "productive," gives us value. Donald's experience points to what it feels like to absorb a set of goals that will be incredibly difficult to reach because of your social position. He also shows us how racial capitalist policies made it harder for him to reach those goals, not by accident but by design. In the following chapter, I explore how residents' "trash talk" similarly normalized the exploitation and dehumanization of private property relations.

A Different Way

In this chapter, I detailed how residents used the specter of neglect to make sense of their experiences in Cincinnati. They discussed how the city was leaving them behind, and how civic organizations and landlords neglected them. These stories of neglect partially capture the workings of racial capitalism, especially how elite financial interests subsume the needs of poor and working-class people in city-level decisions. But these stories often miss the racist dimensions of these class dynamics and how social institutions play active roles in underdevelopment. While the United States' racist housing policies, including denying access to mortgage loans to predominantly Black areas regardless of their economic standing, are intimately tied to contemporary underdevelopment, we tell simplified stories steeped in antiblack racism. The specter of neglect helped residents of Riverside and Carthage reject the commonsense explanation of downtown's gentrification as an opportunity for profit making that benefits all. While residents identified the inequity in resources across neighborhoods, they did not connect it to underdevelopment.

So entrenched is the relationship between underdevelopment and Blackness that many Americans, especially nonblack Americans, do not question its origin. Urban specters fueled by antiblackness naturalize this relationship, making it "common sense." We then hear (and maybe even say ourselves), "Of course houses are less valued by banks in Black neighborhoods," ignoring how the federal government played an intimate role in creating this reality. Or "Of course new businesses do not want to open in the predominantly Black part of town," eliding the naturalization of both disinvestment and deeply entrenched residential segregation. By focusing on underdevelopment as a relational process of racial capitalism, we can better identify this history and make a connection between the Federal Housing Administration's rating system in the 1930s and why residents associate their poor Black neighbors of Cincinnati with neighborhood decay and pathology.[43]

These are not just historical legacies but also contemporary practices. For example, research by sociologists Junia Howell and Elizabeth Korver-Glenn shows that the home appraisal process itself produces racial inequalities. Modern-day home appraisals rely on the "sales comparison approach," which compares a home to recently sold properties in the same area. Howell and Korver-Glenn argue, "The use of the sales comparison approach has allowed historical racialized appraisals to influence contemporary values and appraisers' racialized assumptions about neighborhoods to drive appraisal methods," meaning that the devaluation of Black homes is not a bug but a feature of the racial appraisal and home-buying process today.[44]

In contrast to most residents I spoke with, Eatondale resident Mark (Black renter, forties) understood how racial capitalism was fueling the simultaneous underdevelopment and revitalization of Cincinnati neighborhoods.

Mark specifically described the funneling of resources to create a new Over-the-Rhine that catered to affluent white residents:

> There's a lot of rich folks in this town. This is one of the most segregated cities in this country. [Put] this place in the south and it wouldn't miss a beat. It's like, okay, we're not lynching you, we ain't riding around on horses in the middle of the night, burning crosses, but you stay here and you stay here. And they tend—white folks tend to, in this town . . . what they want [is] what they get, like Over-the-Rhine. . . . And then all the city's resources goes towards Over-the-Rhine. I don't know how much 50, 60, 70—the streetcar goes around the block. When all these other communities, they need that money. It makes no sense to me. Because some person, 3CDC or whatever it's called, decided we want this area.

Mark's analysis focused on the wealthier white residents' power compared to Black residents in Cincinnati and on how development corporations like 3CDC were working for elite white interests. He tied capitalist accumulation to racism. While he acknowledged that the racism of the contemporary moment was not the same as the terrorism of the Ku Klux Klan's midnight rides during Reconstruction and the Jim Crow era, Cincinnati was still as segregated as any Southern town. Mark's reference to "the South" is particularly meaningful in Cincinnati, where Ohio's "free state" identity is front and center. This is perhaps best captured by the National Underground Railroad Freedom Center, located downtown "just a few steps from the banks of the Ohio River, the great natural barrier that separated the slave states of the South from the free states of the North."[45] While Black people could cross the border from Kentucky into Ohio and no longer be enslaved by whites, they did not experience complete freedom.[46] Like his white counterparts, Mark drew on history to make sense of current neighborhood situations. However, the history he referenced highlighted racism and capitalism as fundamental features of life in the United States rather than a nostalgic view of a class and a race-segregated past.

Mark also explained that it is not just white people who ignore issues of inequality and underdevelopment:

> No one wants to address [this] because they're okay. They're fine. I mean, it could be me, you know. I don't take myself out of that equation. If I'm making $120,000 a year, I'm cool. I mean, I can afford to live down in Over-the-Rhine. . . . Don't get me wrong, it's not just

white folks, it's Black folks too. Being in positions—I'm the mayor of a town, I got a bodyguard, I could get eighty grand a year plus a car allowance or whatever else perks you got, I'm cool. I'm gonna promote this city, and plus, I get to travel the world and the country. He's not gonna stir anything up [*laughs*].

Mark's structural analysis perfectly encapsulates how when we ignore racism *and* capitalism, we misunderstand what is happening in the United States. Racism is not an unfortunate but secondary detail of American life but a central lens through which we can analyze why our neighborhoods look the way they do. At the same time, having a Black mayor (as Cincinnati did from 2006 to 2013) does not mean city leaders will address working and poor people's interests. Elites from all racial groups are incentivized by class interests not to see or discuss class inequality. When we forget the intersection of racism and capitalism, our analysis is incomplete.

The racial differences produced by racist practices and policies, such as redlining and urban renewal, transform economic relations, such as private property, into individual characteristics and choices (e.g., homeowner and renter). Under racial capitalism, we tolerate a lot of human suffering and harm in the name of "progress" and "improvement." Ideologies help facilitate that tolerance. They give us partial pictures of what is happening: the new art scene and great tapas restaurants without the displacement or evictions that came before. They dehumanize previous residents, producing stories about former tenants who "destroyed" their communities without talking about how businesses left after the neighborhood became predominantly Black—itself a product of white flight and urban renewal. These stories about the types of people that used to live there also justify how the city and developers have pushed them out. *They didn't know how to take care of these places. They rioted. They ruined a good thing.* I turn to these stories of ruination in the next chapter.

CHAPTER THREE

Trash Talk and Private Property

Brandon (white resident, nineteen) has lived in Riverside all his life. We met at the local park for our interview. It started to storm heavily about midway through our conversation, but thankfully we were seated under a park shelter. Dressed in a hoodie, Brandon apologized for not choosing a better location. He came across as older than his nineteen years and was more financially stable than most Riverside residents with whom I spoke. Brandon worked as a machinist earning between $55,000 and $59,999 a year. He lived with his parents in a home originally owned by his great grandfather. Proud to be from Riverside, he said that I would likely not hear much bad-mouthing of the neighborhood from its longtime residents:

> I know a lot of the older guys that are still cool, and they want things
> to be good, and they won't talk bad about Riverside because they can
> remember when it was great. And I want—because I don't plan on
> moving out and leaving Riverside. I can't imagine it. . . . I don't want
> to, it's nice. Even though we have the drugs or whatever, the people
> are still good, and it's just a nice community. I wouldn't want to
> live anywhere else, and I don't wanna talk bad about where I live
> because I'm proud of it.

Despite these statements, Brandon lamented many changes in the neighborhood, including a loss of community. He said, "It seems like everyone is, instead of being like one big family, like how it used to be, people are kind of spread apart and worried about themselves, which that's how you got to be." Given the rise in property crime and drug use, he explained that people needed to be more vigilant with one another. Brandon perceived a shift in his neighborhood after the older generation began to pass away. He said, "Those houses went to someone else, and it just—it's bringing in trash, and it's not good. I mean, it's what's killing Riverside really. And I hate, it sucks to say stuff like that." When I asked what makes someone "trash," Brandon quickly responded, "Drugs really. 'Cause, I mean, no one here—everyone lives in here for the same reason. [We're] all working-class people. No one is living high on the hog making a whole lot of money. So, the money thing, that's never a big deal. It's all about how you present yourself. If you don't wanna cut your grass and have kids running around all over the place and be loud and obnoxious late at night and then do drugs on top of that, you're trash. Everyone is going to agree with that. No one wants that in the community." While Brandon initially stated that drugs were the driving force of "trash people" in Riverside, he included behaviors that he found unacceptable, such as being loud at night and not cutting the grass. Echoing research by scholars of the white working class, Brandon used cleanliness "to make judgments, indeed moral pronouncements, about one's intelligence, qualities as a parent, and decency."[1]

Like Federico in chapter 2, Brandon referenced Price Hill to construct white Riversiders as deserving better:

> People are worried about—we don't want to end up like, I don't know, like Price Hill. Like how Price Hill used to be, I mean, this is before my time, but I hear about how Price Hill used to be this great community, it was a bunch of working-class people, and now it's Section 8 housing and, which isn't bad if you need it, but at the same time, people make a lifestyle out of it. . . . if you just drive through Price Hill or Sedamsville for that matter, you can just tell, it's a beat-down community in a way. . . . And then you look at the people who walk around with their pants sagging down and I don't wanna live with this. So, that's what people in Riverside are really worried about. I mean, the drug—that's not helping our cause at all.

Brandon talked about Section 8 housing as having ruined Price Hill because some people treated it as a lifestyle. This is classic antiwelfare rhetoric, reminiscent of the 1980s and 1990s debates about "welfare queens" and "welfare dependency." Brandon's reference to "sagging" pants was also a racially coded term. He described the fear of poor Black people moving into Riverside without explicitly using the word "Black." In Brandon's comments, we see how nonparticipation in productive labor marks one as unfit for inclusion in a civilized neighborhood or "great community."

Agnes (white homeowner, nineties) shared Brandon's devotion to Riverside. After an interview in which she described the loss of businesses and community, and her daughter characterized her new neighbors as "hillbillies," Agnes concluded, "I still like it as well as I did growing up there." When I asked her if that meant the changes she described were not bad, she agreed. Interestingly, Agnes and Brandon's disparate ages demonstrate that loyalty to the neighborhood spanned generations. Dick (white homeowner, fifties) from Carthage also criticized his neighborhood but explained, "I like

Carthage because I grew up there." Arguably, some impression management was going on, with people sharing their concerns but not wanting to present a bad image of their neighborhood or be traitorous to a positive neighborhood identity—particularly not to an outsider like me.

Brandon, Agnes, and Dick were all responding to the territorial stigma of Riverside and Carthage. "Territorial stigmatization" is a term coined by sociologist Loïc Wacquant to capture how "the blemish of place impacts the residents of disparaged districts."[2] While residents identified local challenges, their assessments of their neighborhoods focused on honoring their connection to place. At the same time, we see evidence of what I call "trash talk," which is when residents attempt to relocate their neighborhood's territorial stigma. To wit, residents of Carthage and Riverside blamed their neighborhoods' social ills and demise on "trash," referenced as a catchall for a slew of undesirable traits and behaviors. Sometimes it was about leaving literal trash in public view; other times it was about specific behaviors, such as drug use or "bad" parenting. Meghan—whom we met in chapter 1—used trash talk to chastise her since-relocated neighbors and distinguish them from the typical Riverside resident. When I asked her what she meant when she said they were "somewhat trash," she explained, "Trash, as in, didn't pay the rent, had trash in the house, trash, trash, dogs urinating in the house, and just trash. You know, that kind. Just bad tenants."

While chapter 2 discussed residents' perceptions of neglect and its role in Riverside and Carthage's lower status, neglect was only part of the puzzle. According to residents, this neglect left the door open for undesirables or "trash" to move into Carthage and Riverside. At the same time, residents saw "trash" neighbors as the causes of neighborhood problems. Trash people were both cause and effect of territorial stigma. Rather than have the stigma be intrinsic to their neighborhoods, residents projected it onto bodies from other places, including Over-the-Rhine (OTR), Mexico, and Appalachia. Residents also projected stigma onto people that enacted values and behaviors outside the ideal Riverside or Carthage resident, such as renting or drug use.

With trash talk, residents helped Riverside and Carthage maintain their status as "nice" and "good places" filled with potential—a common refrain among longtime residents in particular. While fighting stigmatization, trash talk helped residents claim ownership over neighborhood space and relabel it as worthy. Trash talk also associated any social ills in Carthage and Riverside with nonowners, those *not* worthy of claiming these spaces. Sometimes these self-appointed neighborhood caretakers were literal owners (of their homes), but not always.

I argue that trash talk in Riverside and Carthage was a rearticulation of settler logics that venerate homeownership, normalize private property relations, and launder Indigenous dispossession. Trash talk also reinforced homeownership as an investment, incentivizing residents to police one another and keep any violators at arm's length. Given the self-interest of protecting one's investment or maintaining a positive self-identity despite neighborhood stigma, trash talk fueled disconnection. In turn, what could help protect residents from neighborhood stigmatization—collective efficacy and action—was impeded by colonial capitalist logics of ownership, and racist and classist devaluation. As such, trash talk bolstered exclusionary practices and boundary maintenance. Importantly, homeowners were not the only ones who participated in trash talk. It was also a local ideology enacted by those who were seemingly subject to its boundaries (e.g., renters, residents of color). In this chapter, I discuss three different ways trash was employed: in reference to OTR and subsidized housing, drugs, and renters. I then zoom out and reframe these discussions of trash by using a racial capitalist lens to help us imagine alternative paths to fighting neighborhood stigma.

Subsidized Housing

Residents from both Riverside and Carthage named subsidized housing and other social programs as causes of neighborhood decline. Renee (white renter, forties) explained Carthage's downturn by commenting on the influx of Black residents whom she presumed to live in subsidized housing, saying, "It's gotten progressively—I mean within the first two years, the neighborhood and actually the—if you ever were to get on the bus, if you'd seen it, in the last three years it's been increasingly becoming more and more Black, which is different. I don't know if it's that they've just all gotten HUD [Housing and Urban Development] housing. I have no idea, but there's a lot more. And yeah, there's drug dealers and things like that. I've had to keep my head down, nose to the ground as if I don't see anything." Her characterization of the neighborhood as "more Black" than it used to be is noteworthy because she later commented on how she did not feel safe in Carthage anymore. Carthage's Black population increased by 163 percent (367 people) between 2000 and 2010. The white population decreased by 14 percent (290 people); yet in 2010, there were still about three times as many white residents in Carthage as Black residents. Renee went on, "The community, in general, you've got a lot of people—I don't know all of what's happened, but

I'd say in the last four years, it's been increasingly worse." So while she did not explicitly draw a connection between Blackness and safety, it was clear that she was not happy about the direction of the neighborhood. For Renee, the changes driving Carthage's transformation were a larger Black population and her increased sense of vulnerability.

Like Brandon, Renee talked about people "living off" benefits. She also disparaged them for participating in informal economies. Renee pointed out how very few people can survive on their government benefits. Yet when people participated in the informal economy to bypass maximum income rules, she framed that as a personal failure. She explained:

> They're living off the money that they get for WIC [federal supplemental nutrition program for Women, Infants, and Children] or food stamps or any of those things, and they're living in the cheapest apartments they can, and then they'll start up an illegal babysitting thing and make money under the table. In the entire region, I'd say there's 60 percent of the people doing that, at least if not more. And then if they have a significant other that they have a child with, they're usually only together like three months. The dads are very rarely involved, and that's the case with almost everyone that I've seen. I think I've met two couples that were married that had kids the whole time.

Renee said she knew all of this information because she walked around the neighborhood for her health. In addition to the dog whistle of food stamps, Renee talked about absentee fathers and unwed parents, two staples of the culture of poverty arguments used to pathologize the Black poor for decades.[3]

While this culture of poverty framework is still popular today, research by sociologists Dave Brady, Ryan Finnigan, and Sabine Hübgen shows that single motherhood is only associated with poverty in the United States because of our social policies. In fact, "if, magically, there were no single mothers in the United States, the poverty rate would still be 14.8 percent. What really differentiates rich democracies is the penalty attached to single motherhood. . . . Our political choices result in families headed by single mothers being 14.3 percent more likely to be poor than other families. Such a severe penalty is unusual. In a majority of rich democracies, single mothers are not more likely to be poor."[4] Again, our policy choices create the shape of poverty in the United States.

Importantly, Renee's comments also speak to another misunderstanding about poverty in this country: that welfare benefits are enough to make someone not poor. They are not. As sociologist Mark Rank argues, "Instead of protecting people from falling into poverty, our social policies are designed to punish people who experience poverty. We do this by making it difficult for people to qualify for safety net programs, and offering only minuscule assistance to those who do. The result is the highest rate of poverty among the wealthy countries."[5]

Returning to residents' perceptions of housing issues, let us turn to Deacon (white renter, thirties). Deacon was staying with his grandmother, who lived in subsidized senior housing. He described Carthage as worse off than when he was younger. He said, "I hate to use the word ghetto, but it seems like it's kind of turned into that." When I asked him what happened to cause that change, he said, "I like to believe Section 8 caused it. I mean truly that and then just the lack of employment. I mean it just brought in just all the bad. It really did." It may be tempting to scoff at Deacon's assertion that Section 8 housing ruined the neighborhood, since he and his grandmother themselves benefit from government-subsidized housing programs. However, to denaturalize this thinking, it is crucial to understand how this is logical for Deacon. The people who Deacon associated with Section 8 housing, or housing vouchers, were not longtime residents like himself and his grandmother, but Black people. Even though he benefited from these programs, he considered himself fundamentally different from those who had ruined the neighborhood, thereby protecting himself against his own critiques. Deacon's remarks echo research on welfare beneficiaries who hold antiwelfare attitudes. They saw themselves as the exception while still buying into classist and racist ideas about welfare recipients' worthiness. In Deacon's case, this rationale also allowed him to locate the problems of Carthage outside of himself and other longtime residents.

EATONDALE APARTMENTS RECEIVED much negative attention from Sedamsville residents, given its location on the Riverside-Sedamsville border. Longtime Sedamsville resident Chelsea (white homeowner, fifties) blamed the undesirable elements of the apartment complex on Over-the-Rhine's redevelopment and the building's shift to low-income housing:

> This apartment building over here when it was first built, it was really, really nice. But through the years . . . when Over-the-Rhine started relocating, that building went up for like HUD or something. So we get a lot of people over there that dealt with people from downtown, and Over-the-Rhine — that was a big drug place. So that's where a lot

of our drugs are coming fr—the people that live down there, you know? They're coming from other neighborhoods now. It's not our people that's in our neighborhood; it's people that's coming from outside the neighborhood and bringing it in. That's the problem.

Chelsea, like Brandon earlier, very clearly articulated the view that the neighborhood's problems were coming from people who were outsiders, not from the community. The reference again to Over-the-Rhine and downtown points to the Blackness of these interlopers without having to name it explicitly. Her reference to HUD is another way to denigrate newcomers as unproductive and poor.

Not everyone agreed that Section 8 was the problem, however. Emily (white homeowner, forties) pushed against her Sedamsville neighbors' correlations between subsidized housing and neighborhood decline:

> If you're a landlord or a tenant and you took care of your property, and we all get along well, there's no problem. But if you're not taking care of your property or if you're doing illegal things, drugs or guns or something like that, that's been the issues of our neighborhood, and I don't necessarily think those are always linked with Section 8. I think that unfortunately people think that they are but I don't necessarily think violence is always a class issue. . . . I don't think the Section 8 part of it is a problem, but if you ask other people in my neighborhood, that apartment complex that I mentioned seems to be the problem area. But again, I don't necessarily think that's because it's Section 8.

For Emily, the issue was actual harm rather than whether or not someone lived in subsidized housing. As she noted, this was a pretty big departure from the "commonsense" explanations her neighbors provided. Seeing landlords as equally at fault challenged ideas about the predictable pathology among renters and those in subsidized housing. Emily's comments offer a small window of opportunity to engage with Eatondale neighbors in a non-adversarial way.

As subjects of building-specific territorial stigma, some Eatondale residents used a type of trash talk that blamed neighborhood problems on resident guests, not on residents themselves. While many residents told me that the building was not as bad as outsiders believed, others located the problems among outsiders. Men who were visiting women tenants were seen as particularly at fault. Cathy (Black renter, forties) said she was not really happy with the neighborhood because "a lot of people like to hang in the parking lot, so I can hear their conversations and music or whatever and cars. It's mainly the people that don't live in the neighborhood, though." Tasha (Black renter, twenties) agreed:

> I think it's the problem with the tenants and the people that the tenants allow in their homes. I know that you're allowed to have guests, but their guests becomes a tenant because they're there longer than thirty days, and they never leave. And they don't have control over their guests or their company, so they destroy our buildings. Or you see that it's secure building; they pick the locks so that it won't lock. They'll trash our buildings. They throw parties in our buildings. They hang out in our buildings. And these are all really grown people that's actually doing this, and they don't even live down here.

Lindsey (Black renter, thirties) also highlighted the gender dynamics of these problem guests. "What the problem is around this area is that girls let guys live with them, who interacts with other women in the complex and then the problems start. So it's about young guys out here with nowhere to live, that's where we have most of the problems in this area that I see, and that's where all the drama and violence tends to come from." Many residents corroborated Lindsey's view that men without places to live attached themselves to women tenants for housing. Many of these men were suspected of selling drugs and providing small gifts to the women in exchange for lodging. Donald (Black renter, forties) claimed, "In the four years that I've been here I've witnessed three, four guys that have never left, but the women have moved out of the apartments. These guys have never moved." While this might just seem like young people having messy personal lives, this dynamic was, arguably, also structured by subsidized housing rules—the most important rule being that anyone with a criminal record is ineligible for Section 8 benefits. Given race, class, and gender disparities in arrests due to policing practices, these policies have an outsized effect on poor Black men.[6] Like all trash talk, this narrative about Eatondale constructed an insider/outsider boundary to combat territorial stigma. At the same time, this construction was based on a narrow view of reality that ignored critical details.

Drugs

White Riverside homeowner Scott (thirties) referred to trash to describe people but specifically used the racist and classist phrase "white trash." People use this phrase to demarcate whites who have not achieved the success associated with middle-class whiteness, defining not just those within the category but also those who place themselves outside of it.[7] Scott complained, "There's just a bunch of white trash around the area. People that don't have jobs. They have a bunch of drug use, and they just go around stealing other people's things. It's not good—people don't care for their homes, their yards look like a mess. Not that we can really talk, but—nobody seems to value their property or take care of it." Interestingly, Scott acknowledged that his yard was not necessarily in pristine condition, but rather than lead to a reassessment of the boundary he constructed, he repeated that the new people did not care about the property, in turn defining himself as someone who did. Scott also explained that these drug users, the source of much crime in Riverside, were people that his wife, a longtime Riverside resident, had known since she was a child. When explaining the cause of the neighborhood's perceived crime problem, he said it was drugs. "They're all just— like the other week, they had people stealing the grates on the side of the streets and probably sell it in the scrapyard to get money for drugs. And the people are, I don't know them personally, but are known in the neighborhood to do that. They're in their mid-thirties and have all been to jail before on multiple drug charges." Scott's comments presented a contrast to residents' insistence that those who were ruining Riverside were outsiders, as we heard from Brandon and Chelsea. Scott indicated that many of those addicted to heroin, and a big target of trash talk, were known by name by longtime Riverside residents.

In Carthage, Deacon discussed coming back home and not knowing what happened to his old friends. He said, "What brought me back was that I'm familiar with the town and some friends were still around, which is—the ones that are still around they're involved with the bad parts, with the bad things in town; the pushing of drugs or the panhandling, stuff of that nature. We're all in our late thirties now, and it's just like what happened?" When I asked what he thought happened, he responded, "Drugs. I mean, it's sad to say. It just destroyed everything."

The way that residents talked about heroin addicts echoed how some discussed Appalachians. While there was undoubtedly more vehemence and vitriol directed at heroin users than at Appalachians, residents also showed tenderness toward both groups. Like many parts of the region, Riverside and Carthage have been plagued by the opioid epidemic and its ramifications. These include public overdoses, property crime, and family reconfigurations due to incarceration, addiction, and death. While it might seem that drug abuse is an equal opportunity experience, the shape of the opioid epidemic and racial capitalism are closely tied. Historian Donna Murch argues, "Racial disparities in health care access, discriminatory prescribing patterns among physicians, and a self-conscious strategy by pharmaceutical companies that cultivated 'legitimate' white consumer markets all contributed to the racial demographics of the opioid crisis."[8] Purdue Pharma's profit-incentive and aggressive marketing strategy is key to the opioid epidemic. Purdue pleaded guilty to federal charges, agreeing to pay over $8 billion, in October 2020. Steven M. D'Antuono, Assistant Director in Charge of the FBI Washington Field Office, said of the settlement, "Purdue, through greed and violation of the law, prioritized money over the health and well-being of patients."[9]

According to Murch, opioids were heavily marketed to suburban and rural markets because white people and their segregated spaces did not conjure racial stereotypes about addiction. In the national imagination, illicit drugs were associated with Black people. So while Richard Nixon was launching the "War on Drugs"—chiefly a war on poor Black and Latinx people—white people were gaining access to opioids via pharmaceutical companies. These differential policies helped create a segregated drug market and the racialized crisis we see today. It also shaped the responses we have seen. As has been well documented, the focus on addiction treatment and noncriminalization for opioid users is a welcome change from the long-standing criminalization of marijuana and crack possession. However, the racial composition of these populations is essential to understanding the shift.

Given the number of Riverside and Carthage residents, particularly white residents, who were affected by opioid addiction, discussion of addicts, even those who committed property crimes, tended to elicit a mix of empathy and frustration. For example, Carthage resident Dick was currently taking care of his granddaughter as part of a negotiation with his daughter:

> I felt bad, I had to take my daughter, who is basically homeless now, she's 25, 'cause she doesn't like to follow the rules. She had my house raided with her and her boyfriend. So I had to eventually put a stop to that, and I said, "but, leave her [his granddaughter] here. There's no reason for her to bounce around." So I talked to the principal [at the local school]. "I'm trying to get custody of her, or shared parent or something. But in the meantime, I'm raising her, so if you have any issues, here's my cell phone. Here's our address. I need to put her into school and on a bus."

As Dick talked about his daughter, he choked up, saying, "I love her, and it breaks my heart, and I'll try not to cry, [*voice breaks*] but it hurts me because I love her so much and I've raised her." Toward the end of the interview, Dick shared that he also had a son who lived in Hyde Park, a wealthy, predominantly white neighborhood on the East Side of Cincinnati. It seemed they were estranged.

Dick was not the only grandparent caring for a grandchild due to opioid addiction. Riverside resident Maggie (white homeowner, fifties) took care of her granddaughter. Her oldest daughter was in a rehabilitation center after time in jail and struggling with opioid addiction. Her granddaughter, Maggie explained, was born at the University of Cincinnati hospital and was in the neonatal unit "for a couple weeks on methadone, and then they released her. She was about three weeks old when I brought her home." Her infant granddaughter still lived with Maggie, and her younger daughter had custody of her oldest daughter's first child.

In Riverside, Marcie (white homeowner, forties) and Collin (white homeowner, forties) also shared the personal toll of the opioid crisis,

> MARCIE: All of the kids that grew up with my kids there are heroin addicts. Almost every one of them.
> COLLIN: It's affected my family, also.
> MARCIE: It's so bad. His mom is raising his nephews.
> COLLIN: It's pretty bad. I fear for my mom being up there, and there's nothing I can do about it. I've actually offered her to move in with us, her and my stepdad and my two nephews to come on.
> MARCIE: And her neighbor is now raising her grandchildren also. That's another child that we knew that we watched grow up who is now a heroin addict, who used to live up here behind us and hung out with the neighbors next to him that we knew were heroin addicts, and now they live in the house next-door to us.
> COLLIN: It's pretty grim.

These stories are not meant to undercut the various ways that residents blamed drugs for neighborhood problems; instead the stories provide context for the complexity of naming drug users as "trash." The term was a pejorative for outsiders. While sometimes people within residents' circles had lost their way, they were not irredeemable trash. The label "trash" was used to police existing insider/outsider boundaries more than it was used to create absolute distinctions. In other words, trash talk was a way of relocating territorial stigma to outsiders, not a hard-line characterization of everyone who participated in a specific behavior (e.g., drug use).

Renters

Antirenter rhetoric in the United States is incredibly normalized, so, unsurprisingly, renters were a focal point of Riverside and Carthage neighborhood complaints. Zach (white homeowner, forties) lived in Carthage and worked in maintenance and remodeling. Like some of his neighbors, he associated renters with filth and literal trash. He suspected that there were a lot of renters nearby because of the amount of trash he saw in the area, saying, "You can tell the houses that people own, like next door—I mean, the people who take care of their yard and they're out there picking up trash."

Patty (white homeowner, seventies) intertwined her trash talk about renters with anti-Latinx racism. She blamed new Latinx renters for deteriorating the cleanliness of the neighborhood, arguing, "I don't want to live in a pigpen." She explained how she approached one of the organizers of a local Latinx organization to provide Spanish-language materials so Latinx residents could "understand some of the rules of being a decent person." She accused the woman she spoke to of getting "very uppity.[10] I believe she's Latino too, and I guess she gets offended that you say anything." She claimed she did not have a problem with Latinx residents who owned their homes, because "they're not filthy." She continued:

> It's the people who rent, and they rent from these slum landlords. And some of them, there's a house a few doors up from me, there must be 25 people in that house. I just can't figure out where they all sleep, and these friends of mine said when they're down in Mexico, they don't have anything, so they're used to it. Where you and I have our bedroom and want to go to our bedroom, they just don't have that, so they're used to it. [11] So they all pile together. That would drive me nuts; I wouldn't be able to do it. But I guess they save on rent and they drive a new car, and they would rather spend it on the car and on the alcohol than a place to live where they can live by themselves. What the difference is between the ones that buy and the ones that don't, I don't know. I haven't figured that out.

Stereotypes about Latinxs "piling together" in homes and spending money on liquor and cars are not new. I found similar characterizations in my research of a multiethnic mixed-income neighborhood in Durham, North Carolina.[12] With these comments, Patty drew on many racial stereotypes, including Latinxs' lack of temperance, ability to delay gratification, and long-term planning. Patty failed to see how many Latinx migrants saved money living with others to send remittances back home. Many such families depend on this money for survival in their home countries due to dire economic situations that the US government is intimately involved in facilitating. While Patty characterized her neighbors as lushes with backward priorities, they sacrificed personal space and comfort for their families and loved ones back home.[13] Her comments also naturalized poverty in Mexico and attached a place-based stigma to Mexican immigrants themselves.

Interestingly, Patty distinguished between renters and owners, saying that not all Latinxs were the problem. Through a racial capitalist lens, we see how a positive framing of Latinx homeowners relies on similar tropes to discussions about immigrants being hard workers and coming to the United States "the right way" (i.e., with documentation). As sociologist Gargi Bhattacharyya argues, "For those hated foreigners moving across the world, only the benefits of their economic contribution can elevate them from the status of insects. Productive work is defence against any slur, an assertion that respect is due."[14] In contrast, white residents did not distinguish between Black homeowners and renters. They associated Black residents almost exclusively with subsidized housing. These narratives normalized the private property relation, a cornerstone of colonial racial capitalism, which I discuss later in the chapter.

In addition to cleanliness issues, residents blamed renters for crime and a sense of insecurity. Helen (white homeowner, sixties) lived in Delhi, a township adjacent to Sedamsville and Riverside. She blamed renters for her new fear of walking around Sedamsville and Riverside:

> The people who own the property, for the most part, are tied to it. And do what they can or whatever. But there's a lot of renters; there's a lot of in and out traffic down there, especially on the side streets. So I got to the point where I was afraid to walk. . . . with the destruction of property and the destruction of community, I think, also came this sense of just—of lawlessness, is what it felt like. Openness. There was garbage on the streets. There was more than just garbage on the streets; there were . . . disgusting things. We were finding dead animals on the streets. I wasn't comfortable anymore.

For Helen, the influx of renters brought a "lawlessness" that made her fearful of the streets she walked on regularly. She also brings up cleanliness—or lack thereof—as an issue, associating trash with destruction.

Douglas (white homeowner, seventies) described transience as an essential difference between those who lived in Riverside when he first moved in and now. He said, "It sounds cruel. I would say when we moved in, there were a lot of the salt of the earth, working class–type people who had worked hard all their lives, maybe were retired, and had kept the neighborhood looking nice and kept their houses nice and so on and so on. And now, it's essentially much more transient people who come and go, and maybe some distant landlord owns the house or in some cases, they got it really dirt cheap, and they don't really take good care of it. So, it's changed in that sense." Here again, rentership is associated with a lack of care and resources to upkeep homes.

How do people know if their neighbors are renters or homeowners? While you could find out through conversations with them or look up public tax information, many residents I spoke with assumed homeownership status based on the behaviors they observed. As such, it can become a self-fulfilling prophecy: if you assume homeowners take care of their properties more than renters, then someone who takes care of their property becomes a homeowner in your mind. And even if you know they are a renter, they become an exception that proves the rule: a "good" renter.

To wit, Hugh (white homeowner, fifties) blamed renters for the "decline" he saw in Carthage. He explained, "There's no government regulation for these renters. They just let these people move in and, unfortunately, some people—they're renters. They don't care whether their lawns look nice or not. They don't care that their house is falling apart, and honestly, there's a lot of slumlords." Pam (white homeowner, sixties) saw renters' lack of investment as related to connection rather than merely aesthetics, saying, "I see potential [in Carthage] because there are a lot of homeowners, and I also see disconnection because there are a lot of renters. And I would say, as a rule, renters don't get invested. That's my gut feeling." Shauna (white homeowner, fifties) had lived in the neighborhood for twenty years and echoed these sentiments, saying, "I believe in owning your home rather than renting because you care more." Importantly, Shauna and her husband bought their current home from her father-in-law, a pathway to ownership not everyone had. Here we see how processes of racial capitalism that historically barred Black people from owning homes in many communities blocked their ability to inherit a home in the present. So the relationship between private property and civic behavior that Hugh, Pam, Shauna, and others saw as "commonsense" excluded Black people without the same access to homeownership as their white neighbors. This is another example of how the past shapes the present. These assumptions about engagement and property ownership are found not just among residents but also in academic research. Brian McCabe's excellent work challenges these ideas. He finds, "Looking broadly across the measures of civic involvement, it turns out that homeowners are not the widely active, deeply engaged citizens we often make them out to be."[15] Rather than homeownership being the key variable that predicted civic engagement, it was length of tenure, specifically living in a community for at least five years.

These dehumanizing beliefs about renters also shaped how landlords approached their interactions with potential tenants. For example, Nick (white homeowner, early thirties), who currently lived in East Price Hill but had lived in Riverside for eight years, was a landlord who owned property and worked for a property management company. In describing his rental screening process, he illuminated how trash talk intersected with racist stereotypes to produce exploitation and dehumanization, of the Black poor in particular.

To start, when looking for new tenants, Nick first posted his property on Craigslist and then fielded phone calls:

I'm pretty good about filtering calls. And most of the times, I let people slit their own throats. You know? If you just talk to someone a moment, especially about, if you've asked more than one or two questions, you can start to paint a picture of that person. And if they're lying, sooner or later, they'll paint themselves in the corner. You know? So I like doing that a lot. If people—I'll say, "Are you under eviction?" They'll say, "No." I'll say, "Have you ever been evicted?" They'll say, "No." I'll say, "Are you currently evicted? Are you currently being evicted?" and they'll stutter. You know what I mean? A lot of people try to use semantics. "He didn't say have I ever—I'm currently." Or, you know, stuff like that. If people become combative at all. If anyone's ever mentioned that they—like, "Oh, we had this one landlord, but I had to sue him," I'll talk to you, but I'm never going to rent anything to you. You know? And the tools Hamilton County provides, especially since this is where I operate out of, Hamilton County, are very powerful. Like I can go to the clerk of courts website, and basically run down; anyone with a valid ID I can check out through the Hamilton County auditor site. I's like, "Okay, you say you lived at 100 River Road," well, I'll go check that out and I'll see if the person you say is the landlord actually owns that property. And then chances are, I can get a phone number from that. So the tools Hamilton County provides me to be able to do what I do are, really makes a lot of aspects of my job extremely simple.

Sociologists Eva Rosen, Philip M. E. Garboden, and Jennifer E. Cossyleon have found similar practices among landlords, arguing that they rely heavily on either algorithms or their guts to screen tenants. Nick's approach used both styles. For example, his reliance on Hamilton County records to notify him of any inconsistencies with prospective tenants' applications fits an algorithmic approach. At the same time, as a small-scale landlord, he made "'gut'-level decisions based on highly subjective—and sometimes illegal—tenant signifiers, including appearance, demeanor, family status, and expressed and ascribed racial identity."[16] For instance, Nick explained that he asked all sorts of questions to get a sense of a tenant's demeanor, both trying to catch them in a falsehood, as well as see if they have had any issues with previous landlords to mark them as "combative."

Nick also did extensive screening in regard to Section 8 housing voucher holders. He said that he did rent to Section 8 holders but was highly cautious:

I'm going to do so, but I'm going to do so under different circumstances and with extreme caution. If you've got Section 8, I want to know why. I want to know how long you've had it. I want to know what type of Section 8 you get. That means what portion do you pay? Stuff like that. If you want to move forward at all, like on our regular property, I'm going to charge a $30 application fee, and I'm going to need you to provide an ID and a month's worth of income. On a Section 8 thing, I'm going to require the same stuff, except I'm going to require an extra $100, and then there's a form called an RTA [Request for Tenancy Agreement]. And it's just this big sheet of paper that I have to fill out—my people have to fill out. That's why I charge more because it's this huge paperwork I have to fill out.

In their research of landlord screening processes, Rosen, Garboden, and Cossyleon found that many landlords approached voucher holders with caution, while others preferred Section 8 recipients. Given his focus on low-income housing, Nick likely could not afford to exclude Section 8 voucher holders, so he used criteria to distinguish between them to minimize his sense of risk, drawing on a "deserving/undeserving" dichotomy in the process.

Nick continued to explain his process, describing his annoyance with the multiple benefits to which many of his prospective tenants had access. It helped him justify his decision to charge them more than market-rate renters to process their applications:

> Then I have to send it [the application] in, and then I have to wait. And this whole time, I can't show the apartment to anyone else. So basically, I have locked it up in there. So what I started doing with these Section 8 people is for every week I have to wait, I charge them 100 bucks. And they don't like that at all. Because they're used to just, "oh, well, this is free, this is free." You have to get—I'll check their income. They'll be getting free housing, they'll be getting free SSI [Supplemental Social Security for disability], they'll be getting free food stamps, and many of them will be on this program that they call PIP [Percentage of Income Payment Plan], to where you can use all of the electric you want, and you only pay $35 a month. So when you start charging these people money that just regular people have to pay—like if I was just having a conversation with a regular guy, and I was like, "Well you know, we're going to charge you 100 bucks to hold the place for the week or two you need us to hold it," "no big deal, that's the charge, man." We're keeping it open for you. It's not like we're showing it to anybody else. We're holding it open for you. They agree, they understand. They see it from the owner's perspective, and they understand, "hey, we're kind of doing you a favor even, in that we're willing to hold something for you at less than cost to us." You know? And the Section 8 person that doesn't take to that well in the conversation, when I have that conversation with them about how it's going to be 100 bucks up front, then 100 bucks per week, as long as it takes, they quickly are turned off and will go to a landlord that has less scruples. So I will do it if they can meet all those terms and they seem happy and approachable.

While Nick said that market-rate renters could see it from the owner's perspective, he also was not charging them $100 per week. This higher rate was reserved for Section 8 voucher holders. He interpreted any incredulity about the charge as a sign of unrealistic expectations and sense of entitlement on the side of Section 8 applicants. However, it could very well be that these applicants were frustrated that their charge was three times as high as that for market renters. Given Nick's belief that these applicants were already getting so much else for free, including housing, electricity, and food, he wanted to ensure that they "paid their way" for the application. While, as Nick alluded, it may seem like meritocracy at work, the exorbitant overcharge was arguably exploitative and punitive. At the same time, when trying to distinguish between a homogeneous pool of tenants whereby traditional measures, such as voucher status, were not helpful in categorizing "good or bad" tenants, Nick used someone's willingness to pay $100 as an informal check for poor tenants specifically.[17] As Nick argued, it was not your ability to pay that made you a good tenant, but your willingness to pay without complaint. He was looking for compliance.

Finally, Nick addressed how racism factored into his decision-making as a landlord:

> But on the same end, I'm not going to set myself up—and being a white guy, maybe reverse racism, is something that it doesn't really affect me, but I definitely have been on Section 8 things with Black people, and they have just been so outwardly racist towards me, in a way that—one of my favorite ones—and I've had this happen with two or three people lately. I think it's because of that Ferguson thing or whatever. I use—like I speak, "We'll shoot for this. Or let's gun for that," or something like this, and I had a couple of people be like, "No, no, no, my hands are up. We don't shoot here, motherfucker." I'm just like, "I'm talking about the time, lady." You know? And I'll speak to people, and I'll be like, "Look, I don't think you would qualify," and they will instantly be like, "Oh because I'm Black?" You know? And I'll be like, "You could be the whitest guy in the world. If you've got three felonies and a pit bull, you don't qualify, Jack." "Well, that's racist." You know? So I do hear a lot of that stuff. I don't know if it's because I have an ear for it—because I listen for it because I don't want to get tangled up in it at all. And if I think that you're going to be someone who's going to be litigious or gonna—because I maintain a license. You know, I maintain a license, and if someone goes to the board and is like, "Oh, this girl was racist to me." This guy—because I have people that work for me too. So I've just trained them really well, we don't want any problems. If people are looking at houses, we only want to work with the people that want to buy. We've got a lot of just lookie-loos, and that's what Section 8 people are a lot, lookie-loos. They think that—because you know, appointments are free. They don't cost them anything. So they'll set a bunch of appointments. They'll generally

cancel those appointments. Or they'll come in, and they'll have unrealistic expectations about something. Like "why is this red on that outlet right there? Are you guys going to fix that?" "No." "Well, why not? I bet"—you know? At that point, I just—I clam up, I nod politely, and show them the door.

While it is not possible for me to verify whether potential tenants told Nick, "We don't shoot here, motherfucker," I think it is more important for our purposes to understand how Nick positioned himself in these comments— as a reasonable guy who Black Section 8 recipients falsely accused of racism. Nick's inclusion of pit bulls alongside felony charges as reasons not to rent to someone point to the ways that landlords make decisions that disproportionately affect Black people without mentioning race.[18] For example, scholar Harlan Weaver has analyzed the connection between pit bulls and Black men in the popular imagination, as well as how advocates have challenged these associations. Nick also discussed how he was sensitive to accusations of racism and had trained his staff to disengage with Black people who seemed litigious or made too many demands regarding a unit. As such, Nick asserted that any claims of racism against him would be unfounded.

At the core of Nick's remarks is an incentive to make money as a landlord. Nick weaved in stories about deservingness and risk to justify his screening policies. He named a variety of differentiation processes, including background checks, home visits, phone conversations, and additional fees, to screen between "good" and "bad" tenants. All of these processes are based on an understanding of homeownership as an investment. Nick's decision-making normalized that housing is something from which he could and should make a profit. His business acumen disguised what was, at its core, an exploitative relationship. His decision to overcharge Section 8 voucher holders in their applications is a perfect example of exploitation. In the following section, I discuss the racial capitalist relations and logics that trash talk reinforced.

Thinking Relationally

While the specter of trash talk helped obscure underdevelopment, as discussed in chapter 2, it also normalized private property and housing as an investment. To say that private property (and by extension, land ownership) is a process of racial capitalism means that it exploits, dispossesses, and dehumanizes by definition. As geographers Malini Ranganathan and Anne

Bonds argue, "This commonsense notion of property as a 'thing' obscures the web of social and power relations that must be performed to produce property as legitimate. Modern property, then, is not only an essential component of capitalist political economy but is also a shifting social formation animated by contextual assemblages of race, class, ethnicity, gender, and citizenship. Theorized this way, property is far from fixed, but rather is an unfolding and continuously enacted set of relations that necessitates and in turn shapes the hierarchical valuation of bodies and places."[19] Rather than consider property a taken-for-granted "thing," I approach property as a relation of racial capitalism that constructs and entrenches race and class inequalities.

Notably, a critical racial capitalist lens must also be one that takes settler colonialism seriously. As Susan Koshy, Lisa Marie Cacho, Jodi A. Byrd, and Brian Jordan Jefferson argue, "Indigenous dispossession is not the precondition for racial capitalism to emerge but always has been part of its very structure."[20] For example, Cincinnati was the site of violent conflict between settlers and sovereign native nations, serving as an early outpost for the western expansion of the colonial United States. The dispossession of native lands and sovereignty, and the racialization and dehumanization of Indigenous communities, fueled the beginnings of Cincinnati as we know it today. But Indigenous dispossession is not only historical; it is a daily act. To wit, the Greater Cincinnati Native American Coalition (GCNAC) is currently working on various projects both to secure resources for impoverished members of their communities and to decolonize occupied land.[21]

Additionally, we must understand settler colonial dispossession as inclusive of the transformation of land into property.[22] In short, private property relations are a colonial racial capitalist construction.[23] As Rob Nichols argues, "Unlike ordinary cases of theft, dispossession created an object in the very act of appropriating it: making and taking were fused."[24] A critical interrogation of private property relations allows us to rethink capitalist conceptualizations of land, ownership, and community relations. For Riverside and Carthage residents, private property was about not just homeownership but also the logics surrounding who could lay claim to a neighborhood. The focus on potential—a reference to an imagined past or future—was about land use, property maintenance, and neighborhood ownership in Riverside and Carthage. These are historical associations, as references to potential were also at the center of land dispossession by settlers.[25] Contemporarily, any squandered potential was attached to "trash" people who were not of the neighborhood. The "true" residents of a community believed in it, as

Brandon argued. Any sort of stigma applied to those who did not truly "belong." But belonging was not available to everyone. Interestingly, it was not only homeowners who engaged in this kind of talk but also renters, as residents of Eatondale used trash talk to distinguish themselves from unhoused guests.

The valuing of homeowners over renters and privileging homeowner rights over all other claims to space also helped elide and normalize racial capitalist relations of property. In *Unsettling the City*, geographer Nicholas Blomley examines the property ownership model that "shapes understandings of the possibilities of social life, the ethics of human relations, and the ordering of economic life."[26] He argues, "Treating property as a spatialized thing, rather than a bundle of relationships, locates its central relationship as that between the owner and the thing owned. The effect is to suppress our understanding of the undeniable and often differential relations between the owner and other people."[27] Trash talk naturalized private property, dispossession, and their accompanying exclusions under racial capitalism, divorcing them from their settler colonial roots and venerating them as ultimate goods.

What happens when we apply a relational analysis to ownership and private property? We begin to see urban dynamics in new ways. For example, a relational analysis helps us understand how tenants and landlords are definitionally bound together and that exploitation is the foundation of their relationship. Borrowing Erik Olin Wright's definition of exploitation, we see how the tenant-landlord relationship meets the three criteria he uses to define the term. First, he names the inverse interdependent welfare principle, whereby "the material welfare of exploiters causally depends on the material deprivations of the exploited." For example, landlords' desire to make a profit often leads them to deprive tenants of repairs that cost money. While landlords are legally obligated to make repairs, the experience of Riverside and Carthage tenants shows how the reality often falls short of the ideal. Second is the exclusion principle: "the causal relation that generates principle (i) involves asymmetrical exclusion of the exploited from access to and control over certain important productive resources." As Wright himself notes, property rights often enforce this principle. That means tenants are categorically excluded from gaining access to the property that landlords own due to state-granted rights. Tenants are also excluded from access to any wealth that the property they live in accrues due to exclusion from property rights. Third is the appropriation principle: "the causal mechanism which translates (ii) exclusion into (i) differential welfare involves the appropriation of the fruits of labor of the exploited by those who control the relevant productive resources."[28] In their study of rental markets, sociologists Matthew Desmond and Nathan Wilmers found that landlords "extract higher profits from housing units" in poor neighborhoods, overcharging their tenants compared to market rents. Desmond and Wilmers frame this as an exploitative dynamic in which landlords extract surplus value from poor renters, the key to the appropriation principle.

In addition, applying a relational analysis allows us to flip the standard narrative on the tenant-landlord relationship. It denaturalizes tenants as problems and brings landlords into the analytical fold. Interestingly, residents' views of landlords were one of the paradoxes of the data. While some landlords or "slumlords" (as a few residents called them) were the subject of resident derision, renters were more likely to be targeted as the locus of neighborhood decline. Those landlords that were absentee or owned multiple "problem" dwellings, such as John Klosterman in Sedamsville, were the most likely to be framed as problems.[29] Why did landlords mostly escape the ire of residents who rail against rental properties? Patty's comments, in particular, were illuminating in this respect:

> I said to him [the man that owns the house behind me], "Don't you care who you rent to?" He said, "I live in Wyoming [a city just north of Carthage]. I don't have to look at it." I thought that was a brilliant answer. So the city did get after him and make him fix his garage, but as far as people he rents to, he wants as much money as he can get for every apartment that is rented, and so does every other landlord that rents along there. I don't think they care who they rent to. How many times can you rent something and then have to redo the whole place because it's so tore up? How can you possibly make money doing that? But they must be able to. And they charge them whatever they want because this is America, and they can charge what they want.
> I can't remember what his first name is. Is it [landlord] Rich Jaffey? I told him about the people across the street. Well, this owner professed to be such a Christian, $500 a person and no bathroom facilities, no running water? I guess they were responsible for paying the water, and they didn't. They just rip the Latino people off, and the Latino people are used to living in a community in Mexico and places like that where that's what they do. They just trash everything.

While Patty's discussed the landlords, she also shared racist sentiments about Latinx renters. Her issue with landlords was that they did not protect her and

Carthage from the misbehavior of Latinx residents. While Patty acknowledged that landlord Rich Jaffey was acting in poor faith in the neighborhood, she blamed Latinx residents for accepting such treatment.

Patty normalized the dehumanization of Latinx people who live in poverty and that, in effect, she did not blame landlords for taking advantage of the renters' low expectations. While she chastised the landlord, she also acquiesced that who could blame him for wanting to make a buck on lesser people? As she said, "This is America, and they can charge what they want." What is vital to identify are the commonsense understandings that allowed Patty to make this argument. The specter of "trash" normalized private property ownership and transformed a class relation into a values-based one. *Who has access to wealth and why?* becomes *Who is fit to take care of a home?* or *Who is capable of the delayed gratification of saving for a home?* While these may seem like outlier beliefs, even social science research is guilty of laundering these class relations into individual-level characteristics. And we see similar conversations around the lower homeownership rates among millennials in popular media. As some have pointed out, it is not the avocado toast keeping many millennials from buying a home, but skyrocketing home prices, stagnant wages, and crushing student debt.[30]

Finally, a relational analysis allows us to understand owner-renter relationships rather than center on the experiences of homeowners as ideal residents. Brian McCabe's critique of the ideology of homeownership finds that while homeowners may engage in more civic activities, such as attending neighborhood meetings, their participation is primarily fueled by economic interest rather than attachment to community or a greater sense of community responsibility, as civic engagement is often framed.[31] Homeowners' financial investments lead to exclusionary practices that center the interests of property owners over others, under the guise of "civic engagement." Homeownership is so entrenched as an ultimate good in the United States that we fail to see how it inhibits our communities from flourishing. Civic associations do not always produce the community that residents are hoping for, and homeownership can incentivize disconnection to "protect one's investment." Civic engagement, therefore, is not necessarily a universal good, but it is a tool that neighborhood associations often use to reinforce homeowner power. Gwen's experience with the rejected rain shelters (discussed in chapter 2) is a great example of this dynamic. That is not to say civic engagement is not a good or worthy practice, only that it can be used to reinforce existing power as much as to upend it. Too often, it is only the former.

Trash Talk's Consequences

In this chapter, I reviewed how residents talked about neighborhood "trash." In particular, I showed how residents used "trash talk" to blame subsidized housing, drugs, and renters for the territorial stigmatization of Riverside and Carthage. I also explained how this specter normalized and reinforced private property as a racial capitalist (and settler colonialist) relation. While it may seem like these specters only matter for those who use them, that is not the case. We often do not think about how the stories that justify gentrification, for example, haunt the people used as scapegoats. These stories have consequences—not just in the gentrifying neighborhoods but also for the rest of the city.

I found that longtime Riverside and Carthage residents pinpointed former OTR and downtown residents as the source of their neighborhoods' problems. The fact is, however, very few residents I spoke with were from these stigmatized locations. This was especially true of Black residents. They were from Avondale, Walnut Hills, or other Cincinnati neighborhoods. Nevertheless, the territorial stigmatization of OTR and downtown were part of the language of antiblackness in Cincinnati. These caricatures of Black people as the cause of the downfall of once-great OTR and Price Hill followed poor Black people around the city. But even if every Black resident in Carthage and Riverside had previously lived in OTR, this specter would still tell an inaccurate story. When we understand the political-economic processes at play, such as disinvestment and redlining, we see it was not a lack of care from poor people that led to the pregentrification state of OTR. It was a lack of care from the city for poor people—and poor Black people specifically.

Distinctions of "trash people" may seem merely discursive, but they are meant to capture material differences. As we have seen in this chapter, "trash" is often a class and race signifier that launders structural relations of racial capitalism, such as poverty and racial subordination, and expresses them as individual value differences. These perceptions of differences (or similarities) then lead to practices of exclusion (or inclusion). In turn, these practices reinforce the structural relations undergirding the trash specter, such as underdevelopment and private poverty. Many residents, especially longtime white homeowners, used these distinctions because their neighborhoods were more stigmatized, and they were feeling increasingly precarious.

To be sure, the financial position of the working class has changed over the last few decades. According to a report from the Economic Policy Institute, while worker productivity increased 74.4 percent between 1973 and

2013, worker compensation has risen only 9.2 percent. When we look at low-wage workers specifically, their compensation has actually *decreased* over this period by 5 percent. These changes are driven by a decline in union membership, which lead to less compensation for those in and outside unions, and increased compensation for CEOs and other executives.[32]

Increased precarity in the workplace could certainly incentivize residents to be particularly attuned to signs of economic precarity at home. Perhaps unsurprisingly, then, homeownership was critical to how residents understood "trash" in their neighborhoods. They wanted to protect the chief way that most people in the United States save and generate wealth. But while homeownership has been sold as a universal engine for social mobility, for the working class and people of color there are no guarantees, as we saw at the end of chapter 2 with Harry and Miriam's story. Nevertheless, trash people were seen as a threat to the individual asset of housing (normalizing it as a private resource in the process), and to residents' financial security and stability. Structural shifts in work and housing were viewed as individual-level problems. This led to not only trash talk but also active exclusion of those people deemed trash, particularly poor Black residents.

For example, Aisha (Black renter, thirties) recounted what it felt like to be treated like trash when she went to the grocery store in neighboring Delhi Township:

> I could imagine staying in the area as long as they accept us as people, but they don't consider us to be equals. They look at us like we're rats or pieces of trash or something. And it's to the point where, I think that's hateful, where you can go in there and touch something, and if they see you touch it, it's no longer of good use to them. It feel like you're AIDS, like you're infectious or something, like if they touch something in my view, they're gonna catch something. I've seen it, and it's not just the Delhi Kroger's. I've seen it even in the Price Hill Kroger's. I've seen it in other Krogers. I've seen it in—oh! Remke Market, don't get me started. Oh my god. When you go in there—and it ain't very many workers in there. But you just see the way they look at some Black people when you go in there.

Aisha reported that grocery store workers ostracized Black customers through stares. She continued, "You walk in Kroger's, they all staring at you, and it's like crazy. And I be like, 'What the fuck [*small laugh*] are you looking at?' Excuse my language, because I hate that. I'm human just like you. You don't have to stare at me. If there's something you want to say, speak, 'hello, how are you?' So, Delhi is very racist."

Aisha's comments are a good reminder that distinguishing someone as trash is not just a belief but a dehumanization practice that scaffolds racial capitalist relations. For example, Aisha and her Eatondale neighbor Alicia (Black renter, twenties) said they were harassed and stopped en route to the Delhi Kroger by police. Alicia said, "Every time I go up there, I get pulled over." Aisha agreed, saying that targeted police harassment was common in Delhi: "People go up to Delhi in a car, look, and be Black. It ain't necessarily that you gotta [not] have your seat belt on or, you know what I'm saying? They will just pull you over just because of you being Black. Automatically assume you're driving illegally whether it be drugs or that you don't have no license." For Aisha, police harassment aligned with her experiences of Delhi as racist and her treatment as "less than." Her experience paralleled that of many Black Cincinnatians. Research by Eye on Ohio's Open Policing Project found that Black people were stopped at a 58 percent higher rate than white people between 2009 and 2017. This was partly explained by the overpolicing of predominantly Black areas, where "police made 120% more total stops per resident."[33] Disproportionate traffic stops have long been a topic of discussion in Cincinnati, at least since the murder of Timothy Thomas in 2001. In the following chapter, I focus on policing as a racial capitalist relation that structures life in Riverside and Carthage, scaffolded by the same racist and classist dehumanization on which trash talk is based.

CHAPTER FOUR

Security and Policing

Policing is a power relation that creates racist, classist, and gendered harms (among others). I identify it as a racial capitalist relation that facilitates exploitation and dehumanization. To say policing is a relation highlights that it connects groups of actors who have differing levels of power.[1] This relational lens allows us to view policing as more than a stand-alone occupation or organization. We can understand how police harm of civilians, especially poor and Black civilians, is not an aberration but is baked into the policing relation. Policing is also tied to other relations of racial capitalism. As scholars David Correia and Tyler Wall argue, "The *nature* of police is to establish the necessary conditions and relations for the accumulation of capital, as order."[2] In other words, policing is a relation that produces exploitation and dehumanization in its normal functioning and facilitates the exploitative and dehumanizing work of other racial capitalist relations.

In this chapter, I present stories from many Carthage and Riverside residents who witnessed firsthand the failures of policing as the sole source of harm reduction and community justice. They felt exasperated because they perceived a disconnect between how police should work and how they do work. But as policing scholars have found, the public profoundly misunderstands police work in the United States. Most of it is clerical, with police solving few crimes—particularly felonies, such as burglary, murder, or rape. Police are also ineffective at preventing crime, as heartbreakingly experienced by Carthage resident Lourdes, from whom we will hear later. I will demonstrate, as many activists have argued, the falsity of the idea that the police are the "thin blue line" protecting society from absolute chaos. They are generally unsuccessful at stopping crimes from happening, as the experiences of poor and working-class residents in Carthage and Riverside illustrate. In short, "surveillance, policing, criminalization, incarceration, and punishment do not bring us closer to genuine safety because they neither prevent nor interrupt violence. They *are* forms of violence."[3] As scholars and activists have noted, this misunderstanding of how policing functions is patterned and intentional. In this chapter, the experiences of Carthage and Riverside residents present a challenge to this misreading.

Central to my analysis and a revisioning of what policing accomplishes is a distinction between safety and security. I argue that security is an urban specter or ideology that obscures and justifies the exploitative and dehumanizing work of the policing relation. As Mariame Kaba defines it, "Security is a function of the weaponized state that is using guns, weapons, fear and other things to 'make us secure.' . . . All the horrible things are supposed to be kept at bay by these tools, even though we know that horrible things continue to happen all the time with these things in place—and that these very tools and the corresponding institutions are reproducing the violence and horror they are supposed to contain."[4] When we understand how policing is deeply ineffective at keeping everyone safe, we can begin to reimagine the role of police in US society. I argue it is difficult to justify large police budgets and police impunity when we reorient ourselves toward safety and away from security. We begin with Colette's story.

COLETTE (BLACK OWNER, FORTIES) has lived in Sedamsville—adjacent to Riverside—for the past six years. She was a self-described "thugged out nerd" back in school while working as a state-tested nursing assistant (STNA), a job she held for over two decades. Since going part-time, Colette made between $15,000 and $19,999 a year. She purchased her home through Habitat for Humanity and considered herself lower working class. Echoing Riverside residents Carl and Maggie (white homeowners in their fifties), Colette stated that her life would be great if she could relocate her home to another neighborhood. Also, as with Carl and Maggie, her reasons for wanting to relocate were frustrating experiences in her community that endangered her sense of safety. Her most significant issues were noise, specifically loud music and dogs barking next door. However, it was the confrontations with neighbors, advocates, and local police about these issues that exasperated her.

Colette explained that things rapidly deteriorated when she asked her neighbor to turn his music down:

I actually ended up calling the police because he stuck his chest out on one occasion. And on the sidewalk, which is public, walked as if he was going to approach my property, but he never did. That let me know he was basically a punk. I'm not gonna let nobody bully me or run me from my home. Long story short, when I called the police several times, they don't do nothing. They do nothing. They candy-coat the situation. If there's no real threat—I basically ended up telling them one time, "well, are you gonna wait 'til the man comes in my house and shoots me? He says he has firearms; he is crazy, in my opinion. He's threatening, for fact." They did nothing.

In one instance, she contacted the police, who had previously informed her that they had a sound meter that could measure loud noises to see if residents violated "maximum permissible sound levels" as indicated in the City of Cincinnati Code of Ordinances. When the police arrived, she became incredulous at what she perceived as their flippant response. She described how the officers tried to get her to change her sleep routine to accommodate her neighbor's barking dog: "Officer Barry said, 'Ms. Johnson, do you have a basement?' And I said, 'are you suggesting that I sleep in my basement—that I don't have—to appease a damn dog?' [He responded,] 'Well, a few nights a week so you can get good rest.' To me, that was the lowest level of respect that you could give to anybody. I might as well have been the dog. I don't have to say that these two officers were Caucasians, but they were." As we will see, Colette's reaction to this interaction was not just about this moment but also about the persistent and consistent disregard with which she felt police and neighbors treated her. Rather than help her, everyone she interacted with— primarily white people—treated her like she was the problem.

Colette continued:

> At that time, I said, "listen, you guys are not here to solve any situation, I need you to leave." [The other officer,] Officer Smith is a heavier man. He stood in my screen—inside of my door. The big [front] door was open; the screen door was closed. He was on the inside of my house with his arms crossed. And I said, "you don't pay my mortgage, you don't pay my bill, if I asked you to leave, you are to leave." He would not leave. I called 911 on the freaking police. And I told the police when I called 911, I said, "My name is Ms. Johnson. I have two officers, Smith and Barry, in my home. I'm asking them to leave. They won't leave. I don't want to make the six o'clock news: 'Black woman dead in her home and no witnesses.' They have guns, and they are intimidating. I would like for them to leave." That's when they left out the door, and then I hung up with the police. It's ridiculous! The way they treat you. It really is. I shouldn't have to—if I say, "get out my house." That's what the hell I mean. That's what you should do. This is my house. You ain't here to solve shit. You here to tell me to sleep in the basement because the dog won't shut up. You ain't here to tell the owner, "respect your neighbor and shut your dog up sometimes. Don't

bring your dog out after nine o'clock or ten o'clock, or eleven o'clock. Take your dog for a walk." I'm just pretty much disgusted.

Colette eventually filed a protective order against her neighbor at the suggestion of one of the many officers who came to her house after repeated calls. It was the only "decent" interaction with a police officer she had; she noted it was with a Black police officer. She ultimately decided to get the protective order "partly because I was afraid of what he [the neighbor] might do, but I went down there also—a bit part of it was because I was afraid of what I might do to him. I won't lie." Even as Colette followed the advice of local police, she said she continued to be mistreated and disrespected—this time by the judge handling her protective order request:

> The judge or magistrate or whoever, he said, "well, I think it's a little disrespect going back and forth between the two of you." Which was a lie. I felt that the magistrate was biased because he said to [my neighbor] "So, sir, how long have you lived in the neighborhood?" and he said over twenty years. He ends up—the judge says, "So you've seen a lot come and go." I don't give a damn what he's seen come and go. That's not the concern. The concern is this man needs to have neighbor etiquette. He needs to not throw out racial slurs or be threatening, or drive recklessly. I felt like I wasn't gonna get no justice there.

Colette's sense of the courtroom dynamic matches observations by sociologist Nicole Gonzalez Van Cleve. In her award-winning book *Crook County*, Van Cleve found that the courtroom was a site of racial degradation ceremonies. Black and Latinx people were dehumanized and chastised regardless of their status as defendants, victims, or support persons. In contrast, court officials treated white defendants as innocent until proven guilty, worthy of consideration and rehabilitation.[5] So while Colette was the one seeking a protective order, she was framed as equally to blame for her white male neighbor's actions. The judge drew on the neighbor's longtime residence in Sedamsville to frame his actions against Colette, putting Colette's claims to the neighborhood at least partially into question due to her shorter tenure.

It was not just these conflicts with the police and neighbors that frustrated Colette, but also her perceptions of how outsiders interacted with her slice of Sedamsville. She elaborated, "The other day I got home from school, and I stopped at the community center. There's a lady who pulls up, pops her trunk, and feeds the damn [feral] cats out of her trunk, gets in her car, and drives away. I want to tell her so bad, 'take these cats home with you. Don't come over here, and they're reproducing by the millions, and then you go home, and your street is probably damn cat free.' I don't—don't do that in somebody else's neighborhood." But even as she was frustrated, she had yet to approach the cat feeder, saying, "I haven't been able to think about how to do it nicely, so I've never confronted this lady." Colette was conscious of how other people experienced her requests, and she tried to navigate these difficulties with tact.

Unfortunately, one of these cats had recently ripped a hole in her screen door, which made her more frustrated. Her house was only five years old, she told me. "It's not raggedy." As I understood, her home was her sanctuary from what she perceived as an increasingly hostile surrounding. This could explain why she wanted Officers Barry and Smith out when she felt they were not there to help her. While a ripped screen door may seem like a minor problem, it piled on top of repeated instances of perceived disrespect and mistreatment. Nevertheless, as Colette said, she was not one to be bullied or run from her house.

While she could not figure out the right way to approach the cat-feeding visitor, she reached out to the American Society for the Prevention of Cruelty to Animals (ASPCA) for help. Unfortunately, they did not give her the support she sought. Colette reported that they proposed she round up all the cats, bring them in her car, have them neutered or spayed, and then set them free again. She explained, "I am an asthmatic who is allergic of pet dander, don't like cats. I'm not putting these cats in my car! There should be a different resolution." After this suggestion, Colette said the conversation with the ASPCA representative devolved; he told her, "Ma'am, I wish you many cats." She was furious that he would be so disrespectful as she was calling for help. The repetition of this type of interaction—where she reached out for support and was not just refused but disrespected—led Colette to feel not only alone but also wary of others. "A lot of times I fight back tears because I'm tired of crying about this shit. . . . And I don't want to give them that much room in my life or rental space in my head or whatever they call it. I'm sick of it, and I feel like I'm just up against a wall, and nothing's ever gonna be done. Nothing been done so far so."

Asking for help requires vulnerability; it requires the person making the request to acknowledge a need for someone else. It also requires some trust. Colette's vulnerability and expressed needs were repeatedly met with disbelief—of her reality, vulnerability, and trustworthiness. Colette was read as "structurally incompetent," as sociologist and McArthur Fellow Tressie McMillan Cottom has written about in her award-winning book *Thick: And*

Other Essays. When "black women are strong in service of themselves, that same strength, wisdom, and wit become evidence of our incompetence." Police, neighbors, and advocates repeatedly read Colette's advocacy for her dignity, peace of mind, and humanity with skepticism, as if she were an unreliable narrator and her experience was a product of her incompetence. "Being structurally incompetent injects friction into every interaction, between people, and between people and organizations, and between organizations and ideologies."[6] In short, Colette's requests for help repeatedly transformed her into a problem.[7]

These repeated moments of friction led Colette to extreme cautiousness. "Usually, when people walk up on my porch, I can hear it 'cause it's wooden, and I'm paranoid all the time, so I've trained myself to listen for everything. I'm always muting my TV; it's ridiculous how I live here." She self-deprecatingly explained how she almost asked me for identification when I came to her door for our scheduled interview: "I'm so glad I didn't do you like this, but when you first came, I'm so paranoid." She said she never has uninvited guests in her home and has had strangers try to visit and look inside her home a couple of times. She explained, "So when you came, I so badly—you look like the lady on the postcard,[8] and I don't think you would come in here if you didn't have a purpose, but I was so paranoid, like it's one of these neighbors sending their family in here to scope out. . . . So I almost asked you for ID. But I'm glad I didn't." I reassured Colette that it would have been totally fine for her to ask me for identification. She continued, "I know it would have been fine, but still, I didn't—I said, 'this lady is all right. Quit tripping, Colette.'" We both laughed. But Colette's point is profound. Asking me for identification was not just about the act of checking that I am who I said I was. It meant approaching me without trust. Her feeling "glad I didn't do you like this" is about the ID, yes, but it is also about trusting me enough to share her perspective and personal experiences, even after being burned by others. At the end of our conversation, she showed me pictures of her family and repeated, "I don't have many visitors." It was evident that she wanted to be able to share parts of her life with new friends, but the hostility, distrust, and frustration she felt in the neighborhood prevented her from getting close to anyone. On my way out, as if to drive home the point, a cat ran across her yard after she opened the front door. She said to me, "you see that cat? I don't want to let him in," and quickly closed the door behind me.

I start this chapter on security and policing with Colette because her experiences help bring into question some of the assumptions of traditional approaches to both topics. Colette seemed to do everything right, speaking to authorities, to advocates, and even directly with neighbors. They repeatedly responded with disrespect and distrust. It led her to feel frustrated and wary, and to become more socially isolated. I argue that the commonsense ways we understand safety in our communities—as tied to policing and punishment—fail to create truly safe neighborhoods. Policing not only limits the kind of safety that residents experience (what Kaba calls "security") but also itself serves as a mechanism of harm. I argue that the specter of security helps normalize that harm by making alternatives seem impossible, even in the face of policing failures. Colette's experiences open the door for us to think of safety beyond the confines of security and the presence of police.

Denaturalizing the specter of security helps us understand ways to redress harm that have nothing to do with punishing and incarcerating individuals but instead rely on building stronger communities and relationships with one another. While popular media often frame abolitionist calls to think beyond policing as unpopular extremist measures, many residents already understood safety beyond security. I discuss how residents of Carthage and Riverside experienced abolitionist possibilities, where harm was addressed outside the carceral system. They illustrate that through abolition, as argued by geographer and prison abolitionist Ruth Wilson Gilmore, "what the world will become already exists in fragments and pieces, experiments and possibilities."[9] I identify resident-created fragments in these two Cincinnati communities.

(In)security

As police abolitionists Mariame Kaba and Andrea Ritchie argue, "The term 'public safety,' as it's currently understood, presumes a need for police, the military, or another security force to prevent people from either outside or within communities from causing harm. This reflects a politics of 'security,' rather than safety. The state produces insecurity through economic and social policies, and then promotes visions of 'carceral safety' that can only be achieved through policing, prisons, and banishment."[10] In other words, racial capitalist relations produced the structural insecurity (e.g., poverty, housing precarity) that Riverside and Carthage residents experienced, yet the locus of this insecurity was relocated—via the urban specter of security—to others based on race and class. As social theorist bell hooks argued, "Fear is a primary force upholding structures of domination. It promotes the desire for separation, the desire not to be known. When we are taught that safety lies always with sameness, then difference, of any kind, will appear as a threat. When we choose to love we choose to move against fear — against alienation and separation. The choice to love is a choice to connect — to find ourselves in the other."[11] Among residents, I found evidence of both fear and love of their neighbors. Unsurprisingly, security logics went hand in hand with fear.

Many residents expressed fears about Carthage and Riverside due to perceptions of crime there. But residents I spoke with were split in their assessment of crime in their neighborhoods. Fifty percent said there was a crime problem, while 48 percent said there was not.[12] Overwhelmingly, residents who did perceive a crime problem associated it with drugs (both the buying and selling) and the ramifications of addiction, such as theft. Sex work was also mentioned by Carthage residents as a pervasive public crime, with strangers approaching a few women residents they assumed were sex workers.

Some residents tried to manage their feelings of fear and insecurity with home security measures. A few felt unsafe even with those measures. For example, Maggie mourned the need for add-ons to address the lack of security she felt in Riverside. She said, "It's really sad that you can't feel safe in your own home; that I have to have security cameras. And, as you can see, my dog, you can hear him but you can't see him because he's a security dog. . . . He actually watches the security cameras, and if there's somebody on [the street], he comes to this door and barks." Morgan (white, sixties), who lives in Carthage, had recently purchased a video and alarm system, and unequivocally stated she did not feel safe in the neighborhood. Hugh (white homeowner, fifties) also had an alarm system and felt unsafe. Colette, unsurprisingly, also did not feel safe in Sedamsville, and said, "To be totally honest, I talk about a pistol, and I'm legal enough to get one. I don't have any felonies. And I'm going to, I just haven't been able to afford one. . . . Real soon, it's gonna be me, God, and a pistol, and my baseball bat, but as you can clearly see I sleep with a baseball bat near my bed."

Conversely, some residents felt safe because of these extra measures. For example, Quinn (white renter, twenties) felt safe in her apartment in Carthage because it was a "secured building." She explained, "In order to get in the main building, you have to have a key. Then you have to go up there to my apartment and unlock my door, so you have to go through two doors before anyone can get it. And I'm on the third floor, too, so I do feel really safe." She then went on to clarify that she still did not go out at night, "During the daytime, I would be out during the daytime until about six o'clock, maybe five-thirty, six P.M. at the latest. After that, I would go in. Don't be out." Edie (white renter, fifties) said she felt safe in the Riverside area "because I have my dog. And I have my big brother and my son's huge."

Whether residents felt safe was not always easy to discern. For example, Eatondale resident John (white renter, thirties) said, "I mean, that's a yes and no" to whether he felt safe. As with Quinn, the most relevant distinction for John's feeling of safety was time of day. He did not feel safe at night, especially as Eatondale was near a wooded area where it was "real easy for someone to come up on you and you wouldn't even know it." Erik (white renter, sixties) said of Carthage, "This block is safe. Going towards Vine [Street], there's incidents, but that can happen in the best neighborhoods." Like John, Erik mentioned that he would not go walking around late at night. Lilian (white homeowner, forties) said that she got a bad feeling when she walked around Carthage at night due to previous "rude" comments that "kind of makes you uncomfortable." She concluded, "I don't know what it is about the nighttime; there's some weird people that come around here." Elisabeth (white renter, thirties) similarly marked Vine Street as less safe than other places, "Some streets feel very safe, some streets feel happy, family-oriented, and some, it just feels like you're sort of unwelcome." Dick (white homeowner, fifties) said that his feelings of safety depended on a few variables, "When there are dealers out on the corner, no. During the daytime, yeah. I feel safe, you know. But at nighttime? When it's dark, and you got tons of people standing at the front of Speedway or on the corners like the prostitutes and the pimps, and stuff, I go ahead and do what I got to do." Dick tied his feelings of safety directly to criminal activities on the streets—whether drug dealing or sex work.

Patty (white homeowner, seventies) also felt "somewhat" safe:

Sometimes I worry about it. We had a rash of burglaries, so I didn't want to leave the house. I was getting to be a prisoner. I didn't want to go out. I tried to make myself go out and hoped nothing will happen. At my daughter's house, they walked in her back door and took her television set. That was the only thing they took. She had a great big flat screen. They walked out with it in broad daylight. . . . they walk around and watch you. The lady across the street, she lost her husband. The next thing I know they stole the copper out of her air conditioner, and did this and that. I mean they're watching us. I don't know where they are. We're not sure who's who. Everybody looks guilty or innocent. I feel sort of semi-safe, I guess.

Patty believed thieves in the neighborhood were well aware of residents' comings and goings. She said her daughter also had a television stolen in broad daylight while she was at work, further evidence in Patty's mind of their observations of residents.

Like Patty, Abby (white renter, sixties) saw daytime as dangerous, too: "The bad ones come out at night. I like winter there because it keeps them inside when it's really cold for the most part. And—but they're out on the streets at night, during the day, constantly. And it's just—it's not a safe place for anybody to live. It just isn't safe." She sometimes took her dogs for a walk down by Vine Street, where she was prepared if anyone harassed her. She explained, "There's always traffic, so all you've gotta do is run out in front of a car if somebody's bothering you. That's my safety net." Abby's statement that she could always jump into traffic—and risk her life—to stay safe from street harassment around Carthage points to how deeply she felt that fear.

Most residents blamed drugs or the economy for the crime in their neighborhoods. To wit, Sue (white renter, sixties) said that Carthage used to be safe, and she tried to make sense of the change during our conversation: "All of a sudden, it wasn't safe anymore, and I don't know what happened. Well, the economy got bad, I think, around then. But, all of a sudden it wasn't safe. So I moved in with my daughter. And I don't know what changed. Then nobody trusted anybody anymore. I don't know if it was the drug thing going on. 'Cause there are so many drugs now in Carthage. You can go down to the bank any time of the day, and they go on the back side. There's drug deals going on all the time."

Conversations about crime often led to discussions about police, with most residents saying police needed to be more responsive to crime in Carthage and Riverside. Helen (white homeowner, sixties) said that the last time she called, it took the police "over an hour to come." Brandon (white homeowner, nineteen) agreed that "the response time for the police down here is slim. Like, they take forever. Which is weird because it's District 3, which is right up in Price Hill . . . a five-minute drive, and they're here." He then blamed this response time on the "huge area" District 3 entailed and the insufficient number of police officers patrolling. Collin, a white homeowner in his forties, explained how "we call the cops all the time. We've called them since we've been here numerous times. And they just don't care to show up on time." His wife Marcie (white, forties) chimed in, "They're too busy." A couple of people mentioned that the police were doing their best under constrained circumstances. As Renee (white renter, forties) put it, "The police are on top of it as much as they can be."

Police departments are citywide organizations with localized implementations. Most major cities have multiple districts to organize resources and police responses. Cincinnati has five police districts; Riverside is in District 3, while Carthage is in District 4. Many residents saw police as an integral part of their neighborhood community, protecting them from increasing insecurity. For example, when I asked Marie (white renter, fifties) if she had ever participated in any neighborhood organization, she responded, "No. Just this here." She then pointed to a pin indicating she had made a financial contribution to the local police. When I asked her how she decided to contribute to the police, she explained:

> Well, me and my sister, we got this thing through the mail. She got one and I got one. And it was saying help out the police department. So, we called about it, to find out how much money goes toward that, and how much goes to somewhere else. Well, 100 percent goes to the police. What it does—it helps them get better vests, bulletproof vests, and helps them to get better uniforms and better cars, everything better. So, we decided to go ahead and chip in together and do that.

Marie lived on a fixed income of between $5,000 and $9,999 and identified as lower class. Yet she still contributed from her limited funds to the local police fundraiser. The Cincinnati police budget was over $220 million in 2014, the year Marie and I spoke. Marie's donation, despite the police's massive budget, points to the efficacy of their messaging. When I asked if she was happy with the police in the area, Marie said she was. She recounted an incident:

> When someone was trying to get in my back door, I called the police, and they were here like that. And whoever it was took off running up in the woods. And when they took off running up in the woods, they told me, they said, "Don't worry, Ms. Michaels." They said, "We'll keep [a] patrol out for the next few nights for you." And I said, "Thank you very much." And they seen the [police fund contributor] pins too, and they said, "We see you donate to the police," and I said, "Well, you don't have to do it because of that." They said, "No, we're doing it because we want you to feel safe."

The police officer's comment that they wanted Marie to "feel safe" speaks to the prevalence of the specter of security. Safety and policing are so inextricable in the national imagination that even when police do not catch the thief (as in Marie's case), civilians experience their mere presence as security. Her view that the police were doing their best with limited resources was not uncommon, echoing conversations across the country that frame police as under siege and needing more support despite ballooning budgets. As sociologist Tyler Wall argues, thin blue line rhetoric frames the police project as a defense of civilization, which is "always incomplete, insecure, and unstable. Of course, it must always be incomplete, because it is through its inability to fully eradicate the bestial trace that police claim a license to endless war in the name of humanity."[13] In other words, rather than challenge police power, police ineffectiveness at solving and preventing crime becomes evidence of their necessity. That logic is integral to the specter of security.

In a similar vein, Dick wanted more resources for policing, which he sensed would help protect the community from crime: "I think we could use more police involvement in the area. I don't think they patrol enough, and that may be because the areas that they do have to patrol, they may not have enough manpower. But more appearance from them maybe would help deter some of this stuff." Dick was referring to drug activity and sex work. In Carthage, part of Cincinnati's District 4, many residents complained about how ineffectually the police handled drug and sex work issues in the neighborhood. Hugh (white homeowner, fifties) described how he saw sex workers at all hours on the street. As for the police, he said, "They obviously don't care. I mean . . . I can identify the people—that's how obviously they are on the streets. You see them every day." Elisabeth also blamed the wave of sex work on the lack of police presence in Carthage: "When they [sex workers] get pushed out of whatever neighborhood, they just come where there's less policing or whatever. And we don't really see a ton of police, so I feel like maybe it's an area where that's kind of thriving right now."

It is not just white residents who were disappointed by police responses. Latino homeowner Diego (fifties) also lamented the lack of response from police and said it was even slower for Latinx residents:

Tú llamas a un policía, "Oiga señor, se acaban de meter a mi casa a robar." Se aparecen en dos horas. . . . en el robo que me hicieron últimamente llegaron detectives, estoy hablando de hace más de seis meses, a sacar huellas, encontraron gotas de sangre por las cosas que me habían estado robando, sacaron huellas aquí, sacaron huellas acá. Dijeron que me iban a llamar para hacer más investigaciones y nunca más regresaron. No les interesa, si es hispano peor, yo no sé si por cuestiones—como el hispano tiene problemas por el idioma, quizás por eso no quieren ayudar porque tienen que traer un intérprete y pienso yo que quizás sea ese el inconveniente, pero no, se apareciera a las dos horas, y yo creo que hasta más tiempo es lo que se demoran. Y eso me ha sucedido en las dos veces que yo he estado ahí. Y no investiga nada, no ves un carro de la policía que esté por ahí chequeando, verificando.

(If you call the police, "Hello sir, they have just entered my house to rob me." They show up two hours later. . . . During the robbery that just happened, detectives came; I'm talking about six months ago. They took fingerprints, they found droplets of blood by the things they had been robbing. They got fingerprints here, over there. They said they would call to do more investigating, and they never returned. It doesn't interest them, and if you're Hispanic, even worse. I don't know if because—since Hispanics have problems with the language, maybe because of that they don't want to help because they need to bring an interpreter, and I think maybe that is the inconvenience, but no, they show up after two hours, I think it takes them even longer. That has happened to me both times that I've been there. And they don't investigate anything. You don't see a police car around checking, verifying.)

Lourdes (Latina homeowner, forties) agreed that the neighborhood needed more police attention. When she first moved to the area, police would respond to her calls quickly, but now, perhaps because residents made so many calls, it took them a while to respond.

Black homeowners were also more likely to rely on the police than Black renters. Miriam (Black homeowner, sixties) said she called the police when the neighborhood conflict warranted it. For example:

There's been problems with a neighbor letting their dog poop in somebody else's yard. And they come to the board. And we send them a letter and try to get them to respect your neighbor. If your dog goes in their yard, go get the poop up. It's that kinda stuff. That's the one thing that will bring somebody to one of our meetings. If they've got a complaint, they will come to the meeting. Like I said, it depends on individual cases. I had crossed the street at one time; there was a group of Hispanics. They would come home. And they would play music loud and sit in the car. I called the police because that's who could handle that one. It just depends.

While dog poop could be dealt with interpersonally, with the assistance of the homeowner's association, noise complaints involving Latinx neighbors rose to the level of police involvement. Angelina (Black homeowner, forties) also felt positively toward the police in Carthage, saying they helped her and her neighbors clean up some of the drug problems on her street: "Lot of our neighbors, we got together, got with drug enforcement and they actually came out and started helping us get it cleaned up." In contrast, Black renters reported unequivocally negative experiences with police, who not only failed to address their issues but also often treated them as suspicious parties in the face of no wrongdoing.

Policing as Racial Capitalist Relation

Policing in Cincinnati

Scholars of policing and abolitionists argue that police surveil and punish to "fabricate order."[14] In other words, the relationship between the police and those policed is characterized by the use of force and punishment to maintain social equilibrium. In the US racial capitalist society, this equilibrium is exploitative, dehumanizing, and dependent on differential valuation across race and class. As sociologist Alex Vitale argues, "The reality is that police exist primarily as a system for managing and even producing inequality by suppressing social movements and tightly managing the behaviors of poor and nonwhite people: those on the losing end of economic and political arrangements."[15] Identifying this overriding objective of policing helps explain the seeming contradiction of overpolicing (of poor Black people and spaces) alongside underpolicing, as reported by many Carthage and Riverside residents.

In Cincinnati, the city and the police force emerged in tandem, with the first city marshal approved the same year that Cincinnati was incorporated, 1819. Interestingly, Cincinnati's was also the "first police force to maintain a regular police force by taxation."[16] But how specifically does policing facilitate racial capitalism in Cincinnati?

First, policing enables class exploitation. The hyperpolicing of poor communities, especially poor neighborhoods of color, produces—by design—a higher number of poor defendants. As scholars have illustrated, policing was historically used to reduce organized dissent against elite powerbrokers and as social control of poor people.[17] The well-documented police crackdown on Over-the-Rhine residents after the 2001 uprisings is one such example. Cincinnati police arrested more than 800 people for curfew violations. At the same time, poor defendants are often subject to more harm than those with the means to pay for bail, for example. According to the Prison Policy Initiative, "Nearly half a million people in the US are currently being detained pretrial—in other words, they are awaiting trial and still legally innocent. Many are jailed pretrial simply because they can't afford money bail, others because a probation, parole, or ICE [Immigration and Customs Enforcement] office has placed a 'hold' on their release."[18] The number of people jailed pretrial has tripled in Cincinnati between 1970 and 2018, according to local advocacy organization the Bail Project.[19]

In addition to separating defendants from their friends and family while awaiting trial, jails are also places of neglect, abuse, and harm. For example, a Reuters investigation found that almost 5,000 people had died in jail while awaiting trial between 2008 and 2019 in the United States.[20] In April 2021, Local 12 News reported on the harsh conditions in Cincinnati-area jails: "a restrictive device called the restraint chair is used every day inside our jails and prisons to subdue and control inmates." The report highlighted the death of Pierre Howell, a thirty-three-year-old inmate who died in 2018 while restrained to the chair. Police falsified reports, claiming to have checked on him every ten minutes, contrary to video footage.[21]

Additionally, asset forfeiture is a policy in which police can dispossess people of their belongings. As the American Civil Liberties Union (ACLU) explains, "Civil forfeiture allows police to seize—and then keep or sell—any property they allege is involved in a crime. Owners need not ever be arrested or convicted of a crime for their cash, cars, or even real estate to be taken away permanently by the government."[22] Section 2981.13 of the Ohio Revised Code delineates ten different law enforcement agency forfeiture funds. Between 2010 and 2015, the thirteen local law enforcement agencies involved in the Hamilton County Sheriff's Regional Narcotics Unit "earned more than $7.5 million in such seizure money."[23] The state legislature passed a law in 2017 that mandated a conviction for seizures under $15,000.[24] Nevertheless, asset forfeiture is still thriving in Cincinnati. A 2017 investigation by Cincinnati alt-weekly *City Beat* found that "the Hamilton County prosecutor's office has built up a $1.7 million pot that isn't posted online or included in county budget documents. It isn't audited and it is used for purchases that don't seem to fit the intent of the law."[25] These purchases included attorney briefcases, office furniture, and consultant fees and expenses for friends and acquaintances. The prosecutor's office does not share official figures, but its website states that "thousands of dollars are seized and forfeited."[26]

The class exploitation of mass incarceration is an extension of policing's harms. The exploitation of incarcerated people includes legalized discrimination in employment and housing, as well as large debts that "a host of agencies" expect prisoners to pay upon release, "including probation departments, courts, and child-support enforcement offices. In some jurisdictions, ex-offenders are billed for drug testing and even for the drug treatment they are supposed to receive as a condition of parole."[27] Exploitation of prisoner labor is also a long-standing practice and directly shaped by policing. One of Cincinnati's first jails was the Cincinnati Workhouse, which opened in late 1869. By mid-1870, over 1,500 people were imprisoned, almost 60 percent of whom were convicted of drunkenness and disorderly conduct. Prisoners "made shoes for the J. P. Hearne Co., castings for the Miles Greenwood Co., and erected new workshops for other manufacturers."[28] Contemporary practices of prison exploitation continue. Wendy Sawyer from the Prison Policy Initiative reported in 2017 that Ohio prisoners averaged $0.10 to $1.23 an hour for their labor. The most common jobs earn the lowest wages and include "custodial, maintenance, laundry, grounds keeping, food service," and other prison-based work. A small percentage of incarcerated people work for private industry.

In addition to exploitation, policing produces dehumanization and reinforces racial and gender hierarchies, among other inequalities. Well-known examples of police brutality and extrajudicial killings spurred the Black Lives Matter movement in the mid-to-late 2010s and the 2001 uprisings in Cincinnati. Rampant sexual assault and racist policies such as stop and frisk are further evidence of the baked-in dehumanization of the policing relation. While it may seem like national conversations about stop and frisk have reached a consensus on its inefficacy and racial bias, that is not the case. As recently as 2021, Hamilton County Prosecutor Joe Deters has remarked that police officers should feel free to use stop and frisk "if these officers think that someone's carrying or they're a danger to the officer."[29] Importantly, open carry is legal in Ohio. Presumably, Deters is referring to carrying concealed weapons without a permit, which is illegal—although one can imagine that openly carrying a firearm would not result in fewer stops and less dehumanization at the hands of police for poor Black Cincinnatians. Indeed, it was in Ohio that twelve-year-old Tamir Rice was murdered by police while playing with a toy gun at a Cleveland recreation center. But the letter of the law is not the basis of stop and frisk's logic. It hinges—like policing—on antiblack dehumanization.

The harms of policing are not equitably experienced, with poor Black people bearing the brunt of the racist and classist US criminal justice system. Scholars, such as historian Simon Balto, have identified antiblackness as a critical logic of policing across the United States.[30] Cincinnati is no exception. In fact, in 2001 a lawsuit filed by the ACLU of Ohio and the Cincinnati Black United Front sought "both a court order requiring the police department to alter its practice of targeting minority citizens for harassment based on their race and money damages for certain plaintiffs." A Department of Justice (DOJ) investigation into the Cincinnati Police Department (CPD) followed and eventually produced a Memorandum of Agreement (MOA) between the DOJ and CPD. Part of the MOA was the creation of a new database to better monitor patterns in police stops and arrests. In popular and scholarly writing, Cincinnati has been upheld as an exemplar of community responsiveness and police reform.[31] However, the daily experiences of residents in Riverside and Carthage indicate that antiblackness and punitive policing are not elements of the past but are woven into the fabric of policing in Cincinnati and across the United States.[32]

Policing in Riverside and Carthage

Despite an increase in accountability being a stated goal of the MOA, as seen in the creation of more publicly available statistics, many Riverside and Carthage residents identified a lack of accountability in their experiences with CPD. Rather than being a shortcoming of "bad policing," lack of accountability is a feature of policing in the United States. We see it in policies, such as qualified immunity, where citizens cannot sue public officials—including police officers—unless there is an existing case with the exact circumstances where the court ruled the official's behavior was unconstitutional. In practice, US laws largely protect police officers against civil suits. The disconnect between the experiences of Carthage and Riverside residents and their expectations of police caused the residents significant frustration. These expectations are shaped in part by the common ways we speak about police, including fictional media portrayals that grossly misrepresent the day-to-day of policing and news reporting.[33] To wit, Riverside resident Douglas (white homeowner, seventies) said that he felt safe because he purposefully did not watch the news, which warps individuals' sense of safety: "I do [feel safe]. I'm not—I don't like television. And honestly, if you don't look at television, you're going to feel a lot safer. Television is notorious for giving people insecurity. And television magnifies every crime into a major social problem when, actually, it's often just an isolated instance. And we had, as I say, we've had a guy that was arrested last week in the neighborhood and his brother has quite a record, but it's just basically breaking and entering and things like that. There's no violence. We feel safe in our home." However, expectations are also shaped by what police say to residents and how they see police interact with other residents. To illustrate this point, we revisit Carl and Maggie.

Carl and Maggie were active neighborhood "watchdogs" and complained that nobody responded to their calls. They said both city services and local police were nonresponsive.

> CARL: Every time we get a decent cop down here, they transfer. Now there's just nobody to call; nobody listens. I've gone out and filed complaints at District 3. I've gone up to District 3. They pulled in my yard and done drug deals. [I] told her to go out with a ball bat and bust their headlights out. I had to put a gate up down there to block them from pulling in down there.
>
> MAGGIE: We've actually had to call the police and waited and waited and waited. Called them back, and they said, "Well, somebody has responded to that call."
>
> CARL: And nobody ever showed.
>
> MAGGIE: "No, they haven't because we've been sitting out here waiting." "Well, would you like to talk to a supervisor?" Well, we don't feel like we can do that because we've already been threatened to have our house burned [after a conflict with neighbors escalated at a civic club meeting]. We've got enough targets around here. I feel like we've been targeted by them next if we complain.

Carl and Maggie then shared the story of their neighborhood police officer, Darrell Beavers. When Darrell first arrived in Riverside, he shared various phone numbers with Carl to contact him, assuring Carl he would be available. Carl reported that Darrell said, "I promise you I'm gonna handle all this and you're gonna have a quiet summer." Darrell turned out to be less reliable than he had promised. He was eventually convicted of creating a fake police substation on a local property to have sex with a minor; he was forty-five at the time.[34] Maggie concluded, "Where do you turn when you get no help from the police?"

Claudia (white homeowner, sixties) said in Carthage, "We don't see the police much, and I've complained about that numerous times." As in many other neighborhoods, including Riverside, Carthage residents complained about scrap metal theft. When I asked who Claudia complained to, she explained:

> Right to the police department, to the chief's office, and to city hall as well. I call several city council members since we don't have particular people covering a certain neighborhood so you just have to make phone calls to. So I chose . . . somebody from each party so I'm being partisan. [*laughs*] And everybody's sympathetic and empathic about the situation, and you know, "have I filed police reports?" I got tired of filing police reports, quite frankly. I got tired of it. I was calling the police every two weeks. It was ridiculous. I finally stopped. I said I'm tired of it. I'm tired of calling the police.

Claudia understood that District 4 is large and as a result, "Carthage gets probably second shrift."

Similarly, Ben (white renter, fifties) did not know where to turn after feeling ignored by the police in Carthage. He theorized, "I've been a victim of a crime recently and they swept it under the rug probably because I have a police record." He also said this neglect affected his wife and daughter, whom a neighbor stalked.

> BEN: People want a better community; it seems like the police don't care.
>
> SARAH: So, do you have any ideas about how to fix that? Do you have any sense of what should happen?
>
> BEN: Overhaul the police station? I mean I made a complaint to city hall, and it went nowhere.
>
> SARAH: And what was your complaint specifically?
>
> BEN: That they simply didn't do their job and didn't care. "Sergeant will get back with you within a couple of weeks." It's been like more than three weeks now.
>
> SARAH: And this is after they haven't responded to your February burglary?
>
> BEN: Right. And I didn't complain to the city for a month because they were supposed to bring out a police lineup and all this stuff. And I would like to say "well, it was because I had a police record" but then I remember my wife and daughter being victims; they didn't care about that either. And the lady across the alley, she's older than me,

and I know she don't have a police record. They don't care about her getting ripped off either. It's not just me.

Ben explained, "I've lived in all five police districts. And this is the laziest police district I've lived in. . . . The police don't want to do any—they want you to do all the police work." He said it took the police "three hours to answer a call" because "they don't care."

Donald (Black renter, forties) also complained that the police wanted residents to do their jobs for them. He explained what happened when he called to report drug dealers in Eatondale Apartments:

I called the cops before, and I told them that there was drug dealing going on in the parking lot. And there was a guy, he had cars lined up in the parking lot. And you know what he told me? The police told me, "do you know his name? Can you take down the plates?" And I said, "Well, no because I'm standing right here in the window, and I don't want these people to point right at me because I'm in the window, and they know who I am. These guys know that I live down here." And I told the cops, "If you guys want to do your job, all you have to do is go out there to the parking lot and don't let anybody out. And then you go and search those cars, and once you get them, eventually they'll tell on the drug dealer because they don't want to get caught anyways." . . . And it's just like I don't want to be the person that keeps pointing and pointing and pointing, and it's not my job. If I get paid for it, then I'll do it. Because then I wouldn't fear them, but I'm not the police. So there's no reason for me to police my building because it's going to eventually end up I'm going to have to fight somebody.

Donald pointed to the dangers of collecting evidence for police as a civilian, such as getting embroiled in a physical altercation with suspects. In fact, this type of dangerous entanglement happened to Carthage resident Lourdes.

Originally from Guatemala, Lourdes was in her early forties and lived in Cincinnati for almost twenty years. She considered herself working class and made just under $30,000 as a teacher's aide, although her family owned a neighborhood business as well. Lourdes bought her home in Carthage in 2001 and lived there with her husband and two teenage sons. When I asked her to describe the kind of people who lived in Carthage, she said that there was a racial mix—Latinxs, whites, and Black people. She commented that Black people were more likely to move around than other groups. She then explained that she had "malas experiencias" (bad experiences) with Black youth in the area. She said when she worked in a store nearby multiple youth assaulted her,

> Tuve muchos incidentes y fue la razón porque yo tuve como un trauma y no me siento muy confiada con ellos porque me golpearon y nos asaltaron muchas veces, eran jóvenes. Ellos venían a vivir un tiempo y luego se iban o se mudaban a otro lugar. Y he tenido muchas malas experiencias con ellos, para el 2003 casi siempre vendían drogas ahí en la esquina, se estaban negociando ahí ellos. Pues nosotros siempre llamábamos a la policía y yo creo que fue una de las razones por las que ellos entraron a golpearme una vez, porque ellos se dieron cuenta que yo siempre llamaba a la policía y les gritaba. Pero yo no sabía que ellos iban a tomar represalias conmigo, porque yo siempre salía y cuando venía el carro de la policía yo salía y le decía, "Él fue, ahí viven." Yo salía pues a decirles y un día fue que me entraron a golpear. Entonces por eso he tenido alguna mala experiencia. Ya no trabajo ahí, pero desde esa vez me quedé como muy traumada. Y después otra vez también aquí entró un hombre y asaltó a mi hijo y también eso me da pues miedo. . . . No me siento tan segura todavía, tengo un poco de miedo; pero yo misma estoy tratando de quitarme el miedo y de decir que no todas las personas son iguales.

(I had a lot of incidents, and that was the reason that I've had like a trauma, and I don't feel too comfortable with them because they hurt me and they assaulted us many times. They were young. They came to live here for a short period, and then they would move somewhere else. And I've had a lot of bad experiences with them. Around 2003, they almost always sold drugs there in the corner. They had their business there. But we always called the police, and I think that's one of the reasons that they came in to hurt me one time because they realized that I always called the police and yelled at them. But I didn't know that they were going to retaliate against me, and when a police car drove by I would tell them, "It was him, they live there." I would go out to tell them, and one day, they came in to hit me. And so because of that, I've had a bad experience. I don't work there anymore, but since then, I've been traumatized. And another time another man entered and assaulted my son and that also made me scared. . . . I still don't feel that safe, I am a little bit afraid. But I'm trying to get rid of the fear myself and say that not all people are the same.)

Ten years after the incidents took place, Lourdes still felt traumatized. While she tried to let go of the fear, it shaped her interactions with her neighbors. There is a dual sadness in her story: the first is the violence Lourdes endured and the difficulties she continued to experience after being assaulted. The police, whom she was trying to assist, did not protect her. The second is the limited redress available under the current carceral system. These are the same reasons that abolitionists call for the end of policing: "survivors [of violence] deserve *more* safety and *more* options for healing and transformation — and we recognize that police were never created to provide them."[35]

Even if the police had caught the young men who assaulted Lourdes, would that heal her wounds? Would that make her feel safe enough to return to her old workplace? And what about the young men? What is the just way to address the harm they caused? The current system relies on subjecting those who cause harm to "social death" as argued by sociologist Joshua M. Price.[36] We often think of police as preventing crime, but as scholars and abolitionists have argued, that punitive approach fails to address the root causes of crime. The criminal/victim dichotomy provides a narrow lens through which to understand the assault that Lourdes experienced. It should never have happened; that is clear. Having more police, however, was not likely to have prevented it either. And if we think of the humanity of the assailants alongside that of Lourdes, we are led to different considerations that help us understand harm prevention holistically. It focuses less on crime and more on creating the conditions to reduce harm — both the interpersonal and the structural. As argued in *No More Police*, "This knowledge — that supporting communities with resources rather than exacerbating conditions that produce violence through criminalization is the most effective strategy for decreasing violence — is precisely what is driving demands to defund and abolish police."[37]

In 2014 and 2015, when I conducted interviews in Cincinnati, the approved public safety budget for the 2014 fiscal year was over $220 million, which was over 60 percent of the general fund operating budget and 22 percent of the city's total operating budget. Of that, $6 million was allocated to public safety overtime, while overtime for all other city employees was denied. To be frank, if $220 million is not enough for police to respond effectively to community harm, shouldn't we evaluate their role in society? In what other industry does repeated failure despite growing budgets and investment justify increased expenditures? When we denaturalize policing and security as the only ways to respond to harm, we can also ask what other ways communities could address their needs with this money. Abolitionists provide us with many ideas, including decriminalizing drugs and sex work, job creation programs, better mental health resources for distressed community members, violence intervention programs, and more affordable housing. This holistic approach to harm reduction and safety takes the root causes of crime seriously and rejects carceral logics that focus on punitive responses and criminalization.

When discussing police abolition, detractors often point to the inevitable chaos of losing the police for protection. However, as police abolitionists (particularly those specializing in gender violence reduction) argue, victims of abuse cannot currently rely on the police to help them. Abby provides us with an example of what this disengagement looked like in Riverside and Carthage, with dire consequences. When she witnessed domestic violence on the street, she turned away: "I watched some guy, she was a prostitute, and I guess she wanted to go home or not work, and I watched him out my window blocking her. He was on a bicycle, of all things, god, and he was blocking her. She was trying to get away from him, and he punched her. And I thought, 'I'm not getting in on this. I'm done with calling the police. I'm not doing this anymore,' and it's nothing unusual." When the police were not effective at stopping "the scary, awful, monster people," many residents became disenchanted that anything could be done.[38] Abby's assessment that witnessing domestic violence and not intervening is "nothing unusual" is a good illustration of that sense of despair.

Carthage and Riverside residents also identified how our reliance on police exacerbated existing inequalities and vulnerabilities. For example, in recounting his experience in Carthage, Diego explained that it was not particularly positive. He had been robbed three times in the last two years. He had also lived in a few other areas in Greater Cincinnati, including Price Hill. In these other locations, he described what he said was an unspoken truth about life in Cincinnati for Latinxs, which is abuse at the hands of their compatriots. Diego explained:

> Esos hispanos cuando están acá muchos años y han adquirido sus propiedades, pero a veces abusan de la gente nueva que llega. Son abusivos, quieren vivir de ellos de todo, les quieren vender todo, hay cosas que las consiguen regaladas y no se las regalan. Se las venden, teléfono, todo.
>
> (Those Hispanics who have been here many years and have acquired properties, they sometimes abuse the people who have just arrived. They're abusive, they want to live off of them, they want to sell them

everything, there are things that they get for free, and they don't give away for free. They sell it to you, phones, everything.)

When I asked Diego if he thought others experienced similar abuse, he hesitated, saying that experiences are personal and some people prefer not to share these things. Then he said yes, he did think it happened a lot, and detailed threats he had received from fellow Latinxs in Cincinnati:

> Y amenazas, yo he recibido amenazas, "Te voy a denunciar a la inmigración." Te amenazan así descaradamente, te lo digo sinceramente, son hispanos mismos. Duele decirlo pero esa es la verdad, abusan de su compañero hispano y eso lo vas encontrar en cualquier lugar, hay demasiado abuso y precisamente por la situación legal; precisamente se aprovechan de eso. Como saben que no sé puede defender, que el idioma es otra limitante, una serie de cositas.

> (And threats, I have received threats, "I'm going to report you to immigration." They threaten you that shamelessly. I'm telling you honestly, it's Hispanics themselves. It hurts to say it, but it's the truth. They abuse their fellow Hispanic, and you will find that in any place, there's too much abuse, and precisely because of the legal situation, they take advantage of that exactly. Since they know you can't defend yourself, that language is another limitation. It's a series of things.)

Diego's experience illuminates how racial capitalism works. The class exploitation that his property-owning compatriots enacted on Diego and others depended on their shared racial differentiation as Latinxs. In other words, their exploitation was possible because of racial and ethnic segregation, both in housing and networks. The segregation of immigration networks meant that compatriots often depended on one another for information and resources. The threats to call the police or immigration officials secured his compatriots' ability to exploit Diego and others. His description of the relation between himself and fellow Latinxs fits the definition of "exploitation" by Marxist sociologist Erik Olin Wright, in which the exploited and exploiter are bound together. As Diego put it, more established immigrants wanted to live off of him and other recent arrivals. Diego's experience not only illustrates how some Latinx residents used the threat of police to facilitate exploitation of others, but how a solitary focus on policing for community safety can further marginalize vulnerable community members. In other words, with the police as the sole outlet for safety, where could Diego and others turn for protection from exploitation?

Across town in Riverside, Donald's girlfriend Tasha (Black renter, twenties) described how the police exacerbated a difficult situation and failed to address her situation. She chronicled harassment by her neighbors, which included threats for being suspected of complaining about them. She and Donald had indeed complained to the property manager, called the police, and even filed a restraining order against one neighbor's partner who threatened Donald with violence due to a conflict with Tasha. However, when the police responded, they framed Tasha as a problem, saying that she was calling to complain too much. She said:

> I had one time where . . . the police was talking about taking me to jail and I couldn't possibly understand why when I was the one getting harassed. [. . .] The officer was trying to take me to jail telling me that I'm calling too much and it's not that serious. I'm up here like—I mean because I was sitting on my couch and I see some smoke coming through my door, so I'm thinking somebody's trying to poison me or anything. So I get up, and it's somebody blowing marijuana in my door. Just standing right there blowing it in my door, banging on my ceilings, doing all of that just because they're just trying to be bullies.

The police response to Tasha was not an isolated incident and was shaped by city policy. When police receive too many calls about a property, the city designates it a "nuisance." Many cities have ordinances to fine and penalize landlords for these repeated phone calls. In 2014, the city deemed Eatondale Apartments a nuisance property. The consequences of these policies, while meant to motivate landlords to address problems with tenants appropriately, can be dire for residents seeking redress for harm. Sociologists Matthew Desmond and Nicol Valdez found that landlords seeking to avoid these nuisance fines in Milwaukee evicted residents who filed complaints or called the police.[39] This practice meant that many residents, including women experiencing domestic abuse, had to choose between eviction and reporting. They often chose to stay quiet to maintain their housing, risking their physical safety. In contrast, Tasha reported that the police chastised her for calling them too frequently rather than calling property management.

Additionally, those who experienced harm at the hands of the police were not always intimately involved in an incident as "perpetrators" or "victims" but became collateral damage nonetheless. Aisha (Black renter, thirties) felt the punitive nature of the state in multiple stages and from multiple agencies, which eventually resulted in Hamilton County Children's Services removing her son from her care. She explained, "I was coming out one day, and I don't know if you seen this story on the news, but we had a girl here by the name of Tameka Spears." Tameka Spears was a young mother arrested for robbing a local Kroger grocery store and leaving her child in the store. Aisha continued,

> This girl is light-skinned. She Black but she's light complexion, I mean really light, looks nothing like me. . . . I was coming out [of my apartment] one day and going to Child Services because my son had his weight problem. I think at the time when he was a baby, he was probably what you call hypoglycemic now. I never knew the term when he was a baby, but I'm thinking that's probably what he had. One day I was going out to go take him to a WIC [Women, Infants, and Children nutrition program] appointment so that we could find out why his weight was going up and down. [As I was heading out to the appointment] The Feds had hit this building. Can I tell you when I was standing on my apartment, that front porch, [*softer*] do you hear me when I say bum-rushed me. When I say bum-rushed me, I mean bum-rushed me and had me out there for hours.

Aisha explained that she told the police officers she had to get to a necessary appointment, as missing it could result in her losing custody of her youngest son. They did not listen. "They weren't listening to me at all. So I'm asking them, 'Well can y'all call the social worker at the hospital?' They refused. They wouldn't call her. So when I called the lady to report it she thought I was lying, of course. Guess what, my baby got tooken. He did. I took it in stride, but still to this day it's crazy, because I should have never had to go through something like that."

In addition to looking nothing like Tameka Spears, Aisha explained that she had identification on her because she was prepared for her appointment. From her perspective, if the police had searched her or asked for identification, she would have easily been able to identify herself to the officers and make her appointment. "He wasn't paying that no mind, or the fact that I'm telling them you could result in my baby getting tooken, and he didn't care. It's like they didn't care. You know how hard it is to be Black and stay in this area you staying in with a strong back?"

When we spoke, Aisha still did not have custody of her then-five-year-old son. She said that once Children's Services took him away from her, they identified many medical problems. She insisted that these were genetic issues and not a result of negligent parenting, as Children's Services claimed. She said that she was filing a civil suit; from her perspective, it was a strong case. She said that the only reason her son was not at home was because of racism. She explained that she had white friends whose children have had health issues, and the children have never been taken away or parents jailed. Aisha concluded, "My heart is wounded, and I keep going." Her experience of police mistreatment was not only about misidentification and wasting her time at the moment. It exacerbated the already existing stress and challenges she faced as a parent. From Aisha's perspective, the police did nothing but make the situation worse for her and her son.

When we begin to understand safety as more than security—not as the police and prisons keeping us safe from monsters, but each of us working together to keep each other safe from all harm, including the harms of racial capitalist exploitation and dehumanization—we move from a place of despair to a place of collective hope. An abolitionist future relies on building cultures and structures of care that address all our human needs; it does not mean turning our backs on one another in despair. And while these abolitionist possibilities may seem unrealistic, they already exist in Carthage and Riverside. And probably where you live, too.

Abolitionist Possibilities

Police abolitionist Mariame Kaba has argued, "The idea that cops equal security is difficult to dislodge. To transform this mind-set, where cops equal security, means we have to actually transform our relationships to each other enough so that we can see that we can keep each other safe. You cannot have safety without strong, empathic relationships with others. You can have security without relationships, but you cannot have safety—actual safety—without healthy relationships."[40] While it is difficult to disassociate safety from policing in the United States, many Carthage and Riverside residents understood the importance of relationships for safety. For example, when I spoke with mother-daughter duo Anita and Cathy, Anita (Black renter, twenties) shared that sometimes she does not feel safe in Eatondale. Addressing Anita, Cathy (Black renter, forties) responded, "She got me, so she's safe. She's safe. She has me." But it was not only family relationships on which residents relied for safety. Janessa (Black renter, thirties) also lived in Eatondale and said she felt safe because of her relationships with neighbors, "I know that if anything was going to happen or anything, my neighbors would have my back. I have no problem with believing that at all. You know, this building at least. Everyone in this building. And the same, vice versa." Timmy (white renter, twenties) also observed that the safety of Carthage was because of his fellow residents, saying, "Everyone's really cool, and they look out for each other. If they see something that doesn't look right, they'll be like 'hey, something about this.'" His partner Skylar (white renter, twenties) agreed, saying she felt safe in the neighborhood. Importantly, all of these residents were renters, showing that those who are not homeowners built relationships of care and reciprocity with their neighbors, counter to much common sense about their "investment" in where they live.

Sedamsville renter Stefanie (white, thirties) provided an excellent example of the abolitionist possibilities that already existed in Cincinnati. She did not rely on the logics of security or policing but used empathy and reciprocity as guiding principles. For example, when approaching drug use in her neighborhood, she argued:

> Maybe have an open mind and say "well, I don't know what that person's been through in life, but I'm gonna let 'em know if they need me I'm here for 'em." And then once I let 'em know that, and then I see some things I don't really like, it's easier for me to approach them about the things I don't care for once they get to kinda know what I'm about first. And then I feel like once people respect you, that's all you need in life is to get a point across, is a little respect and trust, and to say "you know, I'm not here to, to pry or get your kids taken away, or any of that, I'm here 'cause I care." And they know that. They know I'm not—I don't call the cops. I do what I need to do myself. I don't call 241-KIDS [Hamilton County's 24-hour hotline to report suspected child abuse and neglect].[41] I take care of things directly.

Stefanie's approach to her neighbors echoed abolitionist approaches that focus on relationship building to foster mutual respect and create safety. When I wondered how widespread this attitude was, Stefanie explained that her neighbors generally did not take this approach—out of fear: "I think they're afraid to be called names, or, a snitch, or—'cause a lot of them will call the cops and not tell who they are, or come out, they'll be afraid to make a report. That's not doin' nothin'. When you make allegations against someone, if you're not gonna justify 'em, what was the point to begin with? Or calling 241-KIDS and not continuing with the process, what have you done, you've just—you make yourself feel better? I'm not sure, but you never change the situation at all." She argued that fear kept residents from enacting an ethos of care and reciprocity, and in the end, it maintained the status quo. Making an anonymous call did not address residents' problems; in Stefanie's view, neighbors were not helping one another.

While she pointed to the fear of being found out as a "snitch," Stephanie showed that being upfront with neighbors led to deeper connections, "Some of the people here that I've had to approach with problems are some of the people that become the tightest with me, and they actually might get help, or do something differently, or they see I'm a member of AA [Alcoholics Anonymous] and I've had people want to get sober, and—It's a great thing, it's like you know, I don't claim to be perfect, I don't try to act better than anyone, I've been real successful and I've been real down on myself in life, so I understand both ways." Stefanie's own experience with substance abuse seemed to play a role in how she approached social problems in her neighborhood. She grew up as a self-proclaimed "redneck" and said her upbringing was "very close-minded." She recounted that she became friends with the Black women in her building out of a shared sense of need: "We didn't seek each other out, but it happened out of need. I asked to use her washer when mine was broken, and then I bought one. And then her dryer broke, and she asked to use mine, and I said, 'of course.' I got to learn what she's about and she got to learn what I'm about." These are the kind of reciprocal relationships that are possible when residents talk to one another.

Gina (white renter, fifties) explained that good neighbors are those that make you feel safe, and that building trust is essential for good neighbor relationships, saying, "My mom, her neighbor's, like I said, has been there for a long time. . . . we gave her the key so [if] ever something would happen or she wasn't answering the phone she can go check on [my mom]. So that's a good feeling to know that you can trust in." She explained that this trust went both ways, as her neighbor also trusted Gina and her mom to keep her and her home safe:

> When she goes on vacation with her son, she'll come and ask us, "Can you keep an eye on our house?" You know? Just make sure they have lights all around and stuff, just kind of keep—I mean, that trust factor that's a good thing to have with your neighbors, you know what I mean? You wanna feel like you can leave and you know your house is safe or something happened that there's somebody close by

that you can call on and it's kind of cool that you see—you know their children, and you see their children have children, and they grow up, and you know them by name, and you know the generations on, and that's cool.

Kim (Black homeowner, sixties) similarly described her immediate neighbors: "I do know my neighbors, and they know me. And what I love about it is we all got our own lives. We speak. We invite each other over if we're having something like a barbecue or something like that. We got your back. We're like a little neighborhood watch type of thing, but everybody minds their own business." While they have each other's backs, they also gave each other space, an example of how more connection does not mean you have to be best friends with your neighbors. Kim and her neighbors found the balance that worked for them.

In addition to the ways that residents challenged commonsense ideas of security and fear, some also had experiences with challenges to carceral logics, whereby police and judges did not meet every crime with a punitive response. White homeowner Todd (fifties) has lived in Carthage for six years and was originally from the West Side of Cincinnati. In preparation for the Fourth of July holiday one year, he tested some new fireworks. Section 3743.65 of the Ohio Revised Code makes consumer fireworks possession (let alone fireworks use) in Ohio illegal for nonprofessionals. If you purchase consumer fireworks in Ohio, you must take them out of state within forty-eight hours. As Todd was testing his fireworks, someone called the police. Todd explained what happened when the police officer approached him in his front yard:

> "You should not be shooting a gun." I said, "no, sir, I'm shooting off fireworks." He said, "what are you doing?" I said, "I got a bunch of new ones, and I'm testing them." He said, "do you have any more?" I said, "I've got one that I'd like to test." He sat in his car and watched me. He said, "yeah, I'm going to be here on the Fourth of July to watch." He was just kidding around. He called the rest of the dogs off, but we had—I was straightforward with the man. I wasn't trying to hide nothing. I had it all over the driveway. What am I going to do?

Indeed, it would have been hard for Todd to lie, given that there was evidence of his illegal fireworks use all over the driveway. Here we see how despite committing a crime in plain sight, the officer used his discretion to not charge Todd with one, assessing this as a no-harm situation and even finding enjoyment in Todd's law-breaking. This parallels abolitionist Angela Davis's point in *Are Prisons Obsolete?* that "the category 'lawbreakers' is far greater than the category of individuals who are deemed criminals."[42] As such, Davis invites us to question "why 'criminals' have been constituted as a class and, indeed, a class of human beings undeserving of the civil and human rights accorded to others" when we have all likely broken the law at some point.[43]

Cait (white homeowner, sixties), talking to me along with Elsie and Kevin (also white homeowners in their sixties), also recounted a story to show how residents of Riverside showed up for one another. It is an excellent example of how rehabilitation can happen outside of carceral logics:

> CAIT: I wanted to tell you about one of the things that happened. When we were probably in our 20s and 30s, this one guy was growing up. Elsie and I had known his dad. My mama knew his uncle. We knew his cousins, and they were all in prison and jail, all of them. So his young boy was living with his mom, and then when he was like seventeen—you think Bobby was like seventeen or nineteen when he got in trouble for stealing?
>
> ELSIE: He was probably eighteen, right on the border.
>
> CAIT: Anyway, so everybody in the community—and I'm talking about all of them, like fifty, sixty signatures—all signed these papers and went to his court hearing to talk to the judge—we sent it first—to try to get him released into the custody of a few people in Riverside to give him a chance. Because we told him this is generation after generation and jail and prison, so this young guy didn't have a chance. He's raised by his mother, and then she got real sick. His brother went to jail. It was—for rape or something. The whole thing was just crime; they were all crime. And so they gave him a second chance. I signed a paper saying I'd be responsible for him, and several other people did, too. And he had to be accountable to us. And we had already talked to him. And so he agreed to all this stuff because—I think her name was Judge Marie somebody or other— But she said: this is your only chance. If you screw up or mess up, you're going back in, and you're not coming back out. You're gonna be in there for ten years. Well, he hung in there. He was accountable to everybody, and he made it. And he's still living down there in Riverside, and he's had a job, and his kids are like from six [years old] to twenty-two or something. He has stayed out of trouble. He got a job down there at the nursing home, and he's been there ever since.

KEVIN: He's the main maintenance man.

CAIT: Everybody knows he will help you with anything. When I couldn't get my furnace started, I called him, and he came over and helped with that. But he will help anybody.

KEVIN: In an emergency and when they can't afford it.

ELSIE: But he says people on the river are always happy to give. They're there. They'll help you out.

CAIT: But we stood up for him, and he was okay, but it's like people in other communities, they don't have that opportunity. If you steal, if you do something bad, you're on your own. But down here when you know somebody, and you see the kids being raised, and you know what kind of past they've had and what's going on, and so he was saved. And he is special to us. And I go and talk to him, Elsie talks to him, Kevin does, everybody else in the community. Everybody knows him because he knew he was indebted to everybody. And he's been good ever since; had that child ever since.

KEVIN: Now he's on the watch in the neighborhood.

One of the critiques of our criminal justice system is that in its punitiveness, it is not rehabilitative and, in fact, actually multiplies harm.[44] Rather than reduce a person's likelihood of committing another crime, our prison system strips people of their humanity, dignity, and social support.[45] We often accept this as the necessary punishment for criminal behavior. However, Cait's story points to how in many white communities, the police and criminal justice system treat people with rehabilitation in mind, and that with community care, accountability and rehabilitation are possible outside of the carceral state.

A Different Path

While Colette was subject to harassment in her neighborhood and felt incredibly alone as a result, she also shared a story of how she and another neighbor, Danny, patched things up after falling out. They had initially stopped speaking because of her issues with neighborhood cats and what she characterized as "disrespect" from him as an animal advocate. But she explained:

We finally made amends when the girl across the street left her babies in the house by theirselves and caught those two child endangerments.[46] What happened is when I pulled up from work, her two-year-old [was] outside with a tank top on [and] no panties, with the pet pit bull. Danny got the pet pit bull away; I brought the baby in the house. I tied her on a pair of panties, one knot on each side. Gave her a ice cream sandwich, went outside. This is after I called 911. When the police showed up, they got the little girl. I don't know, they got the dog—it was two of 'em. They took care of that. Went inside it [and there] was a 1-year-old in the house! That's how the girl caught the two child endangerments. She had since moved. In that situation, Danny helped me, so we kind of made amends.

While they were not on speaking terms before, she and Danny came together to help care for two neighborhood children who had been left home alone by their mother. Colette experienced this moment as an act of care from Danny. It helped her forgive his previous disrespect toward her, and it seemed Danny felt the same way toward Colette. At the same time, calling the police to deal with negligent parenting perfectly encapsulates the limits of carceral systems of punishment. I do not mean this as a critique of Colette or Danny but as a prompt for reflection on the limits of our current system to produce genuine care and healing. With an abolitionist lens, we can ask ourselves, what was the mother in question experiencing, and what help did she need to better care for herself and her children? Two criminal charges would certainly not help her or her children. As Kaba and Ritchie argue, "The family regulation system blames, punishes, and separates families for conditions framed as 'neglect' that are the products of poverty and structural conditions."[47] Can you imagine a better way, whereby Colette and Danny's extension of care would not result in entanglement with carceral systems for the parent and children?

Calls to defund the police have gotten national attention and are worth examining alongside residents' experiences. Defunding the police entails critically evaluating police budgets and diverting funds from police departments to other programs that would benefit community members, including housing, health care, and education. This view of social harm is expansive; it does not look at the immediate determinants of crime (a "criminal" committing a crime), but instead it seeks to address the distal determinants of harm (e.g., poverty, criminalization, policing). Does funding police forces create safer neighborhoods? What I found in my research is that residents both regularly reported police officers not following through on leads and also were incredulous that the crimes they were subject to, such as theft and stalking, were not taken seriously or resolved. There was no justice or resolution. Defunding movements challenge us to imagine responses to harm outside of policing that are committed to harm reduction rather than criminalization. These movements also consider all the harms that have occurred, including social harms done by institutions against "perpetrators."[48] In other words, defunding campaigns ask us to think structurally and systemically to understand the root causes of harm and how the very functioning of our society is implicated in who and what we deem criminal. And with that, they also remind us that this is not the way the world has to be.

Many residents with whom I spoke identified a variety of social ills and wanted more policing as a result. That is not surprising, given how safety in the United States is entirely subsumed by policing. Yet despite massive budgets, policing is ineffective at dealing with various social ills on the ground. Police also create harm themselves. As I described earlier, policing is a racial capitalist relation that facilitates exploitation and dehumanization. Residents use the specter of security to make sense of the increasing harm they experience in their neighborhoods as victims and bystanders. This specter defines harm solely as criminal activity, obscuring the exploitation and dehumanization of racial capitalism that produces insecurity itself. As others have argued, policing cannot be reformed because dehumanization, violence, and social control are foundational to it.

If we shed the specter of security and embrace an expansive vision of safety, we can imagine other possibilities to solve social problems. What residents want is to feel safe, in the complete sense. As Eatondale resident Estelle (Black renter, twenties) put it, "That's what's important to me— somewhere to feel comfortable and safe with my kids, and clean, so if they wanna go outside and play, I don't have to worry about them getting hurt or anything." How do we reduce the harms that so many face? As I presented in the final section above, residents themselves have already taken steps toward abolitionist futures of harm reduction. In each of these examples, relationships of care, trust, and reciprocity served as the foundation. While these small windows into a different future inspire me, they were few. In the next chapter, I discuss how respectability, antiblackness, and suspicion were norms in Riverside and Carthage, leading to exclusion and disconnection among residents. But let us not forget these few encouraging examples as we enter the next chapter. They will help us remember there is a different path.

CHAPTER FIVE

Respectability, Antiblackness, and Suspicion

In the face of racial capitalism—via relations of underdevelopment, private property, and policing—Riverside and Carthage residents were left to deal with its harms. Abolitionists have argued that a politics of care is necessary to challenge racial capitalism and its consequences. Christopher Paul Harris defines a politics of care as "a world undone." He explains, "to undo towards an otherwise world is to refuse our violent and totalizing system of knowledge anchored in and (re)produced by antiblackness, racial capitalism, and cisheteropatriarchy."[1] In the previous chapter I discussed the abolitionist possibilities that fit within this framework of care, but how common was this orientation toward care in Riverside and Carthage?

I argue that most residents relied on racial capitalist norms of respectability, antiblackness, and suspicion when interacting with one another. These norms were directly related to the racial capitalist specters of neglect (respectability), trash talk (antiblackness), and security (suspicion) discussed in previous chapters. In other words, these norms are behavioral enactments of these specters or local ideologies. Residents executed these norms (or expected ways of behaving) when approaching their neighbors. The relationships produced by these racial capitalist enactments were sometimes reciprocal and maybe even protective, although largely exclusionary across race and class lines. These race- and class-segregated relationships helped transform racial capitalism's material exploitation, dispossession, and differential valuation into distrust of the "other" and boundary policing. For example, rather than see underdevelopment residents saw neglect, and in response they enacted norms of respectability that exacerbated underdevelopment's harm and maintained its structure. While these individualist and exclusionary responses were logical under racial capitalism and gave people short-term gains, these responses also helped maintain its structure in the long term. We are much less able to address systemic harms if we approach them as individual concerns or zero-sum games. In this chapter, I examine how Riverside and Carthage residents created and maintained relationships amidst norms of respectability, antiblackness, and suspicion.

Respectability

Respectability as a concept is perhaps most associated with respectability politics, which dictate that by "presenting oneself in a way that is pleasing to members of the dominant group, one will be able to assuage their fears about one (and one's group), and as a consequence, racial animus will dissipate among White Americans."[2] Only Diego (Latino homeowner, fifties) engaged in respectability politics, as we will see below, but many residents enacted norms of respectability. In my findings, norms of respectability were behavioral expectations of middle-classness as a signal of worthiness and distinction. They resulted in care that was conditional, dependent on these class performances. This class-based norm, however, interacted with the norm of antiblackness. This interaction produced the exclusion of poor Black residents from respectability, regardless of their behavior, and reified the harms of racial capitalism to which Black residents were already subject. I discuss these patterns below.

I argue that norms of respectability produced self-disciplining behaviors in some poor residents and residents of color to gain material and emotional resources from the white middle class. Diego was one of the first people I interviewed in Carthage. He received my Spanish-language postcard in the mail, and we set up a meeting at a library near his new home. While he still owned his home in Carthage, he had recently moved to Springdale, a northern suburb of Cincinnati. Diego was acutely aware of the stereotypes about Latinx migrants and the fears of some longtime residents about their arrival in Carthage. As a result, when he first moved to Carthage in 2006, he started a campaign to clean up the trash on his block. Diego invited his neighbors to join him in helping the community. He said they started with their own houses, cutting grass, making things look nice. As a landscaper, he had tools to help out those on his street who did not have the means to maintain their property. As Diego put it, everything costs money. He distributed flyers, and a few of his white neighbors joined him and picked up trash. He said he contacted all homeowners, explaining that he would pick up the trash and dump it in his trucks. He ran this campaign for a year. When I asked him how it went, he explained:

Unos colaboraron, otros no, pero menos colaboraron los hispanos.
Cosa contradictoria que yo les decía, "Muchachos, hagamos esto
porque tenemos que sembrar una buena imagen en esta comunidad

para que ellos piensen que nosotros los hispanos no somos gente rara ni que hemos venido molestar ni a incomodar a nadie. Somos gente que también nos gusta vivir bien y cómodamente aunque sea en esta pequeña propiedad." Pero no, poca colaboración, más tuve colaboración de los americanos; salían a recoger basura, limpiar sus yardas; todo eso lo hicimos.

(Some collaborated, others didn't, but Hispanics were the least collaborative. It's contradictory. I would say, "guys, let's do this because we need to plant a good image in this community, so they don't think that we as Hispanics are strange and that we haven't come to bother or inconvenience anyone. We are people who also like to live well and comfortably, even if it is in a small property." But no, [there was] little collaboration, I had more collaboration from whites; they would come out to collect trash, clean their yards, we did it all.)

Diego explained that he wanted to challenge anti-Latinx stereotypes and prove the collective worthiness of Latinxs to live in Carthage. By cleaning up, they would indicate that they were the "correct type" of Latinxs, which would prompt their non-Latinx neighbors to welcome them. If they worked hard enough, they would earn their place in Carthage. What was interesting is that Diego lamented his Latinx neighbors' unwillingness to participate in his cleanup campaign but later empathized with white residents who could not participate due to financial constraints.

In terms of motivating his Latinx neighbors, Diego used an ineffective strategy. We can see, however, why Diego chose this approach, as he recounted the success and acceptance he experienced in Carthage from white residents in particular:

El americano a mí me ha ayudado un montón.[3] Ahorita yo tengo una posición, no te voy a decir que estoy millonario, vivo cómodamente, tengo mis propiedades, yo he adquirido propiedades, he crecido económicamente. Y gracias a los americanos, me han apoyado, me han dado la mano bastante, menos apoyo he recibido de los hispanos, de mi gente hispana que de los americanos. No todos por supuesto son bondadosos y cariñosos pero te podría decir que las familias con las cuales yo me he contactado, toda mi vida me han apoyado, me han enseñado a trabajar y cómo se hace el trabajo, me han enseñado a ordenar mi vida, me han enseñado a ganar mi dinero, me han apoyado para trabajar.

(The American has helped a ton. Right now, I have a position—I'm not going to say I'm a millionaire. I live comfortably, I have my properties, I have acquired properties, I've grown economically. And thanks to the Americans, they have supported me, they have given me a hand a lot. I've received less support from Hispanics, from my own Hispanic people than from Americans. Of course not all of them are good-natured and kind, but I can tell you that the families with which I've connected, all my life they have supported me, they showed me how to work and how work is done, they've shown me how to organize my life, they've showed me how to make money, they have supported me to work.)

Diego received material and emotional rewards for his actions from white neighbors and professional contacts. While he said his take-home income was between $40,000 and $45,000 a year, his business earnings were between $150,000 and $160,000. It was clear from our conversation that he credited his connections with whites as leading to this financial success.

So while we can explain Diego's decision-making, we can also identify it as a strategy that enacted norms of respectability. In addition, it shaped his relationships with his Latinx neighbors. While Diego saw this "good Latino" script as beneficial to all, he did not identify what it potentially cost his co-ethnics. If white neighbors were so concerned about Latinx residents ruining their neighborhood, Diego's campaign positioned him (and other Latinx participants) as an exception to that logic, but it did not change it. Indeed, his campaign of respectability reinforced the logic. While some Latinx neighbors' refusal to engage with Diego's campaign did not necessarily challenge anti-Latinx stereotypes or respectability either, it was a rejection of the stakes he set.

Diego envisioned a different way forward for Latinx residents in Carthage and Cincinnati. For example, he outlined a training program to help Latinx residents transition to work in Cincinnati:

Gente que viene de nuestros países viene con . . . como te digo, no todos vienen con vicios, algunos vienen con vicios pero viene gente que no está preparada para este país; entonces vienen a aprender. Entonces sabes lo que deberían hacer las comunidades hispanas es brindar punto de apoyo, preparar a la gente, "¿Qué te gusta a ti hacer?" "Perfecto, te vamos a enseñar plomería." Grupos de gente hispana misma que ayuden a esa gente a que se perfeccione en la plomería. "¿A ti qué te gusta?" "La jardinería." "Perfecto, te vamos a enseñar, vamos a buscar gente que te ayude en la jardinería." A ti housekeeping o limpieza de casas, a ti cuidado de niños, tienes habilidades y las puedes desarrollar y sería una gran ayuda y esa gente prácticamente se prepararía y ganaría mejor y se instalaría mejor.

(People that come from our countries come with, how do I say—not all of them come with vices, some of them come with vices, but people come here unprepared. So they come here to learn. So you know what Hispanic communities should do is provide a foothold, prepare people. "What do you like to do?" "Perfect, we're going to teach you plumbing." Groups of Hispanics themselves that help those people become an expert in plumbing. "What do you like?" "Gardening." "Perfect, we're going to teach you, we're going to find people to help you with gardening." "For you housekeeping or cleaning houses, you childcare," you have abilities, and you can develop them. It would be a great help, and those people would prepare themselves and they would earn more and they would integrate better.)

While Diego used a deficit framework to explain the training program, he also saw strength and possibility in Latinx communities. He said he had spoken to people about his idea, including the local carpenters' association. However, it wanted legal documentation for those involved, and he said that was not possible for everyone. This was why he insisted on the program being a Latinx-led community effort. Here we see the limits of respectability as a response to structural disadvantage. As Diego found in the response from the carpenters' association, even with a successful performance, respectability may not be enough to overcome structural barriers, such as lack of legal documentation (itself a function of global processes of labor exploitation, underdevelopment, and extraction).

JENNY (WHITE RENTER, THIRTIES) moved into Eatondale Apartments in 2009 with her nine- and ten-year-old daughters. For our interview, I picked Jenny up at a nearby park. Since it was a bit chilly, she suggested we go up to the McDonald's in Delhi to talk. During our conversation, Jenny repeatedly emphasized that she knew what it is like to be poor and middle class because she had lived on both sides. She identified as working class to explain why she did not have long-term plans to stay in Eatondale, "[I'm] actually a working-class person. I've worked back before I was even legally old enough to work, but I've got back problems so, therefore, I hadn't been working the last couple of years, and I'm hoping I can either get the problems resolved so

I can go back to work or I'm going to have to—well, I've actually applied for disability, but I haven't been approved or anything like that. And those are my only two alternatives because my ex-husband doesn't pay child support." Jenny marked herself as working class to distinguish herself from her poor neighbors, as she lived in subsidized housing. In her search for additional financial support, she found aid at a local church in Delhi. Despite her positive feelings toward her neighbors, Jenny knew that not everyone viewed Eatondale and its residents that way. She said that local churches were hesitant to help Eatondale residents and have even told her not to share their resources with neighbors after she received assistance from them.

> JENNY: I had got some food, and then they gave me some assistance with my gas and electric. I guess because the people down there [in Eatondale] can be very rude and unappreciative—they can be, and I guess they have been in the past, so they've [the churches have] determined based on those previous incidents that they don't want to help anybody in that location.
> SARAH: But they made an exception for you?
> JENNY: Yeah, which I don't, I mean, I was grateful for it, but I don't think that's fair.
> SARAH: So would you say that's generally the attitude people have towards the apartment?
> JENNY: Oh yes, absolutely.

I characterize Jenny's engagement with the local church as self-discipline because she relied on a respectable race and class performance to acquire resources. In the context of this church, respectability aligned with white middle-classness. Importantly, Jenny was formerly middle class. It was clear from our conversation and my observations at Eatondale that she was a well-integrated community member. She showed and received genuine care from her Black neighbors. When describing them, Jenny said, "They're not bad people. They're just people who are struggling and trying to survive, and some of them are doing whatever means necessary to do that, whether it be legal or not." She continued, "I give a lot of respect, I get a lot of respect" and "they definitely are those kind of people that would help me for sure." She said at this stage she could rely on just about anyone in the complex for support.

Despite their shared economic reality, Jenny's performance of respectability depended on her distancing herself from her neighbors to show she was not "of Eatondale." That is both a race-based performance and class-based performance. So, while Jenny had interracial connections in Eatondale, her exchange with the church remade race into a salient category of difference and status. Jenny's respectability enabled her to wield resources her neighbors could not. She could do this successfully because of her middle-class upbringing and whiteness. Class is not just about the money you have—it is also about how the world interacts with you. Based on Jenny's comments, that seemed to mean a performance of gratitude and stating that she viewed poverty as a momentary circumstance for her and her family. To be clear, the church in Delhi necessitated this distinction between *from* and *of* Eatondale. The church incentivized Jenny's performance by providing her with resources that it, in effect, denied to Black residents in need.[4] In other words, Jenny's performance—like Diego's—was a self-disciplining response to racial capitalist ideas and structures of resource distribution that demanded respectability.

To further elucidate the importance of whiteness and middle-classness for receiving charity in the Riverside area, I turn to Jenny's neighbor Aisha (Black renter, thirties). She shared a story about approaching her predominantly white church across the street from Eatondale for assistance. It did not go as well for Aisha as it had for Jenny in Delhi.

> My church—and that's my church, and I hate to say that—[*softer*] it's been times where I took people over there, and they were in need of food and all of that, and churches normally help with stuff like that. There was an incident where me and a girl upstairs that I had grew up with a long time ago, we walked over there to go get food, and the lady told us that the pantry was closed. She said that they closed it down 'cause they didn't have no funds, so we took back, came over here, and sat on the porch. God was telling me to sit on that wall and watch 'cause right after we came out, no BS [bullshit], a white lady walked right up in behind us, walked right to the door, that [same] lady came down with exactly eight bags. I counted eight bags of groceries, and I attend this church on the regular. And even though I know that it's some people that feel some type of way, I don't let it stop me from going to service, you know what I'm saying.

This was not an isolated incident, as Aisha provided another example of how she was denied charity from her church:

> I told them I need help with clothes, all of that, nothing. But I see white people do it and get everything they ask for [*snaps fingers*]. One

girl got a brand-new [*snaps*] living room suite, tables, chairs, all that. Me, [I get told] "I will see if somebody got something and if you get it then it's up for you to check for [bed] bugs."[5] You'll carry it on your vehicle, but it's up to me to check for [bed bugs]?—come on now, is you serious? This is what we deal with.

Aisha spoke candidly throughout our conversation about the mistreatment that Black residents of Cincinnati experienced every day. As her previous statement indicated, she was often incredulous at the denigration to which individuals and organizations subjected Black people, but it was particularly hurtful when it happened while asking for help from her church.

While Diego and Jenny found self-discipline a successful strategy for bonding with white middle-class people, Aisha's example indicates that self-disciplining is a social performance that the audience must accept for it to succeed. It is an assessment of one's behavior and the body that performs it. For example, Aisha attended her local church to fulfill her spiritual responsibilities within a particular set of constraints, namely lack of transportation. She explained, "That's the closest church. I ain't gotta worry about having the bus fare or all of that." While she appreciated the convenience of the location, Aisha observed racist resource allocation rules by her church. She said the people she interacted with and asked for help assumed that she was on drugs and refused to help her despite helping white parishioners. Aisha elaborated, "Most people won't help you. 'Cause they automatically assume drugs, or—you don't know how many times I done been sitting in that church and asked for help and someone looks over and says, 'Yeah, you're from the hood,' And she's a minister! . . . But she's like, 'Well you can pray and this and that,' And I'm like, 'yeah, I'm doing that,' you know what I mean." So while Aisha attended church and was an active member, including singing in the choir, a minister directed her to pray to solve her food insecurity—which Aisha was already doing at church. In this way, Aisha's performance of respectability as a churchgoer and prayerful person was illegible in the white church she attended. Instead, white church members read her Blackness and association with Eatondale as incongruent with respectability, regardless of her self-disciplining actions.

These interactions and disappointments led Aisha to feel frustrated, saddened, and scared at how church members refused to see her humanity. When discussing the block watch that church members organized to watch and pray for the Eatondale building, she explained, "I pray for this building all the time, but this is my problem right here: when you're watching the building, you're not watching it because of the building having mold, mildew, whatever the building need to come down because of health issues. You're watching this building because it's predominantly Black over here. I know that. And it makes me feel [*pause*] scared. You would think that certain people would be scared to live here because of the violence; the violence is one thing. But it's more of a racist neighborhood than anything." Aisha pinpointed the disconnect between her reality and white church members. While they both prayed for the building, she sensed that church members were not praying for the well-being of its tenants. Their disregard for her and her neighbors' humanity scared her, undoubtedly leading to further feelings of disconnection from the broader neighborhood. Aisha's experience shows how norms of respectability and antiblackness can work in tandem to produce exclusion, disconnection, and marginalization.

Antiblackness

One of the norms that trash talk produced in Riverside and Carthage was antiblackness. Antiblackness, of course, is not just a norm or behavioral expectation. Sociologists Moon-Kie Jung and João H. Costa Vargas call antiblackness an "antisocial logic that not only dehumanizes Black people but also renders abject all that is associated with Blackness. This generalized abjection helps us grasp the ways in which, historically and contemporarily, Black people's embattled bodies, spaces, knowledge, culture, citizenship, and humanity have served as the counterpoints to safety, rationality, belonging, and life. Unlike racism, which tends to focus on analogous experiences of oppression, antiblackness stresses the singularity of Black people's dehumanization, antihumanization."[6] I focus on antiblackness as a behavioral norm to show that antiblackness is not only a set of ideas but also a way of interacting with others. As I show next, Black people did not need to be present for antiblackness to structure relationships and behaviors between residents.

Nick (white homeowner, thirties) was a landlord and had previously lived in Riverside. He explained that his recent experiences in Price Hill and Riverside shaped his approach to new people.

I don't know if it's a lack of trust or just a general sense of suspicion all the time. But I think Riverside and Price Hill, in general, have helped ferment that in me, a general sense of—I hate to judge a book by its cover, but I do it every day out here. And if I think I can trust you, I have no problem saying, "Hey, I don't mind sitting down with a coffee and spilling out to you in front of a tape recorder." But if I think you're that guy out there, and I think you're a junkie, I've got no problems running over you with my car if you step in the intersection.

Nick explained that making judgments was part of his day-to-day, and he explained how he made those judgments as a landlord (see chapter 3). While he had no problem trusting me to participate in an audio-recorded interview about his life, he also had no problem potentially killing someone he deemed a "junkie" on the street. This juxtaposition points to the boundary making on which racial capitalism simultaneously relies and facilitates. The trash talk specter dehumanizes and creates the conditions under which Nick felt no qualms about seriously harming another person who impeded his car from driving past. Because Nick viewed drug addicts as "trash," they were less than human to him. While it may seem that his comments have nothing to do with racial capitalism, dehumanization is one of its critical, differentiating characteristics. The boundary work that Nick is doing is less about the race or class identity of the "junkie" (although those markers also help construct some drug users as worthier than others; see chapter 3) and more about how the construction of drug addicts as part of a stigmatized group helps construct Nick as different and motivates him "to take dramatic social action" (i.e., threaten to run them over).[7] This same process of dehumanization underscores and produces the norm of antiblackness.

While antiblackness as a norm is dehumanizing and leads to disconnection for Black people, as we previously saw with Aisha, it can also lead to connections among nonblack people. For example, Nick described how he came to know and appreciate his elderly neighbor in contrast to his more distant relationship with his other neighbor, saying, "I'm on very good terms with my elderly next-door neighbor. I cut her grass. I help her out. She gives me all of these tomatoes and stuff during the harvest. But my other neighbor, he's been there just as long. I don't even know his name. He lives up a little ways, but that would have never taken place where I grew up in Kentucky. Never. Because you just know everyone. You can—you could recognize a last name and be like, 'Oh, well, I know her brother and their father.' Not out here at all." When I asked him why he thought there was a difference in his relationship with the two neighbors, he responded:

The very first day I moved in, one neighbor is—like I'm here and my other neighbor is right here, and then my third neighbor is up the way a little bit. So this guy's kind of far away. He keeps to himself, man, and I'm not going to dispute that. Keep to yourself. Do what you want. He's a big, fat white guy. He's got some Asian wife. I always see her cutting the grass and stuff like that. I've never approached him, I've never talked to him. I've walked my dogs past their house. They don't really acknowledge me. I don't acknowledge them. No big deal. The very first day I moved into my house, my elderly neighbor on the left comes to the fence and says, "I'm just glad to see that no Black guys bought that house." Says that to me, and I'm like, "You're going to be all right." And it wasn't long before that, that she was coming out with sweet tea and pitchers of this. And I would just want to reciprocate. I would offer to cut her grass.

His response "you're going to be all right" seemed to signal that the elderly neighbor would not need to worry about Black men being around while Nick lived there. That initial exchange made way for future encounters where they established reciprocity. In this way, his neighbor's antiblack comment facilitated the securing of support from Nick—and vice versa. Her statement seemed to endear her to him.

He continued:

She told me about her situation to where she would have—she called them repairmen—just jerks off the street, come and cut her grass or whatever and stuff like that. It didn't sit with me well at the time because I've seen a lot of these people. And they'll come to my door too. They know not to come now because I don't buy. But I just was like, "You know, you don't need to be hiring these guys off the street." Some guy will charge her ten bucks to cut her front lawn. Another guy will be like, "Oh, it's thirty bucks, and you've got to reseal your driveway. I'll do that for one hundred right now." So I just took over a little bit of that. And then, through that, she introduced me to some other—her relatives that actually live on the street.

In short, the initial exchange, characterized by his neighbor's racism, helped Nick and her connect in the longer term. Nick watched out for her, and she helped integrate him into the neighborhood with her family. While Nick's relationship with his neighbor may seem incongruent with his previously expressed distrust, I argue they are two sides of the same coin. The trash talk that shaped his understanding of drug users and most residents also shaped how he understood his elderly neighbor as an exception. "Trash" is a relational construction. In other words, his bonding with his neighbor was not a challenge to the logics of racial capitalism that relied on trash talk and antiblackness, but a reinforcement of them. As he explained later, his relationship with her was very much an exception to how he interacted—or rather, did not—with his other neighbors.

Norms of antiblackness also shaped residents' vision of care. For example, Dick (white homeowner, fifties) imagined a community where neighbors cared for one another and spent time together. He envisioned community businesses contributing to events where neighbors could unite and support one another.

> That's the way I think communities should be. Have a big cookout.
> I don't know—Carthage could get donations from the bank and a
> couple of businesses. Just to buy some hot dogs and hamburger
> patties, and get a big grill and just have a free cookout for everybody to
> mingle, some picnic tables. I would gladly walk up, "hi neighbor, my
> name is Dick. I live at such and such." You know, get to talking and
> maybe see what the area needs. See how do other people feel—if they
> need help with something. I would rather help an old person that has a
> sink leaking, costing them tons of money instead of getting it fixed
> 'cause they can't get it fixed than them be struggling because they ain't
> got the money to buy something else.

Dick proposed a way for neighbors to connect and support one another and seemed enthusiastic about this possibility.

In this same discussion, Dick lamented what he saw as the self-absorbed reality. But his focus on selfishness relied on racist and classist stereotypes about welfare recipients:

> I think now, it's so much me, me, me, me, like people on the system,
> on welfare. Well, "I get a check every month, I get food stamps
> here, I live on Section 8 housing. I only pay $20"—but you got a
> $300 phone. I got a $60 phone. It's just some people's way of thinking.
> I understand some people the way they're raised, they may not know
> any different, may not know any better, but still it's your work ethics.
> You gotta realize, you're walking around with nails done, hair done,
> and a $300 phone, but yet my taxes is paying for your welfare. Is that
> wrong? [laughs]

Dick had just mentioned wanting a community where he and his neighbors cared for one another. He even provided an example of helping unhoused people get back on their feet by sharing his housing and food with them. At the same time, he viewed the state providing benefits to the poor via welfare programs as unacceptable. He tied this unacceptability to his perceptions of inappropriate spending among poor people. How he knew these individuals were poor was not clear. Arguably Dick assumed they were poor because they were Black women, given his references to "nails done, hair done." As sociologist Tressie McMillan Cottom wrote about in *Thick: And Other Essays*, Black people's consumption is deemed problematic at many turns in part because of their presumed poverty.[8] She writes, "Much like we interrogate what a woman was wearing when she was raped, we look for ways to assign personal responsibility for structural injustices to bodies we collectively do not value. If you are poor, why do you spend money on useless status symbols like handbags and belts and clothes and shoes and televisions and cars? One thing I've learned is that one person's illogical belief is another person's survival skill. And nothing is more logical than trying to survive."[9]

Dick's comments also belie how some nonblack people's visions of care and community are exclusive of the Black poor. This categorical exclusion provides the nonblack poor with relative but meager rewards, and upholds and obscures the structural arrangements that enable their exploitation as poor people. This is not false consciousness but, as sociologist Stuart Hall argues, a partial recognition of material reality. While antiblackness protects whites from some harms under racial capitalism, such as targeted police violence, it also subjects them to other harms. Dick's heartbreak over his daughter's opioid addiction and involvement with the criminal justice system is an example of one such harm. So while the specter of trash talk and norms of antiblackness may be short-term strategies for resource hoarding under racial capitalism, especially for working-class whites, these strategies keep in place the racist and classist relations from which residents are trying to shield themselves in the long term, ensuring their continued exploitation and dehumanization.

Suspicion

Suspicion is the third neighborhood norm, a product of the specter of security. A norm of suspicion shaped how many Riverside and Carthage residents, principally white residents, approached their neighbors—with distrust, fear, and belief in their badness. This was especially true if they had nonwhite or poor neighbors, although not always. Suspicion intertwined with ideologies of homeownership as well, where renters seemed to be treated with more suspicion than property owners. This is not surprising, given how ideologies of homeownership entangle tenure status with morality.

Abby (white renter, sixties) used urban specters to evaluate her neighbors and enacted norms of suspicion and fear with her Latinx neighbors. These behaviors helped her maintain a sense of her previous status despite her downward mobility. Carthage was not a neighborhood in which Abby ever wanted to live. She grew up in the "Fairfield-Hamilton area," suburban communities north of Cincinnati. When I asked her how she came to live in Carthage, Abby explained that a taxi driver had misled her. After suffering a stroke and living in a nursing home that raised her rent, she needed to relocate quickly. "I knew Hartwell and Carthage from thirty years ago, which is nothing like that now. And instead of taking me the way I asked him to, [the taxi driver] took me in a different way, and I didn't realize that I wasn't in Hartwell. So I ended up in Carthage." When I asked her the distinction between living in Hartwell and Carthage, she explained:

> ABBY: Living in Carthage is something that I have never encountered before, and I pray to God that I never encounter it again. I'm getting out of there, hopefully by September, and I will never even drive through that neighborhood again. I just won't.
>
> SARAH: Okay. So what is it specifically that you're unhappy with?
>
> ABBY: First of all, the streets are dirty, people throw junk everywhere. They throw tires wherever. Nobody ever cleans anything up. When people move they just sit stuff out on the sidewalk. I mean, everything from couches to bloody mattresses, you name it, it's out there. And there's a little store two blocks down. I can't—this is just unimaginable to me. I can't walk down the street. I don't normally look like this. When I moved here, I had my hair colored and fixed. I wore makeup. I wore my nice clothes. After about two months I realized, if I was gonna survive, I was gonna have to look like everybody else. So I bought old clothes, and I don't put on makeup. I don't do anything.

In Abby's characterization of why she found Carthage untenable, she relied on trash talk and suspicion. It shaped her self-presentation and sense of self. Abby felt the local police abandoned her, leading to additional fear and distress. To wit, she said she had been attacked twice and did not call the police, as they "don't even come down through there unless something major happens." Abby then shared that there were sex workers "all over the place" and that men had propositioned her when she was walking around the neighborhood. She said a neighbor warned her not to go out to the parking lot behind the building at night because people gather to drink and do drugs. He similarly warned her not to walk around at night "because I would get hurt."

Abby's description of Carthage was grim, and it is no surprise she was unhappy there. Clearly, she did not want to identify with Carthage or anyone who lived there. Even the way she told the story of how she ended up moving there—the fault of a taxi driver who would not listen—evaded the more difficult reality that her medical history and its financial strain limited her housing options. Rather than grapple with how illness and our capitalist health care system played a role in her current housing situation, Abby drew on a different thread to make sense of her life. She distinguished herself from those she saw as beneath her through racial devaluation and used racist logics to explain how Latinx residents in her building were to blame for its various problems. She wanted to make it clear that she was not like them.

In response to her need for status differentiation, Abby enacted norms of suspicion and fear with her neighbors that reified racial differences. While Abby's status as one of the few white residents of her apartment building meant that she had the opportunity to build cross-race ties like Jenny did in Eatondale, Abby used fear and suspicion of difference to guide her interactions with her Latinx neighbors. She was not looking for connection but status. Reifying racial boundaries helped Abby maintain the status of whiteness when economic markers were not obvious or present, given that she lived in the same building with Latinxs. For example, Abby shared a story about how she chastised a Latina neighbor's children for only intermittently speaking in English to her.

> One night I went there, they knocked on my door, and I didn't know what they wanted because when you talk to them, their parents have taught them to act like they don't know how to speak English. They do. Because they go to school. And they wouldn't say anything unless they wanted to play with my dog, and they'd ask me. And I told them one day, I said, "If you won't speak to me in English whenever I talk to you," I said, "Then I'm not gonna let you play with my dog whenever you can speak English." And I said, "You speak English to me all the time, or I won't let you play with my dog."

Abby presented this experience as an example of the boundaries she had to set with neighbors. She seemed proud of how she, amidst chaotic life circumstances, stood up to perceived Latinx hegemony in her building. Telling the kids to speak English was a way to assert control and reestablish her dominance despite being a numerical minority in the building and economically equal to her neighbors. Many assumptions underlie her response to the children, but the main is that their parents told them not to speak English as a scam or form of dishonesty. Anti-Latinx racism via suspicion of the children facilitated the status distinction that Abby's class could not provide her. While this provided Abby a psychological wage and brief emotional respite, it ultimately obscured and maintained the exploitation of our class system, where medical debt and disability status can lead to displacement and housing insecurity, and where migrant labor is undervalued and exploited. A racial capitalist lens allows us to weave these connections to understand how Abby and her neighbors came to live side by side in a poorly maintained building in Carthage, while also allowing us to be attuned to differences in experience and vulnerability.

Abby's interactions with her neighbors make sense if we do not see Latinx children as children but as coconspirators or deviants in the making. Our contemporary racial structure, in which Latinx people are deemed suspect and criminal, produces emotions of fear and, in the case of children, disgust at their innate deviance. As sociologist Eduardo Bonilla-Silva puts it, "Once a group is racialized as 'savage' and 'dangerous,' its members are feared and seen in need of supervision and civilization."[10] In short, Abby's approach to the children was in line with the specter of security and norm of suspicion.

It is, of course, possible that Abby approached everyone around her with suspicion. However, that did not seem to be the case. Later in the interview, she described how she had a conflict with two white neighbors who asked to borrow money: "I used to loan it to them, but then they wouldn't ever pay me back, not once. And the only time they would come around is when they wanted something. And I just quit opening the door, and I talk to them if I see them in the hallway, but other than that, I don't have anything to do with them." Even though she perceived wrongdoing by her neighbors, she did not address it directly with them. Additionally, to lend her neighbors money in the first place, Abby needed to trust them, not treat them with suspicion. Notably, the two neighbors she lent money to were two of very few white women in the building. While Abby initially said she avoided these neighbors, she later referred to one of them as a friend. Arguably, the race of her neighbors played a role in how she assessed deviance and punishment. Abby is not unique in this regard. In a system of racial capitalism like ours, racial differentiation and devaluation are guiding logics and practices that facilitate and obscure class exploitation. In Abby's case, racial differentiation promoted her self-making and shaped how she approached her neighbors amidst economic precarity.

Of course, racial sameness did not protect everyone from being approached with suspicion. Carthage residents Skylar and Timmy (white renters, twenties) were treated as suspects by some of their "nosy" neighbors, although they laughed it off.

> TIMMY: When we first moved in, when we first got there, I was approached by at least three or four of 'em, but like coming up to me like "who are you, what are you doing at that house?" because no one had lived there. So they felt like I was breaking in or something, and I was like "no, I mean I have the key, [*laughs*] no I'm not breaking in." They were—so that's an example [of neighbors being nosy].
> SKYLAR: It's just kind of funny. They're curious maybe.

Nevertheless, despite these interrogations about who they were, Skylar and Timmy's interactions with their neighbors turned into positive connections. Timmy explained, "Once they figured out we weren't like breaking in, yeah, they were fine [*both laugh*]." Skylar then explained that "especially a specific person on our street has been very nice to us and anything we need he helps us out, so. Like he, Thanksgiving he gave us a whole box of food and everything, which was really nice. He went out of his way to do that. So it's really nice." Their experience shows that suspicion can transform into care, unlike Abby's exchange with her neighbors.

Race and class differences seemed to be a catalyst for suspicion. Riverside residents Iris (white homeowner, thirties) and Jake (white homeowner, twenties) show how these assessments happened. Iris first moved to Riverside alone, renting one floor of a large house. After Iris and Jake met, Jake moved in to escape his messy roommates. When their landlord decided to retire in Florida, she offered Iris and Jake the chance to buy their home before putting it on the market. They decided to take the opportunity. Now homeowners, they lived with their infant son and Iris's mother, who helped care for him. At over $80,000, Jake and Iris's household income put them far above Riverside's mean and median.

It was clear that Iris and Jake did not feel like typical Riverside residents. When I asked them to describe their neighbors, Iris said, "Wow. Different from us." They described the neighbors behind their home as the exception. When I asked why, Jake said it was because the neighbors had talked to Iris and him. Iris then added:

IRIS: If we're going to get real, it's social cues. Like what they wear, how they speak. They seem like they're educated and somewhat financially stable, I guess. Whereas maybe some other people, if we were just going off of looks—

JAKE: And they're hands-on with their kid. So, for example, last year, they were very nice when we saw them out sledding.

Jake also described how he saw the father and son doing yard work one day while outside, and that "the son is really nice talking to his dad about stuff." Iris said that while there are not many children close to their home, further into Riverside there are many children who play out in the street; "it looks like they're not supervised, and that's kind of dangerous."

Sociologist Annette Lareau introduced the concept of concerted cultivation to describe the hands-on approach that middle-class families take to develop their children's skills and talents. According to Lareau, "Discussions between parents and children are a hallmark of middle-class child rearing."[11] Lareau contrasted this parenting style to an accomplishment of natural growth model that was more common among poor and working-class families, where children had more control over their time and less entitlement. Lareau wrote, "For them, the crucial responsibilities of parenthood do not lie in eliciting their children's feelings, opinions, and thoughts."[12] With Jake's focus on the pleasant conversation between father and son, and Iris's discussion of unsupervised children, Jake and Iris called upon these classed ideals of parenthood to distinguish their family and their neighbors from working-class Riverside. They met these different parenting styles with suspicion, mostly keeping to themselves. Here we see how suspicion is not just a feeling but also a behavior.

As an exception to their rule, Jake did connect with their neighbor Joshua. When Joshua walked by their home to get to the Speedway gas station, Jake and Joshua chatted and have since shared a few beers outside. Jake mentioned that Joshua worked at a casual dining chain restaurant.

JAKE: I did learn some details about his life during my time hanging out with him. And his brother was found floating in the Ohio River, murdered.

IRIS: You didn't tell me that.

JAKE: He told me he wanted to find the person who did it and kill them.

IRIS: That's understandable.

JAKE: Yeah. But it kind of scared me a little bit. Like, I wanted to give him a chance. And then I started being worried that I had given him a chance and gotten close to him. But ultimately, I feel okay about it.

IRIS: You looked him up on Facebook.

JAKE: I looked him up on Facebook. He likes family. He likes his family.

IRIS: And he said that he also played basketball with some of the kid neighbors over on this side.

JAKE: But I feel like maybe some people here might have participated in the stuff that we think about inner-city people doing, like using drugs and selling drugs, getting into trouble, stealing stuff, robbing people. Because of out of necessity possibly.

Jake's perception of the different class statuses between himself and Joshua played a role in his evaluation of Joshua's comments. He felt afraid; it did not seem like he feared for his safety, but that he more feared the unpredictability of Joshua's behavior. In other words, would Joshua *actually* murder someone? Given that Jake immediately commented on people in the neighborhood being involved in illegal activities, he took Joshua's response seriously.

While Jake's social interactions with Joshua were an exception to his general isolation from neighbors, their budding relationship was limited and caused Jake stress.

IRIS: I think, also, because we are so busy, we are fine with our social circle being tight and small like it is. We just probably don't get enough time alone as it is anyway. And so if we expand that and start knocking on neighbors' doors, then people might show up unexpectedly.

JAKE: That was the thing about Joshua. He was calling and texting me, asking to hang out. I'm like, no, it's eleven at night, and I'm a father, and I have to work all the time. So no.

SARAH: And what was his sort of response to that?

JAKE: That's what I didn't like. It was like pushback, like I was obligated to hang out with him. And he's not my friend. He's an acquaintance at this point. So that's not cool.

When we spoke, it had been a month since Jake had seen Joshua.

When I asked Jake what he would do if he had a problem with a neighbor, he said, "I would probably just get anxious and stress out about it and ask someone for help. Or advice. . . . And we would probably start thinking about moving sooner." Iris chimed in, "I'm more of a proactive confront and engage type of person. But again, it depends what it is. If it's a situation that could escalate into any sort of fear or bodily harm, then yeah, I definitely would think about moving." She went on to say that if it were a minor issue, such as someone having a problem with their dogs barking, she would deal with that head-on. She then clarified, "I don't think we're going to have any problems, honestly." I argue that Jake and Iris's ability to start somewhere new shaped their interactions with their neighbors. They did not feel much urgency to connect or stay in Riverside because they were financially secure and well connected beyond the neighborhood. They could take or leave Joshua, and if he caused them distress, they had no incentive to maintain ties to him or even to their neighborhood if things escalated.

What I find noteworthy is not that Jake and Iris were uninterested in being friends with their neighbors—they certainly did not need to be—but that they did not feel any incentive to connect with them at all. I argue that this is profoundly shaped by how we think and talk about homeownership under racial capitalism. Focusing on private property ownership directs us inward and reinforces outward norms of suspicion. When we frame the supposed wealth creation of homeownership as the highest consumer good and exercise of freedom, it incentivizes independence despite homeownership's relational reality. These are not ideas that Jake and Iris created but that are embedded in all aspects of life in the United States. As political scientist Jared Clemons argues, this individualist approach is endemic to how we understand the role of the state under neoliberalism: "While Keynesian capitalism—or, more fittingly, the New Deal order—operated under the assumption that the government played a role in providing labor (workers) with a safety net to protect from the market's excesses, neoliberal capitalism holds that the state has no such obligation; instead, individuals can, through the development of their human capital, become their own safety net."[13] How we frame homeownership, and that homeownership is how most Americans hold wealth, certainly reflects this arrangement. Relatedly, as discussed in chapter 3, homeowners need renters to help reify the privilege of homeownership. In this way, norms of fear and suspicion are not just a product of the specter of security but also shaped by the economic relations of homeownership and private property. Urban specters obscure racial capitalism's interdependency and convince us we do not need each other, yet the opposite is true.

Moments of Care

In this chapter, I present how the urban specters of neglect, trash talk, and security shaped how Riverside and Carthage residents related to one another and their neighborhoods. I specifically focused on norms of respectability, antiblackness, and suspicion that produced patterns of exclusion and division in the neighborhoods. I trace how these three urban specters led residents to boundary policing and disconnection. Importantly, these were individualist responses to systemic harms, leaving racial capitalism's logics and functioning in place.

To be clear, it is not that Carthage and Riverside residents did not care for each other. Case in point, below I include three examples of residents who shared resources and reached out to neighbors in need.

Carthage resident Ben (white renter, fifties) said that he knew his neighbors and spent some time with them despite not speaking Spanish. He even helped them when they lost electricity one night:

> The one neighbor over in apartment D, I've been in their apartment one night on a Friday night, and we drank some beer. And I had a kid translate, was about eight years old and he was translating. But there was one from New York who spoke English real good. And then the neighbor upstairs from me—those [neighbors in apartment D] are Guatemalan. The neighbors upstairs from me are Mexican. And, well, their electrical was out, so I ran an [seventy-five-foot] extension cord for them. . . . Duke Energy got his electricity on that Monday. He said, "I'll be alright." [I responded,] "Well, do you have a refrigerator? With food in it? Well, plug your refrigerator and TV up."

Ben said his neighbor was very appreciative. He presented it as an obvious gesture, saying, "You don't want to leave your refrigerator unplugged with food in the freezer."

If there was any pattern of care across both neighborhoods, it was caring for the elderly. Todd (white homeowner, fifties) helped out his elderly neighbors with their lawn. Todd said, "I've got nine yards on that street [that I take care of]. They basically—they're a little too old to be out there pushing a lawn mower, so I'm out there pushing a lawn mower for them. That's the way I look at it." He explained that he did not ask for a payment, but "if they give me a little gas money, they give me a little gas money. That's about it." Todd did not just help his elderly neighbors, however. He also helped out fellow truck driver and neighbor Eddie:

> Me and Eddie—we've got something totally in common, we both drive. We both drive. He gets Monday and Tuesday off, I get Saturday and Sunday off, but when we meet up, we're pretty good. He'll come

over and help me if he sees me struggling with my backyard, and I'll go over and help him. One day it was going to rain, and I said I've got to go help him. He's not going to get this done. I helped him with the lawn mower, and here he is, trying to go, and it's starting to come down. I got mine out, and we got it done real quick. It cost him a six-pack.

Todd and Eddie's shared work, truck driving, fostered their connection. That evolved into helping each other out with work around their homes.

Lastly, Carthage resident Erik (white renter, sixties) had lived in Carthage for six years. He explained that he would like to move closer to his sister in Montgomery, a city north of Cincinnati where the median household income was over three times that of Cincinnati. However, he remained in Carthage because that move "takes money." While this desire could have led him to isolate himself amidst resentment, he was well connected with his landlord: "I love to death my landlord and landlady. We became very close. They do favors for me, I do favors for them; we get along." When I asked what kind of favors he and his landlords did for each other, he said, "If I need something at the store and a couple weeks ago in appreciation I ordered pizza, the deal at LaRosa's is three for $19.50, for three mediums, so I got them one and kept two, stuff like that. I'm into electronics, so if they have a question or different things we talk, stuff like that. They'll get my mail and my paper if my knee is bothering me, and I'll do things—you know, so it's a good relationship."

Interestingly, all three of these examples of care came from white, working-class men, a group that is not necessarily associated with caregiving. There is, of course, a big difference between interpersonal acts of care and a structural politics of care. That may seem obvious, but distress about the distinction was at the core of many pieces about Donald Trump-supporting loved ones during his presidency (*"How could my loved one, who is kind to me, vote for Trump?"*). As many people seemed to learn, individuals can be courteous interpersonally and still support politics of harm, destruction, and exploitation. In contrast to these interpersonal acts, a politics of care is "animated by a desire for something else, something more, the practice and process of undoing and then remaking the world offers the possibility of a different kind of relation, an unbounded with and for on the other side of domination."[14] Most moments of care in Riverside and Carthage did not meet the standard of creating a new world. However, we can imagine how acts of reciprocal care and resource sharing—of money, transportation, time, and expertise—become first steps toward rejecting norms of respectability, antiblackness, and suspicion. This deeper, collective, countercultural work of a world undone is possible when we understand our interdependency outside of the partial stories of urban specters and their norms of exclusion and disconnection. To combat racial capitalist relations of dehumanization and exploitation, we need a "radical interdependency" where our relationships to one another are grounded in what bell hooks defines as "the will to nurture our own and another's . . . growth, revealed through acts of care, respect, knowing, and assuming responsibility." [15]

Carthage residents Harry and Miriam (Black homeowners, sixties) had a strong desire to connect with their neighbors. The alienation they felt from those around them was palpable. When I asked them what made a good neighbor, Miriam responded, "You'd like to think that your neighbor's looking out for you enough to know who you are and speak to you." Harry quickly added, "I don't have good neighbors. I can tell you that." In the conclusion, I explore the dreams that residents shared, like Harry and Miriam's desire for deeper connection, and possible ways to make them a reality.

Urban Exorcism

Urban Specters is a story about how residents in two working-class Cincinnati neighborhoods used local ideologies to justify and explain their life circumstances. These specters were partial recognitions of the actual material conditions in which residents found themselves. I described three specters, the racial capitalist relations they helped to normalize and obscure, and the norms they produced. By pairing ideologies and structural relations, I presented an innovative case for how ideologies justify, obfuscate, and sustain material conditions of racial capitalism that produce exploitation and dehumanization.

In chapter 2, I discussed the specter of neglect and how residents often discussed the ways they were left behind—by the city, landlords, and civic associations. I also traced how residents were subject to underdevelopment and segregation, relations that created the "neglected" conditions of Riverside, Carthage, and other Cincinnati neighborhoods. In chapter 3, I focused on the specter of "trash talk" and private property ownership as a process of racial capitalist exploitation, dispossession, and devaluation. I described how residents talked about subsidized housing, drug users, and renters to lay claim to neighborhoods experiencing territorial stigma. Trash talk was a distancing tactic used to blame transient interlopers for neighborhood problems. This tactic also maintained the system that produced this neighborhood stigmatization.

Chapter 4 documented how residents discussed security in Carthage and Riverside, and it drew a distinction between security and safety in line with abolitionist thinking. I considered the harms and failures of contemporary policing and how residents were already enacting abolitionist possibilities. Lastly, chapter 5 bridged urban specters with residents' behaviors. I identified three norms (respectability, antiblackness, and suspicion) that stemmed from the ideologies and relations of racial capitalism. The norms produced exclusion and boundary policing among residents, especially across race and class lines.

Urban specters haunted the imaginations of residents, shaping not only what they saw but also how they interacted with one another. It is no surprise that, plagued by the harms of racial capitalist relations, many were looking for relief. But rather than seeking to reduce the harm in their neighborhoods and expelling the demons of racial capitalism, residents were looking to extricate themselves from these communities. The more I spoke with residents, the more I noticed that moving away was a common refrain. You may have noted this as well. Abby wanted to get out of Carthage as soon as she was able. Harry and Miriam would have liked to move, but that was not possible without a significant loss of money. Carl and Maggie would have happily relocated their home to another neighborhood if they could. If Iris and Jake ever had a large enough conflict with a neighbor, they would move. Even Meghan, who was very happy in Riverside, said she would have moved if there had ever been an issue.

Many other residents also dreamed of relocating. Some renters wanted to head "back home," such as Akilah, who planned to return to Detroit, Michigan. Others wanted to move to totally new cities, such as Federico, who said, "Austin, Texas, is what's standing out so far because they're conservative and freaky at the same time. That's me." Bonnie and Deacon both mentioned Florida. Julius was thinking about Charlotte, North Carolina. Aisha said she would move if she could, "maybe to Kentucky or something." Milton just wanted to get out of Riverside, while Maggie wished to leave the city of Cincinnati altogether. Neither had a particular destination in mind. Skylar and Timmy were interested in moving to Hyde Park or the Kenwood area on the East Side. Elisabeth was not sure if she'd stay in Cincinnati long term, but if she did, she would like to move to a different street within Carthage.

A few homeowners also mentioned wanting to get away. Hugh wanted to leave Cincinnati, saying, "If I didn't have a dog, I would be already gone." He explained he did not want his dog to lose the yard, so he'd wait to move until after his dog passed. Cindy also imagined moving away in the next five to ten years, "but it's more a age thing." Her husband had difficulties climbing steps, so their two-story home was not their best long-term option. Erika dreamed not of moving but of buying out her neighbors so *they* would move. She said if she won the lottery, that was the first thing she would do. She would offer $100,000, which she said was about double the home's market value.

Colette loved her home and wanted to "put it on wheels and move it." When I asked where she would go, she said she was unsure. She concluded, "I wish I could live in a bubble in my own damn universe. That's the only safe haven, besides a pistol and God being on my side. That's my only safe haven and you can't live in a bubble in your own universe." Colette's comments get to the heart of the matter: People wanted to move toward comfort and safety. Their neighborhoods did not feel safe, and they wanted to get to a place where they could thrive.

Similarly, Donald and Tasha dreamed of a place to call their own. As Donald explained, "I don't want to be filthy rich. I just want to be comfortable." His dream of comfort included a riding lawn mower. "I just want a lawn mower I can ride in on my own yard, yeah—and I could fix my one-story house and get on the roof, a basement, everything just right there for me. Do you know what I mean? It's like a home. That's basically the way I see it." Tasha similarly framed her dream as not ostentatious but comfortable, "Maybe a two-story home or something. Nothing real big, just something that's comfortable, you got a front and backyard, just so you can feel that open space and don't feel the four walls like, is hitting you sometimes. So that's how I feel sometimes when I sit at my house too long by myself. I'm like, oh gosh, I feel like I'm gonna suffocate in here."

The impulse to move away to escape poverty and disinvestment is not unique to Riverside and Carthage residents. It permeates how we think about poverty in the United States. Poor neighborhoods are seen as decayed places, made that way by a set of circumstances—most often their residents. We rarely identify the government policies, economic realities, and business decisions that led to these circumstances. And if we do, we present them as less relevant than the cultural traits of the poor people currently occupying these spaces. This focus on residents relieves governments from having to invest in these spaces and further justifies their disinvestment after the fact. This logic also motivates antipoverty housing policy that centers on the "deconcentration" of poverty. The Moving to Opportunity Program is an example of one such program. Its premise is that relocating poor residents to a nonpoor neighborhood will improve their life outcomes. The results of such programs have been mixed, with some relocated residents moving back to their original neighborhoods. One key element that policy makers overlooked was the importance of long-standing social ties to residents' well-being.

Undoubtedly, many Riverside and Carthage residents' desire to move was about the difficulties of living in neighborhoods described as "poor, crime-ridden, and unsafe," as Collin characterized Riverside. But let us think about those descriptions critically. If a neighborhood is poor, crime-ridden, and unsafe, what does it need to transition out of those categories? Rather than move the people, how do we change the space? How do we exorcise the exploitative and dehumanizing relations that cause so much harm? What policy solutions can you imagine that would treat residents with respect and dignity, and support their flourishing regardless of class, race, or immigration status? How do we build the kinds of neighborhood spaces whereby residents do not dream of moving away?

We must remember that poverty—for individuals and neighborhoods—is not a necessary characteristic of modern living. It is a policy choice.[1] We choose it daily with our economic priorities and policies. When we understand our current society as a series of daily decisions, it is easier to reject that this is the way it needs to be or will always be. Or that only some people deserve safe and affordable housing, health care, and fresh food. We can choose for it to be different. Undoing these decisions is not easy, but it is possible if we work together to make it so.

Throughout *Urban Specters*, I have tried to showcase the small ways that residents imagined and attempted to build different realities for Carthage and Riverside. For example, Diego envisioned a job training program for newly arrived Latinx migrants, while Gwen lobbied for better neighborhood infrastructure for public transportation. Unfortunately, neither of these proposals was successful due to barriers from local associations. Jenny saw a lot of need in Riverside, particularly for folks in Eatondale Apartments. She wanted more centralized help for the poor:

> There should be a little more offered down for where we're at, like community-wise. . . . there is transportation problems that people have with being down on the bottom of a hill and bus services, it's like every two hours and one doesn't—there is only one bus to Delhi a day. . . . There is a few people that you know have health problems, that can't physically do it, things like that, and I've noticed, as far as community resources go, there really isn't anything available to us that would—like some of the churches and things like that don't really help.

Jenny saw the needs for community-wide social safety nets to help with food, transportation, and health services. Many residents in Riverside brought up the lack of transportation as a problem.

In short, residents can diagnose neighborhood troubles and envision a different way of being. They can make their neighborhoods and communities into places of flourishing and care with the necessary support. A big part of that support is financial and infrastructural—the job of government to meet the needs of its constituents—but it is also interpersonal. As we've seen, dismantling the harms of racial capitalism is primarily about relations of exploitation, dispossession, and dehumanization, but it is also about the stories we tell about how the world works and how individuals relate to one another. As such, the work of abolition is both material and ideological.

When thinking about racial capitalism, it can be tempting to feel nihilistic. How can we possibly abolish a system that is so entrenched in the fabric of our cities, institutions, and even dreams? I have spent multiple chapters chronicling racial capitalism's machinations and ideologies. Challenging racial capitalism is no small feat; it is a multilevel and multisite fight made even more difficult because "capitalism offers itself as the best cure and consolation for the injuries it has inflicted."[2] So, where and how do we begin? To answer this, I turn to abolitionists who have been grappling with these questions for decades.

We start with a vision of what we want.[3] And we start locally. Envisioning a future outside of racial capitalism's ravages is the first step to making it a reality. We employ our radical imaginations to foresee something that may appear impossible now—and we do not let that impossibility stop us from taking the next steps toward it. Before we can build the alternative, we have to imagine it. But as historian Robin D. G. Kelley argues, "It is not enough to imagine a world without oppression (especially since we don't always recognize the ways we ourselves practice and perpetuate oppression). We must also understand the mechanisms or processes that not only reproduce subjugation and exploitation but make them common sense and render them natural."[4] *Urban Specters* is an attempt to take stock of where we are to better understand the path forward.

While abolishing racial capitalism may indeed demand we "change everything," the building blocks of that change are already here.[5] "Abolition is building the future from the present, in all of the ways we can," according to Ruth Wilson Gilmore.[6] That also means we start where we are, literally. As Gilmore argues, "All liberation struggle is specific to the needs and the struggles of people where they are, and that 'where' has many, many dimensions."[7] Better cities for all—ones that meet residents' needs and facilitate their growth and flourishing—are indeed possible. We have some ideas of what that might look like in Carthage and Riverside. What would you need to make that true of where you live? Equally as important, what would your neighbors need?

Urban specters present a vision of a siloed world where racialized and classed others are the locus of social ills. These stories have limited vision. Narratives of neglect, trash, and security ask us to pull away from one another to keep ourselves safe and afloat. They normalize hierarchy, exclusion, and disconnection. When scholars, advocates, and abolitionists present alternatives to racial capitalism, critics frame them as naive. The irony is that these alternatives start from a clear-eyed view of how racial capitalism works and harms us all. Racial capitalism creates an interdependency based on harm, exploitation, and dehumanization. Our task is to challenge this interdependency with a new vision, a radical reimagining of relations that we create together, piece by piece.

Acknowledgments

> Writing is always a brutally social process that is
> rude enough to masquerade as a solitary one.
> —TRESSIE MCMILLAN COTTOM, *Thick*

I would first like to thank my editor at The University of North Carolina Press, Lucas Church, who has been a champion of this book since he first read the proposal. It is wonderful when you work with someone who has complete trust in you and fully supports your vision. Thank you also for understanding the struggles of pandemic parenting. Your compassion and solidarity were incredibly meaningful to me as I pushed back deadlines amidst impossible circumstances. This is my second time working with UNC Press, and it is a fantastic team. Thank y'all for everything you've done to make *Urban Specters* possible. Thank you also to Erin Greb Cartography for creating the beautiful maps included in this book.

I have had the immense privilege of working at three institutions while researching and writing this book (also an indication of how long I've been working on it). Thank you to my colleagues at the University of Cincinnati, my first job and the place where I first felt like I could really trust myself as a scholar—a testament to the supportive, collegial environment. Thank you to my amazing Team Tenure writing group: Danielle Bessett, Erynn Masi de Casanova, and Rina Williams. Thank you to the Kunz Center for Social Research and the Cincinnati Project, the Taft Research Center, the Third Century Faculty Research Fellowship, the University of Cincinnati LEAF Grant Program, and the College of Liberal Arts Dean's Research Fund for their financial support. Thank you also to Chloe Connelly, who helped with interview transcription, and Littisha Bates, who generously shared her expertise on Cincinnati public schools. And thank you to my senior colleagues for their mentorship and support, especially Jeff Timberlake, Anna Linders, Earl Wright II, and Jennifer Malat. A special thank you to Jennifer, who read the full manuscript and provided crucial comments and local knowledge that pushed me to sharpen my analysis.

Thank you also to my former/always advisor Eduardo Bonilla-Silva. Eduardo saw me present on this work early on in Cincinnati and was so excited about it, he sent me a message that I still have saved on my phone. Thank you for always believing in me and being a champion of my research. This book would not have been possible without your mentorship and guidance. I'll keep trying to earn that 10/10.

To my colleagues in Sociology and Critical Ethnic and Community Studies at the University of Massachusetts Boston, thank you for your support of my work and solidarity. I am especially grateful to Sofya Aptekar, Liz Brown, Andrea Leverentz, and Leslie Wang for their friendship. Thank you to the College of Liberal Arts and the support of the late David Terkla, who was dean during my tenure there. I also would like to thank my colleagues in the Faculty Staff Union—organizing alongside you taught me a lot, and I'm grateful to you.

Thank you also to my colleagues at Brandeis University. It has been a joy to jump into work with you all, and I look forward to many years of building together. Thank you to Dean Hodgson and the College of Arts and Sciences for your support of this book via a Senior Research Semester. It provided me with invaluable time to focus on finalizing this manuscript. I'd also like to thank the college for the Co-Curricular Funding that allowed me to connect with Mo Torres, who later was one of my book workshop participants. I would also like to thank Jenny LaFleur for sharing her time and expertise with creating maps. And a special thank you to Lauren Crosser, Rachel Guaderrama, and Sanchita Dasgupta, who read the manuscript and provided insightful feedback that helped me tighten my language, and who also gave me a much-needed vote of confidence as I sent off the final draft.

I was privileged to be able to host a book manuscript workshop and invite three brilliant sociologists, Jose Itzigsohn, Louise Seamster, and Mo Torres, to read my book. Their comments were invaluable, showing me the parts of the book that were compelling and, importantly, the parts that needed work. I completely rewrote the book based on their feedback, landing on the current structure. Thank you, Jose, Louise, and Mo, for your expertise and honesty that pushed me to be better. Thank you also to Carina Ray for her advice on how to most successfully organize this workshop.

Thank you to my friends whose support continues to buoy me. I am lucky that I have friends across my many stages of life. Although I won't name them all here, thank you for your friendship, for your check-ins, and for bringing me moments of joy, especially over the last few not-so-joyful years. I'd like to give a special thanks to Elizabeth Hordge-Freeman, whose positive reaction to my new organization gave me the boost I needed to keep going amidst messy and vulnerable rewrites. Thank you also to Elizabeth Korver-Glenn, whose friendship has felt like a cosmic gift. Thank you for reading this book despite your own full plate and being a consistent source of support as I finished this book.

And to my dear friend Candis Watts Smith: you are a gem. I shared the first version of this manuscript with Candis in April 2021. I was a year into pandemic parenting and a new job, trying to make a book come together in sixty- to ninety-minute writing sessions a couple of times a week. While my first draft stunk (I'm paraphrasing), Candis gave me the ego boost I needed to know that while it wasn't happening right now, it would. And because she is indeed the best, Candis read *Urban Specters* again as I worked on final revisions. I'm grateful to you, friend. Thank you.

To my parents, Lydia and Oscar, and my siblings, Oscar, Jill, Carla, Luis, George, and Molly—thank you for all the ways you care for me. Thank you also to my mother-in-law Fran, whose help was essential, especially as I finished the third draft of this book. Thank you for all the ways you've shown up for me, Jonathan, and Ellie, this last year especially. We couldn't have done it without you. Thank you also to my therapist, E. Our work together made this book possible, too.

And, of course, to my favorite people: Jonathan and Elina. Jonathan, thank you for seeing my whole self and for a love that has never been *in spite of* but always *because of*. I love you and our beautiful life. And to our sweet Ellie Belly: Thank you for helping me be brave and reminding me that work isn't everything. It's an honor to be your mama. I love you always.

Methods

Recruitment

The basis of my data collection for *Urban Specters* was semistructured interviews with Carthage and Riverside residents in fall 2014 and spring 2015. In addition to speaking with residents of these two target neighborhoods, I talked to a handful of residents in neighboring locales, including Sedamsville, Delhi Township, and Elmwood Place. In total, I interviewed 117 residents. My interviewing of residents of nearby areas is a result of my recruitment strategy. I used the Every Door Direct Mail feature of the United States Postal Service (USPS) to recruit participants. This feature allows you to choose a zip code and select whether you want to deliver your mail to every residential and/or business address in that area. The benefits of this feature are that the USPS delivers your mail at a reduced postage rate and that you can target every household in a geographic area without knowing who lives there. Zip codes are not a perfect match for neighborhood boundaries, which is why I also interviewed some residents of nearby neighborhoods. I use these interviews when relevant, particularly when they can contextualize the narratives of Riverside and Carthage residents. Zip codes, however, were still a pretty close approximation for Riverside and Carthage.

I created a postcard advertising my study in Riverside and including that I would pay residents $15/hour to speak with me. For context, the minimum hourly wage for nontipped employees in Ohio increased from $7.95 to $8.10 while I was in the field. Using a new recruitment technique, I was unsure what kind of response I would get after dropping off my postcards. The following day, I went to my office and had ten voice mail messages waiting for me. I was delighted and overwhelmed. The calls and voice mails kept coming, and I eventually interviewed fifty-eight residents of Riverside and sixteen from the surrounding area. Initially, I interviewed multiple people a day, including one day I scheduled four, but that interview load proved to be too demanding. I loaded my schedule because I worried that residents would stand me up if the time between initial interaction and scheduled interview was too long. This was because some residents did not have regular phone access, and it was hard to reach them in the first place. But I needed to balance that fear with my capabilities and data integrity. After a month, I targeted two interviews a day (one in the morning, one in the afternoon).

In Carthage, I used the same recruitment strategy with minor tweaks. I initially sent the postcards out in Spanish, hoping to recruit Latinx residents first. Based on ethnographic methods advice arguing that researchers should start recruitment with the most vulnerable population, I hoped that Latinx residents would be more amenable to participating if I focused on them to start. I then sent recruitment materials in English. I am not sure how helpful this recruitment strategy was, and I have no counterfactual with which to compare it. However, it is possible that some English-speaking residents were more hesitant to speak with me after seeing the postcards in Spanish. One white participant greeted me with "hola" upon my arrival for our interview, telling me he had seen and mostly understood the Spanish postcard. When I first sat down to talk with Eric, he greeted me with "How are you?" I responded, "I'm doing well, how are you?" He then said, "Or, should I say que pasa?" I replied, "yeah," and just kind of laughed. While he seemed hesitant in our interview to say anything that could be construed as anti-immigrant, he was very open about how other people talked about Latinx communities to him (see chapter 1).

I concluded my Carthage fieldwork after interviews with forty-three residents. Forty lived in Carthage, and two lived in neighboring Elmwood Place. I also interviewed a former Carthage resident who moved to Springdale, about twenty minutes north of Carthage. Interviews ranged from twelve minutes to over two hours, although most lasted between forty-five and seventy minutes. I conducted interviews in residents' preferred language. Most Latinx residents chose to be interviewed in Spanish.

Access

I am always amazed and grateful that people share their stories with me. As a qualitative sociologist, I am also curious about why they do so. This curiosity led me to coauthor an article with my close friend and graduate school cohort-mate Elizabeth Hordge-Freeman about conducting fieldwork in multiethnic spaces.[1] I aim to be courteous, empathetic, and a good listener as a researcher. But why people speak to researchers is never just about what researchers do. It is also about who researchers are. Hordge-Freeman and I argue that thinking critically about how researchers perform and are also perceived as credible and approachable can be a more helpful reflection on positionality than a list of demographic characteristics.

My job helped mark me as credible, although this was not straightforward. At the time of my fieldwork, I was a thirty-year-old assistant professor in my third year on the tenure track. Residents were curious about my job and often asked about it at the end of our conversations. Eatondale Apartments resident Mark commented, "Thirty and a professor. That's impressive," while Tasha's eyes widened when she asked me what I did at the university. Lashonda inquired, "Do the kids listen?" after asking me how long I had been a professor, which was likely a comment on my youthful appearance at the time. While my affiliation with the University of Cincinnati may have made me credible in the eyes of some, others were not sure who was behind my project. For instance, at the end of our interview, Christopher asked me if the city was behind my research despite the informed consent form and recruitment postcard including my university affiliation. When I clarified it was the University of Cincinnati, he asked whose money I was using to pay participants. He queried, "This isn't coming out of your pocket is it?" I assured him it was paid for by a grant, and he responded, "Okay, good."

My ability to pay participants was likely the most important reason people reached out to me. It also lent credibility to my project, that I was not trying to scam them. My race, class, and gender performances also shaped my credibility and lent my project legitimacy. While outsider status is a complex construction—and there were many ways that I was not of Riverside and Carthage—my middle-class feminine whiteness marked me as a credible outsider that folks could let inside of their homes and lives. This was true even in predominantly Black Eatondale, where I was legible to residents as a professional doing home visits. Some who saw me around the apartment complex assumed I was a caseworker.

My approachability was also about performance, not just perceptions. For example, I first met Janessa when I came to Eatondale to schedule an interview with Aisha. As I was asking around for Aisha, a few people sitting outside asked me about my study. One person was amazed at the $15/hour pay rate and said he was interested. I started to give out business cards, and Janessa informed me, upset, that she called me and I had not returned her phone call. She didn't need a business card, she explained. I became somewhat flustered but then stopped myself from explaining and just apologized. I told her I was happy to schedule something with her if she was still interested. I then decided that I could just schedule the interviews rather than wait for people to call and schedule. I proceeded to schedule everyone, and Janessa was first in line. As soon as I apologized, her demeanor changed. By owning my mistake and apologizing, I became approachable. During interviews, I follow the path of least disturbance. I do not attempt to challenge the beliefs or experiences of the people I am interviewing. I ask clarifying questions but do not challenge beliefs or ideas I disagree with, embodying what Hordge-Freeman calls "critical accommodation."

My performance of femininity certainly mattered in constructing me as both credible and approachable. And even before people met me, this was signaled by the professional, smiling photograph on the postcard. It also shaped people's concern over my safety, particularly in their parting words to me. I imagine my short stature (five foot three) also mattered here. For instance, Federico, who lived in Riverside, asked me how long I had been studying Cincinnati. When I told him I was just getting started with my project, he responded, "You poor girl." When I asked him why he said that, he responded, "I'm just kidding." But the day after our conversation, he emailed me and added at the end, "Be safe as you navigate through the locals." White Eatondale resident John similarly said, "You stay safe in this area, okay?" as I departed. Donald escorted me to my car to ensure no one in the parking lot bothered me.

Eatondale resident Lindsey also asked me if I had any protection with me. She asked at the end of our conversation, "Are you packing?" I showed her my pepper spray keychain and said, "I have this, but I figure the people letting me into their homes don't have anything to hide." She nodded, seemingly satisfied with my answer. She then said, "'Cause people around Delhi don't come around here." Unlike the men who commented on my safety, Lindsey's comments were about perceptions outsiders have of the apartment complex. She also grouped me alongside the white, middle-class people of Delhi. Non-Eatondale residents to whom I spoke confirmed Lindsey's perceptions, warning me about the apartments. For example, when I spoke with Meghan, she mentioned that I should not interview anyone who lives in Eatondale. It all started when I asked her if she saw interracial interactions in the neighborhood. She said there might be some in certain areas:

MEGHAN: If you go up towards Fairbanks, there's that whole apartment, that Eatondale apartment building, that's all African American too, so.

SARAH: But there's not necessarily any interaction between the Eatondale residents and the rest of the neighborhood?

MEGHAN: No, no. Stay away from there.

SARAH: Okay. Why?

MEGHAN: A lot of drugs.

SARAH: A lot of drugs out there?

MEGHAN: There's always cops up there. That's just a bad, bad, bad. If anybody says, "Meet me at Eatondale," don't do it.

SARAH: Okay.

MEGHAN: Just letting you know.

Meghan's comment especially struck me because I had started that day at Eatondale to interview Cathy and Anita. Meghan ignored that there were drugs all over Riverside. But her warning that I would not be safe there was likely more about the demographics of who lived there, given her transition from interracial interactions to danger.

A Note on White Latinidad

I have written previously about my field experiences as a white Latina, whereby residents perceive me as a white woman.

Actually, I have never written in my work that I am a white Latina. I have called myself a white-passing Latina and a light-skinned Latina, but never a white Latina. I rejected that label for a long time. I thought white Latinxs were the kids I went to school with in Miami, Florida, whose parents instructed them to select both Hispanic and white on demographic forms regardless of what they looked like. Or people who felt no tie to or pride in their Latinidad. That was how scholars seemed to interpret identifying as white and Latinx—as a distancing tactic from brownness and Blackness. That was never me. As a kid, the forms I filled out had Hispanic as a racial-ethnic category, so I always chose that. I identified as Nicaraguan. It was not until I left Miami for college that I understood myself differently.

I embraced the Latina label when I went to school at a predominantly white college. And I mean predominantly white in the strictest terms. White, non-Hispanic students were over 90 percent of the student body. As you can imagine, it was a culture shock; my high school was over 90 percent Latinx. I initially didn't mind being an oddity. I felt special amidst the many white students from New England and the tristate area, a boon for a middle child.[2] But that got old fast. And then I felt angry. Thus, a sociologist was born.

But now, almost twenty years later, I identify as a white Latina. I don't flinch or cringe when I say it—and trust me, that took some time to accomplish. By claiming a white Latina identity, I realize that I am not denying my Latinidad or trying to distance myself from it. I am following the lead of Afro-Latinxs whose work and advocacy highlight that our experiences are not the same. By not naming our whiteness explicitly, white Latinxs participate in the delegitimization of Black Latinxs via an exclusive "race-less" Latinidad.[3] As a sociologist of race, I certainly knew that my whiteness mattered. It's been a cornerstone of my research agenda. But I also continued to cling to the pan-ethnic identity as my racial identity. Owning that label without a racial signifier felt like rejecting whiteness and assimilation. But that's not how structure works. I can still experience microaggressions, be proud of my Latinaness, and be a white Latina. But if I'm going to be upfront about the systemic privileges of whiteness I wield, especially as a tenured professor, "white passing" and "light skinned" just won't cut it.

Not all non-Latinxs see me in the same ways they see white non-Hispanics. But as both Aisha's "no offense, but this is a white world" comment and Patty's attempt to distinguish me and her from her Mexican neighbors (see chapter 4) indicate, most people in Riverside and Carthage did see me as a non-Hispanic white woman. But non-Latinxs also sometimes mark me as racially different. For example, when I met with Agnes and her daughter Grace, at the end of the interview they asked me where I was from because, as Grace said, she heard a little bit of an accent. It was clear from the way she asked the question that she wanted to know where I was *from*. I said I grew up in Miami but my family was from Nicaragua. She then asked when my parents came to the United States, and I said in the mid-eighties. She responded, "Oh okay, so you were born here," but I corrected her and told her I was born in Puerto Rico and came to the United States when I was two. She then asked me how I like the states. I responded, "You know, it's basically all I've ever known, so I like it."

We often miss in our everyday conversations and even sometimes in scholarly discussions that racial identity is an identity that speaks to a set of power relations. It is not an intrinsic set of characteristics defining "the real you." I identify as Nicaraguan American, but was born in Puerto Rico. Spanish was my first language, yet I sometimes struggle to come up with Spanish words. All of these are facts about me, but they don't tell you much about the treatment I receive in the classroom, at the grocery store, or in the field while conducting research. Perhaps most importantly, identifying myself as a white Latina reminds me that racial identities are social and should foundationally be about solidarity.[4] I don't mean the solidarity that panethnic ties often rely on, whereby we do not talk about how some of us benefit from the oppression of others under the same umbrella. I am talking about solidarity that takes power, colonialism, and antiblackness seriously. That's the Latinidad that I want but have undermined. I am indebted to Afro-Latinx scholars, especially the Black Latinas Know Collective and Paul Joseph López Oro, whose work has challenged me on this point in particular.[5] I had become so focused on legibility, people seeing me as I understood myself, that I lost sight of the political consequences. Heeding the words of Shireen Roshanravan, "The goal of coalitional boundary crossing is not vertical communication with the state or general public, but rather horizontal communication with those with whom one seeks to build new horizons of liberation."[6] Rather than see my illegibility as a problem for myself, I will use it to be a "problem for power."[7]

With this reorientation of my identity, I now interpret Grace and Agnes's comments differently from when the conversation took place. This exchange, whereby my accent and birthplace marked me as other, does not make me white-passing or off-white. These moments of exoticization are part of the white Latinx experience, and they can be difficult. At the same time, I am still a beneficiary of systemic whiteness, classism, and their attendant logics. In other words, how would I have had to signal my credibility and approachability with a different class or race position?

So, as in my previous work, I am studying whiteness as a system of power relations and using my "epidermal capital" (as my advisor used to call it) to do so. But this is not undercover work because I am off-white and people are misidentifying me, as I used to argue. I can do it because I have access to white spaces as a white upper middle-class Latina.

APPENDIX B

Interview Questions

1. How long have you lived in the neighborhood?
2. Do you know anything about the history of this neighborhood?
3. Have you lived in other neighborhoods/areas in Cincinnati before?
4. Were there other areas you were looking at closely when you chose to live in [neighborhood]?
5. Why did you move here? What were you looking for in terms of house/ apartment complex/neighborhood?
6. Do you rent or own? If own, how long have you owned your home? If rent, who is your landlord? Do you know if they own other property across the neighborhood?
7. What do you know about landlords in this neighborhood? Do you have any kind of relationship with them?
8. Do you live with anyone? (If children, probe about age and schooling.)
9. What kind of people would you say live in the neighborhood? How would you describe the residents to someone who doesn't live there? (Probe: demographics, class, occupations, household/family type)
10. What kind of people live on your street/in your building?
11. Who are your neighbors? Are they renters or owners?
12. Would you say the neighborhood has any leaders? Who would you consider a leader? Why?
13. Are you involved with any neighborhood-specific organizations (like the civic club/league)? If yes, why did you choose to join? Do you attend meetings regularly? If not, have you been asked to join any?
14. Have you ever been involved in any neighborhood-wide efforts to address specific issues or problems?
15. How do you spend your free time? Are there areas not directly in the neighborhood that you spend a lot of time in?
16. What areas do you consider to be a part of the neighborhood (specific streets, businesses)? Where would you draw the neighborhood boundaries? (Draw on map.)
17. Do you have a dog? If so, do you take him/her on walks? (Draw on map.)
18. Do you think neighbors spend a lot of time interacting socially? If yes, where do these interactions happen?
19. If you had a problem with a neighbor or in the neighborhood, how would you handle it? (Probe: individually, go to property management, police) Have you ever had any problems in the past? How did you handle them?
20. What do you think makes someone a good neighbor? Do you have good neighbors?

21. Do you think other neighborhoods in Cincinnati look like this one, or is [neighborhood] different? How so?
22. Do you see interracial interactions in the neighborhood? Like, white and Black people hanging out together, for example? Where do you see this? Do you have a specific example? If you don't see it, why do you think that is?

Before we wrap up, I have a few survey questions I'd like to ask you. You don't have to answer any questions you don't want to, and your responses are anonymous.

- What three words would you use to describe your neighborhood?
- Where do you buy the majority of your groceries? (Store name and location)
- Which statement best describes your relationship with your immediate neighbors? We do not talk to each other; we say hello when we see each other; we have conversations outside our homes when we see each other; we make plans to spend time together every once in a while; we regularly make plans to spend time together.
- Do you feel safe in your neighborhood?
- Do you think your neighborhood has a crime problem?
- If yes, what do you think is the main source of your neighborhood's crime problem?
- Do you have any good friends that you feel close to?
- About how many good friends do you have?
- I would like you to think about your five closest friends. Are they male or female? What is the racial-ethnic background of your five closest friends? Do your five closest friends live in your neighborhood? How often do you visit or see your five closest friends?
- Do you agree or disagree? Because of past discrimination, employers should make special efforts to hire and promote qualified women.
- How important is the issue of race relations to you?
- On the average, Black people have worse jobs, income, and housing than white people. Do you think these differences are: mainly due to discrimination; because most Black people have less inborn ability to learn; because most Black people don't have the chance for education that it takes to rise out of poverty; because most Black people don't have the motivation or willpower to pull themselves up out of poverty?
- Some people say undocumented or illegal immigrants help the economy by providing low-cost labor. Others say they hurt the economy by driving wages down. Which is closer to your view?
- If you were asked to use one of four names for your social class, which would you say you belong in: the lower class, the working class, the middle class, or the upper class?
- How old are you?
- How do you identify racially and ethnically?
- What is the highest level of education you completed?

- What is your occupation?
- In which of these groups did your total family income, from all sources, fall last year before taxes?

23. I am trying to get a sense of who lives in this neighborhood and what the experiences of residents are. Are there people that you think I should talk to or that would be willing to speak with me?
24. Okay, and my last question: is there anything we didn't talk about that you think I should know to understand what it's like to live in [neighborhood]?

APPENDIX C

Interviewee Demographics

TABLE C.1 Interviewee Demographics

Name	TS#	Age	Self-ID Race/Ethnicity	Edu*	Occupation~	Income (in 1000s)	Class ID^	NBH**
Abby	R	62	White	SC	Medical transcriptionist	$15–19.99	LC	C
Adele	R	—	—	—	—	—	—	R (E)
Adolfo	O	48	Mexican	SC	Mechanic	$30–34.99	WC	C
Adri	R	31	Latina (Mexican)	LH	SAHM, PT restaurant work	$30–34.99	UC	C
Agnes	O	92	White	HS	Retired	$15–19.99	MC	R
Aisha	R	31	Black	HS	Unemployed	$15–19.99	LC	R (E)
Akilah	R	29	Black	LH	Temporary work	<$1	UC	R (E)
Albert	R	35	Black	HS	Unemployed	$10–14.99	WC	R (E)
Alicia	R	27	Black	HS	Housekeeper	$5–9.99	LC	R (E)
Andrea	R	70	Mixed	SC	Retired	$20–24.99	MC	C
Angelica	R	42	Caucasian	C	Delivery driver	$5–9.99	LC	RA
Angelina	O	42	African American	AS	Claims processor	$50–54.99	WC	C
Anita	R	—	—	—	—	—	—	R (E)
Antonia	R	—	—	—	—	—	—	R (E)
Barb	R	58	Black	HS	Care worker	$15–19.99	WC	R
Ben	R	51	White	HS	Machine operator	$15–19.99	WC	C
Bernice	R	72	Mixed	SC	Retired	$20–24.99	R	C
Brandon	N	19	White	TS	Machinist	$55–59.99	WC	R
Cait	O	65	Caucasian	C	Social worker	$10–14.99	WC	R
Camille	R	23	African American	LH	Telemarketing	$1–4.99	WC	R (E)

(continued)

TABLE C.1 Interviewee Demographics (*continued*)

Name	TS#	Age	Self-ID Race/Ethnicity	Edu*	Occupation~	Income (in 1000s)	Class ID^	NBH**
Carl	O	52	White	HS	Heating & AC	$60–64.99	LC	R
Carmen	O	44	Hispanic (Bolivian)	HS	SAHM	$40–44.99	WC	C
Cathy	R	43	Black	HS	Unemployed	—	MC	R (E)
Chelsea	O	55	White	LH	Housekeeper	$10–14.99	LC	RA
Cherise	R	30	Black	SC	Unemployed	$1–4.99	MC	R
Christopher	O	58	White	HS	On disability	$10–14.99	WC	RA
Cindy	O	48	White	AS	Administrative Technician	$75–79.99	WC	R
Clare	R	45	Human	AS	Unemployed	$25–29.99	LC	R (E)
Claudia	O	67	Caucasian	C	Retired	$45–49.99	MC	C
Colette	O	42	African American	SC	STNA, CS	$15–19.99	WC	RA
Collin	O	40	White	LH	Forklift driver	$40–44.99	WC	R
Craig	R	25	African American	C	Property manager	$30–34.99	WC	R
Damian	R	55	Black	SC	Mortgage loan officer	$15–19.99	MC	R
Deacon	R	36	Caucasian	SC	Mover	$20–24.99	MC	C
Dean	O	63	Polish	SC	Carpenter	$50–54.99	WC	R
Denise	O	37	African American	C	Program coordinator	$35–39.99	WC	C
Dick	O	50	Caucasian	LH	Laborer	$10–14.99	LC	C
Diego	O	59	Mestizo (Peruvian)	SC	Landscaper	$40–44.99	MC	SP
Donald	R	46	African American	HS	Unemployed	$1–4.99	LC	R (E)
Douglas	O	72	White	GS	Editor	$40–44.99	R	R
Edie	R	53	White	HS	Cleaning technician	$5–9.99	WC	R
Elisabeth	R	37	White	C	Copy writer	$35–39.99	MC	C
Elsie	O	64	White	TS	Nurse's aid	$40–44.99	MC	R

TABLE C.1 Interviewee Demographics (*continued*)

Name	TS*	Age	Self-ID Race/Ethnicity	Edu*	Occupation˜	Income (in 1000s)	Class ID^	NBH**
Emily	O	40	White	AS	Paralegal	$35–39.99	WC	RA
Erik	R	69	Caucasian	SC	Mortgage broker	$25–29.99	WC	C
Erika	O	43	Mennonite/ White	SC	SAHM	$55–59.99	MC	R
Erin	O	56	German Irish	HS	Banker	$50–54.99	WC	R
Estelle	R	29	African American	AS	SAHM	$1–4.99	WC	RA
Eve	O	82	Irish American	SC	Retired	$25–29.99	WC	C
Evelyn	R	23	White	HS	Unemployed	$5–9.99	WC	R (E)
Federico	R	48	Italian	HS	Promoter	$5–9.99	WC	R
Felipe	O	53	Hispanic (Honduran)	HS	Carpenter	$15–19.99	MC	C
Frances	R	—	—	—	—	—	—	R
Gina	R	53	White	AS	Home senior care	$15–19.99	WC	RA
Grace	O	—	—	—	—	—	—	RA
Gwen	O	62	White	GS	Retired	$30–34.99	LC	C
Harry	O	69	African American/ Black	SC	PT delivery, retired	$55–59.99	WC	C
Helen	O	61	German Appalachian Caucasian	GS	Counselor	$45–49.99	WC	RA
Hugh	O	56	Caucasian	SC	Customer service	$50–54.99	WC	C
Iris	O	37	White	TS	Compliance manager	$80–84.99	WC	R
Ivory	R	25	Black	HS	Nursing home worker	$1–4.99	WC	R

(*continued*)

TABLE C.1 Interviewee Demographics (*continued*)

Name	TS#	Age	Self-ID Race/Ethnicity	Edu*	Occupation~	Income (in 1000s)	Class ID^	NBH**
Jake	O	26	White	C	Sales	$80–84.99	WC	R
Jamal	R	40	Black	AS	Cook	$30–34.99	WC	RA
Janessa	R	36	Black	SC	STNA	$25–29.99	WC	R (E)
Jenny	R	36	Caucasian	SC	Unemployed	$5–9.99	LC	R (E)
Jill	R	59	American Indian	SC	Nanny	$15–19.99	LC	R
Jimmy	R	52	Black	SC	Unemployed	$1–4.99	LC	R
John	R	33	White	HS	Unemployed	$10–14.99	LC	R (E)
Julius	R	35	African American	TS	Electrician	$5–9.99	LC	WH
Kalisha	R	21	Black	HS	CS	—	MC	R (E)
Kareem	R	19	Black	HS	Temp work	<$1	MC	R (E)
Kay	R	32	White	GS	Genetic counselor	$100,000+	UC	EP
Keisha	R	38	Black	HS	Temp work	$1–4.99	WC	R
Kevin	O	65	Cherokee Indian, Russian, Scottish	SC	Sales	$40–44.99	WC	R
Kim	O	62	African American	SC	Nonprofit work	$20–24.99	WC	C
Lamar	R	48	Black	SC	On disability	<$1	MC	C
Lashonda	R	21	Black	LH	Warehouse worker	$5–9.99	WC	R (E)
Lilian	O	43	White	AS	Quality technician	$65–69.99	WC	C
Lindsey	R	36	African American	LH	Unemployed	<$1	MC	R (E)
Lisa	R	45	White	SC	CS	$5–9.99	LC	R
Lourdes	O	43	Latina (Guatemalan)	C	Teacher's aide	$25–29.99	WC	C
Luke	R	52	African American	AS	Housekeeper, cook, cashier	$30–34.99	WC	C

TABLE C.1 Interviewee Demographics (*continued*)

Name	TS#	Age	Self-ID Race/Ethnicity	Edu*	Occupation~	Income (in 1000s)	Class ID^	NBH**
Maggie	O	50	White	HS	SAHM	$60–64.99	LC	R
Marcie	O	45	White	HS	Warehouse worker	$40–44.99	WC	R
Marcos	O	19	Guatemalan Latino	HS	CS	$25–29.99	WC	C
Margaret	O	29	Black	AS	CS	$50–54.99	WC	C
Marie	R	52	White	LH	On disability	$5–9.99	LC	RA
Mark	R	49	African American	SC	Forklift driver, CS	$20–24.99	WC	R (E)
Meghan	O	54	Caucasian	HS	Assistant manager	$25–29.99	WC	R
Milton	R	—	—	—	—	—	—	R
Miriam	O	68	African American/ Black	SC	Retired	$55–59.99	MC	C
Morgan	N	69	Caucasian & Cherokee	SC	On disability	$5–9.99	WC	C
Nick	O	33	White	TS	Real estate	$45–49.99	WC	RA
Pam	O	60	German	AS	Nonprofit work	$35–39.99	WC	C
Patty	O	71	German, Jewish, English	C	Social worker	$15–19.99	WC	C
Paul	R	31	White	GS	Pharmacist	$100,000+	UC	EP
Philip	O	87	White	GS	Retired	$100,000+	MC	RA
Quinn	R	22	White	HS	Homemaker	$15–19.99	MC	C
Rachel	R	23	Black	SC	Fast-food worker	$10–14.99	LC	R (E)
Ramona	R	37	Hispanic (Guatemalan)	C	Waitress	$10–14.99	WC	C
Raúl	O	46	Hispanic (Dominican)	SC	Contractor	$20–24.99	WC	C

(*continued*)

TABLE C.1 Interviewee Demographics (*continued*)

Name	TS#	Age	Self-ID Race/Ethnicity	Edu*	Occupation¯	Income (in 1000s)	Class ID^	NBH**
Renee	R	43	—	C	On disability	—	—	C
Rich	R	52	White	C	Project manager	$55–59.99	WC	R
Ruth	R	59	White	SC	Dog trainer & groomer	$15–19.99	WC	R
Scott	O	32	Caucasian	GS	Social worker	$100,000+	MC	R
Shauna	O	57	White	SC	Bookkeeper	$80–84.99	WC	R
Shawn	R	49	Black	HS	Truck driver	$20–24.99	LC	C
Skylar	R	20	White	SC	Childcare, cook	$20–24.99	MC	C
Stefanie	R	36	Caucasian	AS	Unemployed	$10–14.99	WC	RA
Sue	R	67	Irish and German	SC	Retired	$15–19.99	WC	C
Tasha	R	25	African American	SC	Cosmetologist	$1–4.99	LC	R (E)
Timmy	R	25	White	SC	Cook	$20–24.99	WC	C
Tina	O	51	Caucasian	HS	STNA	$50–54.99	WC	R
Todd	O	56	White	SC	Truck driver	$75–79.99	MC	C
Tom	O	74	White	HS	Retired	$55–59.99	WC	R
Victor	R	27	Black	LH	Unemployed	$5–9.99	WC	R (E)
Zach	O	43	Caucasian	SC	Maintenance, remodeling	$65–69.99	—	C

#Tenure Status: R = rent, O = own, N = other arrangement

*Education: LH = less than high school, HS = high school or equivalent (GED), SC = some college, AS = associates degree, TS = trade school, apprenticeship, or certification, C = college, GS = graduate or professional school

¯Occupation: SAHM = stay-at-home mom, STNA = state-tested nursing assistant, PT = part-time, CS = college student

^Self-identified class: LC = lower class, WC = working class, MC = middle class, UC = upper class, R = refused to answer, * = missing data

**Neighborhood: C = Carthage, EP = Elmwood Place, R = Riverside, R (E) = Eatondale, RA = Riverside area, SP = Springdale, WH = Walnut Hills

Notes

Introduction

1. I am not alone in my assessment. Historian Henry Louis Taylor, Jr., uses "duality" to describe Cincinnati's history and its treatment of Black people.

2. Republican George W. Bush won Hamilton County in 2000 and 2004, while Democratic candidates won the county in the 2008, 2012, 2016, and 2020 presidential elections.

3. Penn, "Here's the Weirdest Food"; Hershberger, "How Cincinnati Fell in Love."

4. The Cincinnati Bengals are a professional football team in the National Football League (NFL), and the Cincinnati Reds are a professional baseball team in Major League Baseball (MLB).

5. 24.3 percent of the population lived below the poverty line, according to 2020 Census data.

6. Tweh and Coolidge, "Cincinnati: 20 Years Later"; CFLeads, "A Tale of Two Cities"; Wilson, "A Tale of Two Cities."

7. On the concepts of formation and racial capitalism, see Bhattacharyya, *Rethinking Racial Capitalism*; and Robinson, *Black Marxism*. While the term "racial capitalism" is most associated with political scientist Cedric Robinson, he borrowed it from South African intellectuals in the 1980s. The study of racism and capitalism as interconnected systems precedes Robinson, however, perhaps most notably in the work of sociologists W. E. B. Du Bois and Oliver Cromwell Cox. Rather than frame racism as a product of capitalism, Robinson argues that racialization practices emerged before industrialization from "'internal' relations of European peoples." While many scholars have identified how capitalism uses racial differentiation to maintain itself, Robinson's theory of racial capitalism demands that we contend with racism as an independent yet mutually reinforcing system with capitalism. Historian Robin D. G. Kelley ("What Did Cedric Robinson Mean?") describes Robinson's conceptualization as follows: "Capitalism and racism, in other words, did not break from the old order but rather evolved from it to produce a modern world system of "racial capitalism" dependent on slavery, violence, imperialism, and genocide. Capitalism was "racial" not because of some conspiracy to divide workers or justify slavery and dispossession, but because racialism had already permeated Western feudal society."

8. Bhattacharyya, *Rethinking Racial Capitalism*, ix.

9. Card, *Geographies of Racial Capitalism*. As Gilmore explains in this 17-minute online video, racial capitalism is "not a thing, it's a relation."

10. By material, I mean "the net of constraints, the 'conditions of existence' for practical thought and calculation about society" (Hall, "The Problem of Ideology," 42).

11. I find Stuart Hall's definition of "ideology" most helpful: "By ideology I mean the mental framework—the languages, the concepts, categories, imagery of thought,

and the systems of representation — which different classes and social groups deploy in order to make sense of, define, figure out and render intelligible the way society works" ("The Problem of Ideology," 29). For another example of a place-specific ideology, see Wyndham-Douds, "Diversity Contract."

12. Kaba and Ritchie, *No More Police*, 15–16.

13. As Ruth Wilson Gilmore ("Making Abolition Geography") puts it, "Abolition is building the future from the present, in all of the ways we can."

14. Riverside and Carthage are bordered by locales that are not part of the city of Cincinnati. Riverside is bordered to the north by Delhi Township, a suburb of Cincinnati, and Carthage is bordered to the south by Elmwood Place, an unincorporated village.

15. When referencing Riverside census data, I always use data from blocks 103 and 104. However, this designation includes parts of Sedamsville and Sayler Park. I choose to use the full census blocks (and not just some block groups or one block) for two reasons: first, to make sure all parts of Riverside are included, and second, to maintain comparability across decennial censuses, including when block group data was not available.

16. Draut, "Understanding the Working Class."

17. The median income was $29,091 in Carthage and ranged from $18,952 to $37,414 in Riverside in 2014. The incomes of residents I interviewed ranged from under $1,000 to over $100,000, although the median was $20,000–$24,999.

18. Indeed, 12.6 percent of Carthage residents and 31 percent of Riverside residents had incomes that fell below the poverty line in 2010.

19. The nine Latinx residents from Carthage comprised 20 percent of my Carthage sample, comparable to the neighborhood's demographics. Throughout the book I introduce residents with a parenthesis after their name, indicating their race or ethnicity, tenure status, and age. For analytical clarity, I use one of three broader racial-ethnic categories for residents — Black, Latina/o/x, or white. While Black and white are racial categories, Latinx is a panethnic category that can refer to someone of any race. According to 2010 Census data the majority of Latinx residents in Carthage racially identified as white (51%) or some other race (40%), reflecting 2010 national trends. While I asked all residents their racial-ethnic identity, most Latinx respondents used a panethnic term (e.g., Hispanic) or country of origin reference (e.g., Guatemalan) rather than existing US Census racial categories. This reflects trends scholars have long found for first-generation immigrants, which comprised the majority of my Latinx interviewees. When I use the term "white" alone, I am referring to white non-Hispanics, and when I use the term "Black" alone, I am referring to Black non-Hispanics. I use Latina or Latino if I know the gender of the person. I prefer to use the gender-inclusive term Latinx when describing multiple Latin Americans and their descendants or referencing this group in general. For those interested in residents' racial-ethnic self-identity, see table C.1 in appendix C. For a deeper engagement with Latinx identity, see appendix A.

Chapter One

1. hooks, "Theory as Liberatory Practice."

2. For more on exploitation, see Wright, *Class Counts*.

3. Nichols quoted in Koshy, Cacho, Byrd, and Jefferson, *Colonial Racial Capitalism*, 5. For more on expropriation and dispossession, see Dawson, "Hidden in Plain Sight"; Fraser, "Expropriation and Exploitation"; and Harvey, "The 'New' Imperialism."

4. Nichols, *Theft Is Property!*, 31.

5. Pulido, "Geographies of Race," 528.

6. Racial capitalism, like many scholarly concepts, is a highly contested theoretical framework. Debates about the origins of racialization, whether capitalism is necessarily racial, and the defining features of racial capitalism span disciplines. While important and generative, those scholarly debates are outside the scope of this book.

7. Catte's historical view of Appalachia helps us reject one-dimensional stories about Appalachians.

8. Obermiller, *Down Home*, 8.

9. Metzl, *Dying of Whiteness*, 6.

10. See Anderson, *White Rage*.

11. Stradling, *Cincinnati*, 110.

12. Stradling, *Cincinnati*, 110.

13. Henry Louis Taylor, *Race and the City*, 157.

14. Hall, "Problem of Ideology," 29.

15. Althusser, "Ideology," 117.

16. Althusser, "Ideology," 118.

17. Gramsci quoted in Hall, "Gramsci's Relevance," 20.

18. All resident names are pseudonyms. I have occasionally changed minor identifying details to help maintain resident confidentiality.

19. Delhi was 94.3 percent white in 2019 and is an independent community, not part of the city of Cincinnati.

20. I interviewed twenty-three residents from Eatondale. Black resident Lashonda (twenties) described these apartments as "its own little town." Yet they were also the focus of negative attention from nearby residents, particularly those in Sedamsville.

21. As scholars of food systems have argued, this is not an accident but a function of the "food apartheid" system we have in the United States (Reese, *Black Food Geographies*). See Mayorga, Underhill, and Crosser, "Aisle Inequality," where we discuss the experience of Riverside residents specifically and Mayorga, Underhill, and Crosser, "'I Hate That,'" for a discussion of middle-class residents in other Cincinnati neighborhoods.

22. For an insightful discussion of how these stereotypes are long-standing and informed by eugenicist ideas, read Catte, *What You Are Getting Wrong*.

23. UACC, "About Urban Appalachians."

24. For an excellent account of how deindustrialization shaped inequality in Detroit, see Sugrue, *Origins of Urban Crisis*.

25. UACC, "About Urban Appalachians."

26. Rhee and Scott, "Geographic Discrimination."

27. *Washington Post*, "Mountain People."

28. *Washington Post*, "Mountain People."

29. Catte, *What You Are Getting Wrong*, 14.

30. See Oliver and Shapiro, *Black Wealth/White Wealth*.

31. Wacquant, "Territorial Stigmatization."

32. Brandon was technically neither an owner nor a renter. His parents owned the home he lived in.

33. Ohio History Central, "Shawnee Indians"; Ohio History Central, "Miami Indians."

34. The Latinx community comprised 3.6 percent of the total city population in 2017, with 39 percent of the Latinx population identifying as Mexican origin and 22 percent identifying as Central American. Guatemalans were the most represented Central American group, at 15 percent of the total Latinx population. Eight percent of the Latinx population identified as South American, with Colombia and Peru being the most common South American countries of origin.

35. According to Ohio's Department of Education, "The Educational Choice Scholarship (EdChoice) Program provides students from designated public schools the opportunity to attend participating private schools. The program also provides low-income students who are entering kindergarten through 12th grade scholarship opportunities" ("EdChoice Scholarship Program").

36. See Gilens, *Why Americans Hate Welfare*; and Rank, Eppard, and Bullock, *Poorly Understood*.

Chapter Two

1. Kenny, *Illustrated Cincinnati*, 129.

2. As NBC News reported, "Beginning in February of 2000, as Timothy Thomas drove his friend's car, Cincinnati police began pulling him over, and ticketing him at an astounding rate. On March 10, Thomas is ticketed for not wearing a seatbelt and driving without a license. Later that same day, Thomas is pulled over again by a different officer and ticketed for driving without a license. In fact, in just more than two months, Thomas was pulled over 11 times by six different white officers and four black officers. They cited Thomas for 21 violations, almost all of them for the exact same things—not wearing a seat belt or driving without a license." (See Larson, "Death of Timothy Thomas.") The number of traffic violations points to a pattern of racial profiling by the Cincinnati police. See chapter 4 for more on racial disparities in traffic stops in Cincinnati.

3. If you want to learn more about this period in Cincinnati's history, watch April Ryan and Paul Hill's excellent 2015 documentary *Cincinnati Goddamn*.

4. The role of the arts and artists in gentrification is a long-standing stream of research; David Ley and Sharon Zukin's work is exemplary. To Julius's point, sociologists Samuel Shaw and Daniel Monroe Sullivan ("White Night") found that in gentrifying Portland, Oregon, participation in the arts festival had little to do with differences in appreciation of art, but was more about the types of people associated with art scenes. In other words, white people were more likely to participate because Black residents felt unwelcome.

5. Here, Julius is not alone. At a 2016 event revisiting the 2001 unrest, Reverend Damon Lynch III said that he received calls from people he did not know who lived in affluent Indian Hill during the riots: "They said, 'Damon, Damon, what can we do? We have to fix this,'" Lynch said. "If there is unrest in Over-the-Rhine, there is unease

in Indian Hill. The symphony is in Over-the-Rhine, and the people in Indian Hill could not go to the symphony" (Curnutte, "Civil Unrest of 2001").

6. Rodney, *How Europe Underdeveloped Africa*.

7. As political scientist Katherine J. Cramer argues, "What might seem to be a central debate about the appropriate role of government might at base be something else: resentment toward our fellow citizens," fueled by "ideas about who gets what, who has power, what people are like, and who is to blame" (*Politics of Resentment*, 5).

8. Butler and Warren Counties are racially and economically very different from Cincinnati. As of 2018, Butler County was 81.2 percent white non-Hispanic, while Warren County was 86.4 percent white non-Hispanic—significantly higher than Hamilton County's 65.4 percent or Cincinnati's 48.2 percent. In 2017, Butler and Warren's median household incomes were $62,188 and $79,397, respectively, while Hamilton and Cincinnati's were $52,389, and $36,429, respectively.

9. Henry Louis Taylor, *Race and the City*, 14.

10. Kruse and Sugrue, *New Suburban History*.

11. Purifoy and Seamster, "Creative Extraction," 52.

12. Kruse and Sugrue, *New Suburban History*, 6.

13. The streetcar has recently been renamed "The Connector."

14. City of Cincinnati, "Background & Benefits."

15. Hall, "Race, Articulation," 341.

16. Riverside has a new school in the former Riverside-Harrison building, a charter school called Riverside Academy that opened in 1999.

17. Shipp, "Cincinnati School Pact"; *Bronson*, 550 F. Supp. 941.

18. Lavelle, *Whitewashing the South*, 147.

19. As Monica McDermott found in her study, white working-class residents in Atlanta framed "rights to white schools, white neighborhoods, and white jobs" as an integral part of white racial identity (*Working-Class White*, 54).

20. Lavelle, *Whitewashing the South*, 139.

21. Rachel Woldoff's book *White Flight/Black Flight* focuses on racial change in a northeastern city. She found that longtime white residents were often reluctant to see neighborhood change as the result of white decision-making. Interestingly, the Black residents that Woldoff interviewed had no trouble identifying the role of white flight and antiblack racism in creating neighborhood change, citing it as the central reason for neighborhood decline.

22. Latinx people belong to all racial groups since Hispanic origin is an ethnic designation in the US Census. Latinx people in East Price Hill primarily identified as "Some Other Race" (54 percent) in 2010. They also identified as white (24 percent), Black (3 percent), or American Indian and Alaska Native (8 percent), and 7 percent identified as two or more races.

23. "Anti-Blackness describes the reduction of Blackness to a category of abjection and subjection through narrations of absolute biological or cultural difference; ruling-class monopolization of political power; negative and derogatory mass media propaganda; the ascent of discriminatory legislation that maintains and reinscribes inequality, not least various modes of segregation; and social relations in which distrust and antipathy toward those racialized as Black is normalized and in which

'interracial mass behavior involving violence assumes a continuously potential danger.' Anti-Blackness thus conceals the inherent *contradiction* of Blackness—*value minus worth*—obscuring and distorting its structural location by, as Ralph and Singhal remark, contorting it into only a 'debilitated condition'" (Burden-Stelly, "Modern U.S. Racial Capitalism").

24. You may wonder whether this decline was real or imagined. In this book, I focus on perceptions of decline and try to contextualize them with nonresident data when possible. Still, the stories that residents tell are meaningful in and of themselves and are the core of my analysis.

25. Riverside uses the term "civic club" for their neighborhood organization, while Carthage describes theirs as a "civic league." Both of these terms refer to the local neighborhood organization run by neighborhood residents.

26. For an excellent analysis of the cruelty and inefficacy of banishment practices on unhoused people, see Herbert and Beckett, "Home for Us."

27. Seamster and Charron-Chénier, "Predatory Inclusion." See also Keeanga-Yamahtta Taylor, *Race for Profit*.

28. Keeanga-Yamahtta Taylor, *Race for Profit*, 5.

29. Marable, *Underdeveloped Black America*, 2.

30. Magliozzi, "Securing the Suburbs."

31. Copper theft was a national problem that even the FBI monitored. "The global demand for copper, combined with the economic and home foreclosure crisis, is creating numerous opportunities for copper-theft perpetrators to exploit copper-rich targets. Organized copper theft rings may increasingly target vacant or foreclosed homes as they are a lucrative source of unattended copper inventory. Current economic conditions, such as the rising cost of gasoline, food, and consumer goods, the declining housing market, the ease through which copper is exchanged for cash, and the lack of a significant deterrent effect, make it likely that copper thefts will remain a lucrative financial resource for criminals" (FBI, "Copper Thefts").

32. Christie, "7.5 Million Homeowners 'Underwater.'"

33. Mehkeri, "Predatory Lending."

34. "In collaboration with HUD, the [National Center for Health Statistics] linked longitudinal HUD administrative data with two cross-sectional health interview surveys across a 14-year period (1999 to 2012): the National Health Interview Survey (NHIS) and the National Health and Nutrition Examination Survey (NHANES)" (Helms, Sperling, and Steffen, "Health Picture"); 16.3 percent of HUD-assisted adults reported experiencing asthma, whereas 8.7 percent of the general adult population reported asthma.

35. Monk, "New Owner Promises."

36. Desmond and Wilmers, "Do Poor Pay More?"

37. "In certain submarkets, a voucher can mitigate the risk landlords feel when confronted with a tenant whose racial or ethnic identity makes them uncomfortable, yet in other submarkets, the opposite is true. In this way, we find that landlords are prompted to put aside certain racial prejudices when they have the right financial incentives, but only when the tenant's behavior and manner defy the landlord's racial stereotypes" (Rosen, Garboden, and Cossyleon, "Racial Discrimination in Housing").

38. I did not investigate whether this withholding occurred, because the veracity of these claims is not the focus of my argument. What matters is the perceptions of residents and how these perceptions reflected and constructed their daily realities. In other words, whether they were written in a handbook or not, residents experienced these policies as real.

39. Soss, Fording, and Schram, *Disciplining the Poor*, 1.

40. See Soss, Fording, and Schram, *Disciplining the Poor*.

41. Bhattacharyya, *Rethinking Racial Capitalism*, 153.

42. Bhattacharyya has written about edge populations as "those on the edge of capitalist formations with occasional entry to insecure waged work and participating in the consumer markets shaped by these productive forces, yet unable to gain recognition or secure entry to the terms of capitalist citizenship in that location. This relegation to the edges of capitalist living seems a good candidate for one aspect of capitalist racialisation. It is this location as almost included and yet on the boundary that constitutes one (often if not always) racialised economic position" (*Rethinking Racial Capitalism*, 26–27).

43. Jason Hackworth similarly traces this association across the Rust Belt, arguing that urban decline was caused by "the withdrawal of capital and people. That withdrawal was planned and significantly facilitated by the attempted actuation of a free-market utopia for fleeing white people. This attempt involved and continues to involve institutions, organization, common purpose, and intent" (*Manufacturing Decline*, 215).

44. Howell and Korver-Glenn, "Increasing Effect."

45. National Underground Railroad Freedom Center, "Our History."

46. Black laws, for example, still legally controlled the movements and behaviors of Black people, limiting their ability to serve as a witness in a court, for example. At the same time, Black men served on the city council of Cincinnati in the late 19th century. Cincinnati had a "dual personality," when it came to its treatment of Black residents. As historian Henry Louis Taylor Jr. argues, "This duality, this dialectic, this contradiction, is central to understanding the history of both Cincinnati and its African American population" (*Race and the City*, xiv).

Chapter Three

1. Kefalas, *Working Class Heroes*, 116.

2. Wacquant, Slater, and Pereira, "Territorial Stigmatization in Action."

3. This historical pattern is perhaps best represented by "The Negro Family: The Case For National Action," better known as The Moynihan Report, written by Daniel Moynihan in 1965. In it he argues, "At the heart of the deterioration of the fabric of Negro society is the deterioration of the Negro family. It is the fundamental source of the weakness of the Negro community at the present time." For an annotated review of the document, see Geary, "The Moynihan Report."

4. Brady, Finnigan, and Hübgen continue, "Denmark, for example, has chosen to provide universal cash benefits and tax credits for children, publicly subsidized child care and health care, and paid parental leave. Because of these generous

social policies, single mothers and their children have a similar level of economic security as other families." For more, see Brady, Finnigan, and Hübgen, "Single Mothers."

5. Rank, "Five Myths about Poverty."

6. Alexander, *New Jim Crow*; Londberg and Walinchus, "Investigation: Traffic Stop Targets."

7. For more on this term, see Isenberg, *White Trash*; and McDermott, *Working-Class White*.

8. Murch, "Race Made Opioid Crisis."

9. Department of Justice, "Justice Department Announces Resolution."

10. It is noteworthy that Patty used the word "uppity," a term historically used by white people toward Black Americans "who violated white expectations of black deference" (PBS, "Lynching in America").

11. For more on this construction of Patty and me as an "us," see appendix A.

12. See Mayorga-Gallo, *Behind the White Picket Fence* and "Estamos a la Fuerza."

13. For more on these transnational relationships, see Abrego, *Sacrificing Families*; and Levitt and Jaworsky, "Transnational Migration Studies."

14. Bhattacharyya, *Rethinking Racial Capitalism*, 65.

15. McCabe, *No Place Like Home*, 96.

16. Rosen, Garboden, and Cossyleon, "Racial Discrimination in Housing," 789.

17. See Rosen, Garboden, and Cossyleon, "Racial Discrimination in Housing."

18. See Mayorga-Gallo, "Whose Best Friend?"; and Alexander, *New Jim Crow*.

19. Ranganathan and Bonds, "Racial Regimes of Property," 198.

20. Koshy et al., *Colonial Racial Capitalism*, 5.

21. Through the Ohio Native Land Initiative, for example, "the GCNAC seeks to establish a broader platform to promote Indigenous perspectives on sacred sites, encourage land rematriation efforts, and assert Native sovereignty as foundational to some of the region's most important natural resources and public spaces" (Greater Cincinnati Native American Coalition, "Ohio Native Land Initiative"). The Fort Ancient sites, or Mound Sites, north of Cincinnati are of particular importance to the coalition. Fort Ancient Earthworks & Nature Preserve is run by the Ohio History Connection, a settler organization started in 1885 as the Ohio Historical Society. The executive director of GCNAC, Jheri Neri, describes her first time visiting the sacred mounds as marked by "non-native reenactors entertaining tourists with a 'Pow Wow' and performing rituals (of questionable European origin) on top of the serpent mound itself" (GCNAC, "Note from Executive Director"). I raise this example to remind us that the occupation of native lands is not a historical occurrence but a daily one.

22. Cited in Koshy et al., *Colonial Racial Capitalism*, 5.

23. For more on the relationship between settler colonialism, racial capitalism, and property, see Koshy et al., *Colonial Racial Capitalism*.

24. Nichols, *Theft Is Property!*, 145.

25. Glenn, "Settler Colonialism as Structure."

26. Blomley, *Unsettling the City*, 3.

27. Blomley, *Unsettling the City*, 6.

28. Wright, *Class Counts*, 10.

29. John Klosterman and his wife were sued by the Justice Department for John's sexual harassment of female tenants over several years. The case was settled with an agreement to pay "$167,125 in damages to former tenants who were harmed by John Klosterman's harassment, $7,875 to another plaintiff in the lawsuit, and a $2,500 civil penalty to the United States. The consent order also bars the defendants from participating in the rental or management of residential properties in the future" (Department of Justice, "Department Settles Harassment Lawsuit").

30. To wit, the *Los Angeles Times* ran a piece by Jessica Roy titled, "Why you can't afford a house (Hint: It's not the avocado toast)" in 2017. For more on student loan debt, see the work of sociologist Louise Seamster and colleagues, including her incredibly eye-opening and informative podcast interview with Tressie McMillan Cottom (Seamster, "Differences between White and Black Debt").

31. McCabe, *No Place Like Home*.

32. As the report explains, "This occurs because collective bargaining not only raises wages for organized workers but also leads other employers to raise the wages and benefits of nonunion workers to come closer to union wage standards. This phenomenon occurs when collective bargaining achieves even modest penetration. The erosion of collective bargaining can explain from one-fourth to one-third of the growth of wage inequality between 1973 and 2007 and had a greater impact on men than women" (Mishel, Gould, and Bivens, "Wage Stagnation").

33. Londberg and Walinchus, "Investigation: Traffic Stop Targets."

Chapter Four

1. Desmond, "Relational Ethnography."

2. Correia and Wall, *Violent Order*.

3. Kaba and Ritchie, *No More Police*, 179.

4. Kaba, *We Do This*, 95.

5. See chapter 2 in Van Cleve, *Crook County*.

6. McMillan Cottom, *Thick*, 93, 95.

7. This also echoes the work of philosopher Sara Ahmed (*On Being Included*) on how naming the problem, such as institutional racism, in an organization transforms the reporting individual into a problem.

8. I sent out postcards advertising my study as a recruitment tool. See appendix A for more details.

9. Gilmore, "Making Abolition Geography."

10. Kaba and Ritchie, *No More Police*, 180.

11. hooks, *All About Love*, 93.

12. The remaining 2 percent were split, saying that crime was a problem in some neighborhood locations.

13. Wall, "Inventing Humanity."

14. Correia and Wall, *Violent Order*, 3; Cacho and Melamed, "'Don't Arrest Me.'"

15. Vitale, *End of Policing*, 34.

16. Greater Cincinnati Police Museum, "Department History."

17. See Vitale, *End of Policing*; and Wall, "Inventing Humanity."

18. Prison Policy Initiative, "Pretrial Detention."

19. Bail Project, "Fast Facts."

20. Eisler et al., "Why 4,998 Died."

21. Pohlman, "Restraint Chair."

22. ACLU, "Asset Forfeiture Abuse."

23. Pilcher, "Federal Seizure Program."

24. Rodd, "Should Police be Allowed?"

25. McNair, "Fund for All Occasions."

26. Hamilton County Prosecutor's Office, "Forfeitures."

27. Alexander, *New Jim Crow*, 154.

28. Hamilton County Sheriff's Office, "History of Cincinnati Workhouse."

29. Kirklen, "Prosecutor Says 'Stop and Frisk.'"

30. Balto, *Occupied Territory*.

31. Semuels, "Broken Police Department"; Schatmeier, "Reforming Police Practices."

32. For more on the relationship between antiblackness and policing in the United States, see Balto, *Occupied Territory*. I discuss antiblackness as a norm of life in Carthage and Riverside in chapter 5.

33. Activists call these portrayals "copaganda—propaganda favorable to law enforcement that inundates mainstream media" (Kaba and Ritchie, *No More Police*, 183). For more on copaganda, see Vakil, "Hollywood's Facing a Reckoning."

34. "Beavers pleaded guilty in June [2014] to illegal use of a minor in nudity oriented material and attempted tampering with evidence. A theft in office charge that would have resulted in Beavers losing any police pension was dropped as part of the plea deal" (Perry, "Ex-officer Going to Prison").

35. Kaba and Ritchie, *No More Police*, 75.

36. Price, *Prison and Social Death*.

37. Kaba and Ritchie, *No More Police*, 83.

38. Kaba, *We Do This*, 94.

39. Desmond and Valdez, "Unpolicing the Urban Poor."

40. Kaba, *We Do This*, 99.

41. "HCJFS has the statutory responsibility to receive and respond to reports of child abuse and neglect in Hamilton County. Specially trained caseworkers staff the hotline. Their questions are designed to collect the necessary information to make an initial determination of suspected abuse or neglect" (Hamilton County Job and Family Services, "Frequently Asked Questions").

42. Davis, *Are Prisons Obsolete*, 112.

43. Davis, *Are Prisons Obsolete*, 112. For more on police discretion as foundational to their power to criminalize and commit violence, see also Cacho and Melamed, "Don't Arrest Me."

44. Kaba and Ritchie, *No More Police*.

45. See Price, *Prison and Social Death*.

46. Child endangerment is defined by section 2919.12 of the Ohio Revised Code as "a substantial risk to the health or safety of the child, by violating a duty of care, protection, or support."

47. Kaba and Ritchie, *No More Police*, 171. For more on the carceral function and abolition of the child welfare system, read Dorothy Roberts, *Torn Apart*.

48. And it is not just institutional harm we must consider, but the interpersonal harm perpetrators have experienced. As Kaba writes, "My friend Danielle Sered has said . . . 'no one enters violence for the first time by committing it.' . . . If that's true, then all this shit that we talk about, these binaries about victims and perpetrators—that explodes it all" (Kaba, *We Do This*, 145–146).

Chapter Five

1. Woodly et al., "Politics of Care," 905.

2. Bunyasi and Smith, *Stay Woke*, 102.

3. When Diego used the term "Americano," he was referring to white Americans, as he later clarified in his interview. When referring to Black Americans, he used the word "morenos."

4. Given my positionality as a white Latina professor, it is unsurprising that Jenny also used this performance with me at the start of our interview. See appendix A for more on how residents interacted with me and how it relates to my race, class, and gender position.

5. Bed bugs are a significant problem in Cincinnati. It was ranked the eighth worst city for bed bugs in the United States in 2021 by fumigating company Orkin, which bases the rankings on treatment rates. See Rice, "Cincinnati Ranks Eighth."

6. Jung and Vargas, *Antiblackness*, 8–9.

7. Wray, *Not Quite White*, 141. Wray argues, "Group effects like boundary work, intergroup conflict, and status differentiation can and do occur whether or not there are 'real' groups standing behind these processes."

8. In her essay titled "The Price of Fabulousness," McMillan Cottom explains, "Why do poor people make stupid, illogical decisions to buy status symbols? For the same reason all but only the most wealthy buy status symbols, I suppose. We want to belong. And not just for the psychic rewards, but belonging to one group at the right time can mean the difference between unemployment and employment, a good job as opposed to a bad job, housing or a shelter, and so on" (*Thick*, 165).

9. McMillan Cottom, *Thick*, 161.

10. Bonilla-Silva, "Feeling Race," 3.

11. Lareau, *Unequal Childhoods*, 2.

12. Lareau, *Unequal Childhoods*, 3.

13. Clemons, "From 'Freedom Now!,'" 2.

14. See Woodly et al., "Politics of Care," 905.

15. For more on radical interdependency, see Card, *Geographies of Racial Capitalism*; in her definition of love, hooks uses the phrase "spiritual growth" while I prefer the more general term "growth" (hooks, *All about Love*, 136).

Conclusion

1. Rank, Eppard, and Bullock, *Poorly Understood*, 64–69.
2. Bhattacharyya, *Rethinking Racial Capitalism*, 165.
3. Kaba, *We Do This*.
4. Kelley, "Twenty Years."
5. Ruth Wilson Gilmore quoted in Kaba and Ritchie, *No More Police*, 39.
6. Gilmore, "Making Abolition Geography."
7. Card, *Geographies of Racial Capitalism*.

Appendix A

1. Mayorga-Gallo and Hordge-Freeman, "Between Marginality and Privilege."
2. And a Leo sun sign.
3. For more on "raceless" Latinidad, see Adames, Chavez-Dueñas, and Jernigan, "Fallacy of Raceless Latinidad." Thank you to my sister Carla for sharing this reference.
4. As Shireen Roshanravan argues about Asian American solidarities with Black people, "Exhibits of coalitional boundary crossing are thus central to this Asian American feminist praxis because they disrupt both state-prescribed hostility toward other communities of color and the heteropatriarchal principle of indifference to those not legally defined as one's own community or kin" ("Weaponizing Our (In)visibility," 263–264).
5. Dinzey-Flores et al., "Black Latina Womanhood"; López Oro, "Performing Indigenous Blackness."
6. Roshanravan, "Weaponizing Our (In)visibility," 266.
7. McMillan Cottom, *Thick*, 28.

Bibliography

Abrego, Leisy J. *Sacrificing Families: Navigating Laws, Labor, and Love Across Borders*. Stanford, CA: Stanford University Press, 2014.

Adames, Hector Y., Nayeli Y. Chavez-Dueñas, and Maryam M. Jernigan. "The Fallacy of a Raceless Latinidad: Action Guidelines for Centering Blackness in Latinx Psychology." *Journal of Latinx Psychology* 9, no. 1 (2021): 26–44.

Ahmed, Sara. *On Being Included: Racism and Diversity in Institutional Life*. Durham, NC: Duke University Press, 2012.

Alexander, Michelle. *The New Jim Crow: Mass Incarceration in the Age of Colorblindness*. New York: New Press, 2012.

Althusser, Louis. "Ideology and Ideological State Apparatuses: Notes Towards an Investigation." 1971. In *Lenin and Philosophy and Other Essays*, translated by Ben Brewster, 85–126. New York: Monthly Review Press, 2001.

American Civil Liberties Union (ACLU). "Asset Forfeiture Abuse." Accessed September 17, 2022, www.aclu.org/issues/criminal-law-reform/reforming-police /asset-forfeiture-abuse.

Anderson, Carol. *White Rage: The Unspoken Truth of Our Racial Divide*. New York: Bloomsbury, 2016.

Bail Project. "Fast Facts." Accessed September 14, 2022, https://bailproject.org /cincinnati.

Balto, Simon. *Occupied Territory: Policing Black Chicago from Red Summer to Black Power*. Chapel Hill: University of North Carolina Press, 2019.

Bhattacharyya, Gargi. *Rethinking Racial Capitalism: Questions of Reproduction and Survival*. Lanham, MD: Rowman and Littlefield, 2018.

Blomley, Nicholas. *Unsettling the City: Urban Land and the Politics of Property*. New York: Routledge, 2004.

Bonilla-Silva, Eduardo. "Feeling Race: Theorizing the Racial Economy of Emotions." *American Sociological Review* 84, no. 1 (2019): 1–25.

Brady, David, Ryan M. Finnigan, and Sabine Hübgen. "Single Mothers Are Not the Problem." Op-ed, *New York Times*, February 10, 2018, www.nytimes.com/2018/02 /10/opinion/sunday/single-mothers-poverty.html.

Bronson v. Board of Education of City School District, 550 F. Supp. 941 (S.D. Ohio 1982).

Bunyasi, Tehama Lopez, and Candis Watts Smith. *Stay Woke: A People's Guide to Making All Black Lives Matter*. New York: New York University Press, 2019.

Burden-Stelly, Charisse. "Modern U.S. Racial Capitalism: Some Theoretical Insights." *Monthly Review*, July 1, 2020, https://monthlyreview.org/2020/07/01 /modern-u-s-racial-capitalism.

Cacho, Lisa Marie, and Jodi Melamed. "'Don't Arrest Me, Arrest the Police': Policing as the Street Administration of Colonial Racial Capitalist Orders." In *Colonial Racial Capitalism*, edited by Susan Koshy, Lisa Marie Cacho, Jodi A. Byrd, and Brian Jordan Jefferson, 159–205. Durham, NC: Duke University Press, 2022.

Cann, Jarrod, and Erick Stoll (directors). *Good White People: A Short Film About Gentrification*. November 27, 2016, https://www.youtube.com/watch?v=xdUsZaJ8ozI.

Card, Kenton (director). *Geographies of Racial Capitalism with Ruth Wilson Gilmore. Online*, June 1, 2020, https://antipodeonline.org/geographies-of-racial-capitalism.

Catte, Elizabeth. *What You're Getting Wrong about Appalachia*. Cleveland, OH: Belt Publishing, 2018.

CFLeads and Greater Cincinnati Foundation. "A Tale of Two Cities: Advancing Racial Equity in Cincinnati." April 19, 2021, https://cfleads.org/cfleads-post/a-tale-of-two-cities-advancing-racial-equity-in-cincinnati.

Christie, Les. "7.5 Million Homeowners 'Underwater.'" *CNN Money*, October 31, 2008, https://money.cnn.com/2008/10/30/real_estate/underwater_borrowers/index.htm.

City of Cincinnati. "Background & Benefits." Accessed June 1, 2021 (site discontinued), available at https://web.archive.org/web/20210309140534/https://www.cincinnati-oh.gov/streetcar/background-benefits.

Clemons, Jared. "From 'Freedom Now!' to 'Black Lives Matter': Retrieving King and Randolph to Theorize Contemporary White Antiracism." *Perspectives on Politics* (2022), https://doi.org/10.1017/S1537592722001074.

Correia, David, and Tyler Wall. *Violent Order: Essays on the Nature of Police*. Chicago: Haymarket Books, 2021.

Cox, Oliver Cromwell. *Caste, Class, and Race: A Study in Social Dynamics*. New York: Monthly Review Press, 1948.

Cramer, Katherine J. *The Politics of Resentment: Rural Consciousness in Wisconsin and the Rise of Scott Walker*. Chicago: University of Chicago Press, 2016.

Curnutte, Mark. "Looking Back at Civil Unrest of 2001." *Cincinnati Enquirer*, February 2, 2016, www.cincinnati.com/story/news/2016/02/02/looking-back-civil-unrest-2001/79650790.

Davis, Angela Y. *Are Prisons Obsolete?* New York: Seven Stories Press, 2003.

Dawson, Michael. "Hidden in Plain Sight: A Note on Legitimation Crises and the Racial Order." *Critical Historical Studies* 3, no. 1 (2016): 143–161.

Department of Justice (DOJ). "Justice Department Announces Global Resolution of Criminal and Civil Investigations with Opioid Manufacturer Purdue Pharma and Civil Settlement with Members of the Sackler Family." Office of Public Affairs, October 21, 2020, https://www.justice.gov/opa/pr/justice-department-announces-global-resolution-criminal-and-civil-investigations-opioid.

———. "Justice Department Settles Sexual Harassment Lawsuit Against Cincinnati, Ohio Landlord." Office of Public Affairs, September 30, 2020, www.justice.gov/opa/pr/justice-department-settles-sexual-harassment-lawsuit-against-cincinnati-ohio-landlord.

Desmond, Matthew. *Evicted: Poverty and Profit in the American City*. New York: Crown Publishing, 2016.

———. "Relational Ethnography." *Theory and Society* 43, no. 5 (2014): 547–579.

Desmond, Matthew, and Nicol Valdez. "Unpolicing the Urban Poor: Consequences of Third-Party Policing for Inner-City Women." *American Sociological Review* 78, no. 1 (2012): 117–141.

Desmond, Matthew, and Nathan Wilmers. "Do the Poor Pay More for Housing? Exploitation, Profit, and Risk in Rental Markets." *American Journal of Sociology* 124, no. 4 (2019): 1090–1124.

Dinzey-Flores, Zaire Zenit, Hilda Lloréns, Nancy López, Maritza Quiñones, and Black Latinas Know Collective. "Black Latina Womanhood." *Women's Studies Quarterly* 47, no. 3/4 (2019): 321–327.

Draut, Tamara. "Understanding the Working Class." *Demos*, April 16, 2018, www.demos.org/research/understanding-working-class.

Du Bois, W. E. B. *Black Reconstruction in America, 1860–1880*. New York: Free Press, 1935.

Eisler, Peter, Linda So, Jason Szap, Grant Smith, and Ned Parker. "Why 4,998 Died in U.S. Jails without Getting Their Day in Court." *Reuters*, October 16, 2020, www.reuters.com/investigates/special-report/usa-jails-deaths.

Federal Bureau of Investigation (FBI) Criminal Intelligence Section. "Copper Thefts." September 15, 2008, www.fbi.gov/stats-services/publications/copper-thefts.

Fields, Karen E., and Barbara J. Fields. *Racecraft: The Soul of Inequality in American Life*. Brooklyn, NY: Verso Books, 2014.

Fraser, Nancy. "Expropriation and Exploitation in Racialized Capitalism: A Reply to Michael Dawson." *Critical Historical Studies* 3, no. 1 (2016): 163–178.

Geary, Daniel. "The Moynihan Report: An Annotated Edition." *The Atlantic*, September 14, 2015, https://www.theatlantic.com/politics/archive/2015/09/the-moynihan-report-an-annotated-edition/404632/.

Gilens, Martin. 1999. *Why Americans Hate Welfare: Race, Media, and the Politics of Antipoverty Policy*. Chicago: University of Chicago Press, 1999.

Gilmore, Ruth Wilson. "Making Abolition Geography in California's Central Valley." *Funambulist* 21 (2018), https://thefunambulist.net/magazine/21-space-activism/interview-making-abolition-geography-california-central-valley-ruth-wilson-gilmore.

Glenn, Evelyn Nakano. "Settler Colonialism as Structure: A Framework for Comparative Studies of U.S. Race and Gender Formation." *Sociology of Race and Ethnicity* 1, no. 1 (2015): 52–72.

Greater Cincinnati Native American Coalition. "A Note from the Executive Director." June 8, 2019, https://gcnativeamericancoalition.com/news/2019/6/8/a-note-from-the-executive-director.

———. "Ohio Native Land Initiative." Accessed September 17, 2022, https://gcnativeamericancoalition.com/ohionativelandinitiative.

Greater Cincinnati Police Museum. "Cincinnati Police Department History—1825 to 1849." Accessed September 14, 2022, https://police-museum.org/greater

-cincinnati-police-history/chronological-history-of-the-cincinnati-police
-department/cincinnati-police-department-history-1825-to-1849.

Hackworth, Jason. *Manufacturing Decline: How Racism and the Conservative Movement
Crush the American Rust Belt*. New York: Columbia University Press, 2019.

Hall, Stuart. "Gramsci's Relevance for the Study of Race and Ethnicity." *Journal of
Communication Inquiry* 10, no. 2. (1986): 5–27.

———. "The Problem of Ideology—Marxism without Guarantees." *Journal of
Communication Inquiry* 10, no. 2 (1986): 28–44.

———. "Race, Articulation, and Societies Structured in Dominance." In *Sociological
Theories: Race and Colonialism*, edited by the UN Educational, Scientific and
Cultural Organization (UNESCO), 305–345. Paris: UNESCO, 1980.

Hamilton County Job and Family Services. "Frequently Asked Questions." Accessed
September 14, 2022, www.hcjfs.org/services/child-protection/241-kids
-frequently-asked-questions.

Hamilton County Prosecutor's Office. "Forfeitures." Accessed September 14, 2022,
https://hcpros.org/divisions/civil-division/forfeitures.

Hamilton County Sheriff's Office. "History: History of the Cincinnati Workhouse."
Accessed February 28, 2022, www.hcso.org/history-of-the-cincinnati
-workhouse.

Harvey, David. "The 'New' Imperialism: Accumulation by Dispossession." *Socialist
Register* 40 (2004): 63–87.

Helms, Veronica E., Jon Sperling, and Barry L. Steffen. "A Health Picture of
HUD-Assisted Adults, 2006–2012." U.S. Department of Housing and Urban
Development (HUD) and Office of Policy Development and Research, accessed
September 17, 2022, www.huduser.gov/portal/sites/default/files/pdf/Health
-Picture-of-HUD.pdf.

Herbert, Steve and Katherine Beckett. "'This Is Home for Us': Questioning
Banishment from the Ground Up." *Social and Cultural Geography* 11, no. 3 (2010):
231–245.

Hershberger, Matt. "How Cincinnati Fell in Love with One of America's Weirdest
Dishes." *USA Today 10 Best*, August 31, 2018, www.10best.com/interests/food
-culture/how-cincinnati-fell-in-love-one-of-americas-weirdest-dishes.

hooks, bell. *All about Love: New Visions*. New York: William Morrow, 2001.

———. "Theory as Liberatory Practice." *Yale Journal of Law and Feminism* 4, no. 1
(1991): 1–12.

Howell, Junia, and Elizabeth Korver-Glenn. "The Increasing Effect of Neighborhood
Racial Composition on Housing Values, 1980–2015." *Social Problems* 68, no. 4
(2021): 1051–1071.

Isenberg, Nancy. *White Trash: The 400-Year Untold History of Class in America*. New
York: Penguin Books, 2017.

Kaba, Mariame. *We Do This 'Til We Free Us: Abolitionist Organizing and Transforming
Justice*. Chicago: Haymarket Books, 2021.

Kaba, Mariame, and Andrea Ritchie. *No More Police: A Case for Abolition*. New York:
New Press, 2022.

Kefalas, Maria. *Working Class Heroes: Protecting Home, Community, and Nation in a Chicago Neighborhood*. Berkeley: University of California Press, 2003.

Kelley, Robin D. G. "Twenty Years of *Freedom Dreams*." *Boston Review*, August 1, 2022, https://bostonreview.net/articles/twenty-years-of-freedom-dreams.

Kelley, Robin D. G. "What Did Cedric Robinson Mean by Racial Capitalism?" *Boston Review*, January 12, 2017, https://bostonreview.net/articles/robin-d-g-kelley-introduction-race-capitalism-justice.

Kenny, D. J. *Illustrated Cincinnati: A Pictorial Hand-Book of the Queen City*. Cincinnati, OH, 1875.

Kirklen, Ashley. "Hamilton County Prosecutor Says 'Stop and Frisk' Is a Solution to Crack Down on Gun Violence." WLWT 5, July 8, 2021, www.wlwt.com/article/hamilton-county-prosecutor-says-stop-and-frisk-is-a-solution-to-crack-down-on-gun-violence/36974371#.

Koshy, Susan, Lisa Marie Cacho, Jodi A. Byrd, and Brian Jordan Jefferson, eds. *Colonial Racial Capitalism*. Durham, NC: Duke University Press, 2022.

Kruse, Kevin M., and Thomas J. Sugrue, eds. *The New Suburban History*. Chicago: University of Chicago Press, 2006.

Lareau, Annette. *Unequal Childhoods: Class, Race, and Family Life*. 2nd ed. Berkeley: University of California Press, 2011.

Larson, John. "Behind the Death of Timothy Thomas." *NBC News*, April 4, 2004, www.nbcnews.com/id/wbna4703574.

Lavelle, Kristen. *Whitewashing the South: White Memories of Segregation and Civil Rights*. Lanham, MD: Rowman and Littlefield, 2014.

Levitt, Peggy, and B. Nadya Jaworsky. "Transnational Migration Studies: Past Developments and Future Trends." *Annual Review of Sociology* 33 (2007): 129–156.

Londberg, Max, and Lucia Walinchus. "Investigation: Blacks, Black Neighborhoods Most Likely to Be Traffic Stop Targets in Ohio's 3 Biggest Cities." Eye on Ohio: Ohio Center for Journalism, December 18, 2019, eyeonohio.com/investigation-blacks-black-neighborhoods-most-likely-to-be-traffic-stop-targets-in-ohios-3-biggest-cities.

López Oro, Paul Joseph. "Performing Indigenous Blackness: Ancestral Memory in the Garifuna Diaspora." Lecture at Brandeis University, Waltham, MA, April 12, 2021.

Magliozzi, Devon. "Securing the Suburbs: How Elites Use Policing to Protect Their Advantages." PhD dissertation, Stanford University, 2018.

Marable, Manning. *How Capitalism Underdeveloped Black America*. Chicago: Haymarket Books, 1983.

Mayorga-Gallo, Sarah. "'Aquí Estamos a la Fuerza:' Interracial Relations in a New Latino/a Destination City." *Sociologica* 9, no. 2 (2015), www.rivisteweb.it/doi/10.2383/81431.

———. *Behind the White Picket Fence: Power and Privilege in a Multiethnic Neighborhood*. Chapel Hill: University of North Carolina Press, 2014.

———. "Whose Best Friend? Dogs and Racial Boundary Maintenance in a Multiracial Neighborhood." *Sociological Forum* 33, no. 2 (2018): 505–528.

Mayorga-Gallo, Sarah, and Elizabeth Hordge-Freeman. "Between Marginality and Privilege: Gaining Access and Navigating the Field in Multiethnic Settings." *Qualitative Research* 17, no. 4 (2017): 377–394.

Mayorga, Sarah, Megan Underhill, and Lauren Crosser. "Aisle Inequality." *Contexts* 22, no. 1 (2023).

———. "'I Hate That Food Lion': Grocery Shopping, Racial Capitalism, and Everyday Disinvestment." *City and Community* 21, no. 3 (2022): 238–255.

McCabe, Brian. *No Place Like Home: Wealth, Community, and the Politics of Homeownership.* New York: Oxford University Press, 2016.

McDermott, Monica. *Working-Class White: The Making and Unmaking of Race Relations.* Berkeley: University of California Press, 2006.

McMillan Cottom, Tressie. *Thick: And Other Essays.* New York: New Press, 2019.

McNair, James. "A Fund for All Occasions." *City Beat*, September 20, 2017, www.citybeat.com/news/joe-deters-assetforfeiture-fund-helps-pay-for-law-enforcement-but-also-for-furniture-briefcases-dues-and-consultants-12231467.

Mehkeri, Zainab A. "Predatory Lending: What's Race Got To Do With It." *Loyola Public Interest Law Report* 20, no. 1 (2014): 44–51.

Metzl, Jonathan. *Dying of Whiteness: How the Politics of Racial Resentment Is Killing America's Heartland.* New York: Basic Books, 2019.

Mishel, Lawrence, Elise Gould, and Josh Bivens. "Wage Stagnation in Nine Charts." Report, Economic Policy Institute, January 6, 2015, www.epi.org/publication/charting-wage-stagnation.

Monk, Dan. "New Owner Promises Upgrades at Problem Property in Sedamsville." WCPO *ABC 9 News*, July 9, 2016, www.wcpo.com/news/insider/new-owner-promises-upgrades-at-problem-property-in-sedamsville.

Murch, Donna. "How Race Made the Opioid Crisis." *Boston Review*, April 9, 2019, https://www.bostonreview.net/forum/donna-murch-how-race-made-opioid-crisis.

National Underground Railroad Freedom Center. "Our History." Accessed March 29, 2023. https://freedomcenter.org/about/history.

Nichols, Robert. *Theft Is Property! Dispossession and Critical Theory.* Durham, NC: Duke University Press, 2020.

Obermiller, Phillip J. *Down Home, Downtown: Urban Appalachians Today.* Dubuque, IA: Kendall Hunt Publishing, 1996.

Ohio History Central. "Miami Indians." Accessed January 5, 2023, https://ohiohistorycentral.org/w/Miami_Indians.

———. "Shawnee Indians." Accessed January 5, 2023, https://ohiohistorycentral.org/w/Shawnee_Indians.

Oliver, Melvin and Thomas Shapiro. *Black Wealth/White Wealth: A New Perspective on Racial Inequality.* 1995. Reprint, New York: Routledge, 2006.

Penn, Farrah. "Here's The Weirdest Food Every State Is Known For, According To People Who Live There." *Buzzfeed*, August 17, 2018, www.buzzfeed.com/farrahpenn/heres-the-weirdest-food-every-state-is-known-for-according.

Perry, Kimball. "Ex-Officer Going to Prison: 'I'm the Boogeyman.'" *Cincinnati Enquirer*, October 30, 2014, www.cincinnati.com/story/news/2014/10/30/former-cpd-officer-sentenced-today/18169601.

Pilcher, James. "Federal Seizure Program That Benefits Cops Called 'Legal Robbery.'" *Cincinnati Enquirer*, September 15, 2015, www.cincinnati.com/story /news/your-watchdog/2015/09/10/federal-seizure-program-benefits-cops-called -legal-robbery/71995798.

Pohlman, Duane. "The Restraint Chair: Investigating Pierre Howell's Disturbing Death in Jail." WKRC *Local 12*, April 30, 2021, https://local12.com/news /investigates/the-restraint-chair-investigating-pierre-howells-disturbing-death -in-jail-cincinnati.

Price, Joshua. *Prison and Social Death*. New Brunswick, NJ: Rutgers University Press, 2015.

Prison Policy Initiative. "Pretrial Detention." Accessed February 28, 2022, www .prisonpolicy.org/research/pretrial_detention.

Public Broadcasting System (PBS). "Lynching in America." On *American Experience*, accessed September 17, 2022, www.pbs.org/wgbh/americanexperience/features /emmett-lynching-america.

Pulido, Laura. "Geographies of Race and Ethnicity II: Environmental Racism, Racial Capitalism and State-Sanctioned Violence." *Progress in Human Geography* 41, no. 4 (2017): 524–533.

Purifoy, Danielle, and Louise Seamster. "Creative Extraction: Black Towns in White Space." *Environment and Planning D: Society and Space* 39, no. 1 (2021): 47–66.

Ranganathan, Malini, and Anne Bonds. "Racial Regimes of Property: Introduction to the Special Issue." *Environment and Planning D: Society and Space* 40, no. 2 (2022): 197–207.

Rank, Mark. "Five Myths about Poverty." *Washington Post*, March 25, 2021, www .washingtonpost.com/outlook/five-myths/5-myths-about-poverty/2021/03/25 /bf75d5f4-8cfe-11eb-a6bd-0eb91c03305a_story.html.

Rank, Mark Robert, Lawrence M. Eppard, and Heather E. Bullock. *Poorly Understood: What America Gets Wrong about Poverty*. New York: Oxford University Press, 2021.

Reese, Ashanté M. *Black Food Geographies: Race, Self-Reliance and Food Access in Washington, D.C.* Chapel Hill: University of North Carolina Press, 2019.

Rhee, William, and Stephen C. Scott. "Geographic Discrimination: Of Place, Space, Hillbillies, and Home." *West Virginia Law Review* 121, no. 2 (2018): 531–609, https://researchrepository.wvu.edu/wvlr/vol121/iss2/7.

Rice, Brianna. "Cincinnati Ranks as the Eighth Worst City in America for Bed Bugs." *Cincinnati Enquirer*, February 1, 2021, www.cincinnati.com/story/news/2021/02 /01/orkin-cincinnati-columbus-cleveland-indianapolis-among-worst-bed-bugs /4338370001.

Roberts, Dorothy. *Torn Apart: How the Child Welfare System Destroys Black Families— and How Abolition Can Build a Safer World*. New York: Basic Books, 2022.

Robinson, Cedric J. *Black Marxism: The Making of the Black Radical Tradition*. 1983. Reprint, Chapel Hill: University of North Carolina Press, 2021.

Rodd, Scott. "Should Police Be Allowed to Keep Property without a Criminal Conviction?" *Stateline*, February 8, 2017, www.pewtrusts.org/en/research-and

-analysis/blogs/stateline/2017/02/08/should-police-be-allowed-to-keep-property
-without-a-criminal-conviction.

Rodney, Walter. *How Europe Underdeveloped Africa.* 1972. Reprint, Brooklyn, NY: Verso Books, 2018.

Rosen, Eva, Philip M. E. Garboden, and Jennifer E. Cossyleon. "Racial Discrimination in Housing: How Landlords Use Algorithms and Home Visits to Screen Tenants." *American Sociological Review* 86, no. 5 (2021): 787–822.

Roshanravan, Shireen. "Weaponizing Our (In)visibility: Asian American Feminist Ruptures of the Model-Minority Optic." In *Asian American Feminisms and Women of Color Politics,* edited by Lynn Fujiwara and Shireen Roshanravan, 261–282. Seattle: University of Washington Press, 2018.

Roy, Jessica. "Why You Can't Afford a House (Hint: It's Not the Avocado Toast)." *Los Angeles Times,* May 15, 2017, https://www.latimes.com/business/technology/la-fi -avocado-toast-millennials-home-buying-20170515-story.html.

Schatmeier, Elliot Harvey. "Reforming Police Use-of-Force Practices: A Case Study of the Cincinnati Police Department." *Columbia Journal of Law and Social Problems* 46, no. 4 (2013): 539–586.

Seamster, Louise. "The Life-Altering Differences between White and Black Debt." Podcast interview by Tressie McMillan Cottom on *Ezra Klein Show,* November 2, 2021, https://www.nytimes.com/2021/11/02/podcasts/transcript-ezra-klein-show -louise-seamster.html.

Seamster, Louise, and Raphaël Charron-Chénier. "Predatory Inclusion and Education Debt: Rethinking the Racial Wealth Gap." *Social Currents* 4, no. 3 (2017): 199–207.

Semuels, Alana. "How to Fix a Broken Police Department." *The Atlantic,* May 28, 2015, www.theatlantic.com/politics/archive/2015/05/cincinnati-police-reform /393797.

Shaw, Samuel, and Daniel Monroe Sullivan. "'White Night': Gentrification, Racial Exclusion, and Perceptions and Participation in the Arts." *City and Community* 10, no. 3 (2011): 241–264.

Shipp, E. R. "Cincinnati School Pact Is Embraced as a Model." *New York Times,* February 17, 1984, www.nytimes.com/1984/02/17/us/cincinnati-school-pact-is -embraced-as-a-model.html.

Soss, Joe, Richard C. Fording, and Sanford C. Schram. *Disciplining the Poor: Neoliberal Paternalism and the Persistent Power of Race.* Chicago: University of Chicago Press, 2011.

Stradling, David. *Cincinnati: From River City to Highway Metropolis.* Charleston, SC: Arcadia, 2003.

Sugrue, Thomas. *The Origins of the Urban Crisis: Race and Inequality in Postwar Detroit.* 1996. Reprint, Princeton, NJ: Princeton University Press, 2014.

Taylor, Henry Louis, ed. *Race and the City: Work, Community, and Protest in Cincinnati, 1820–1970.* Urbana: University of Illinois Press, 1993.

Taylor, Keeanga-Yamahtta. *Race for Profit: How Banks and the Real Estate Industry Undermined Black Homeownership.* Chapel Hill: University of North Carolina Press, 2019.

Tweh, Bowdeya, and Sharon Coolidge. "Cincinnati: 20 Years Later, It's Still 'Two Cities.'" *Cincinnati Enquirer*, August 29, 2015, www.cincinnati.com/story/news/2015/08/30/urban-league-report/71378016.

Urban Appalachian Community Coalition (UACC). "About Urban Appalachians." Accessed September 17, 2022, https://uacvoice.org/about-urban-appalchians.

Vakil, Keya. "Hollywood's Decades-Long Love Affair with Copaganda Is Finally Facing a Reckoning." *Courier*, June 30, 2020, https://archive.couriernewsroom.com/2020/06/30/hollywoods-decades-long-love-affair-with-copaganda-is-finally-facing-a-reckoning.

Van Cleve, Nicole Gonzalez. *Crook County: Racism and Injustice in America's Largest Criminal Court*. Stanford, CA: Stanford Law Books, 2016.

Vitale, Alex S. *The End of Policing*. Brooklyn, NY: Verso Books, 2017.

Wacquant, Loïc. "Territorial Stigmatization in the Age of Advanced Marginality." *Thesis Eleven* 91, no. 1 (2007): 66–77.

Wacquant, Loïc, Tom Slater, and Virgílio Borges Pereira. "Territorial Stigmatization in Action." *Environment and Planning A: Economy and Space* 46, no. 6 (2014): 1270–1280.

Wall, Tyler. "Inventing Humanity, or the Thin Blue Line as 'Patronizing Shit.'" In *Violent Order: Essays on the Nature of Police*, edited by David Correia and Tyler Wall, 13–30. Chicago: Haymarket Books, 2021.

Washington Post. "Mountain People as an Urban Minority." December 27, 1993, www.washingtonpost.com/archive/politics/1993/12/27/mountain-people-as-an-urban-minority/b4ccedb8-4c96-44e7-8a5b-5c47d9167f34.

Williams, David R. "Stress and the Mental Health of Populations of Color: Advancing Our Understanding of Race-related Stressors." *Journal of Health and Social Behavior* 59, no. 4 (2018): 466–485.

Wilson, Kathy Y. "A Tale of Two Cities." *CityBeat*. August 20, 2014, www.citybeat.com/news/a-tale-of-two-cities-12216132.

Woldoff, Rachael A. *White Flight/Black Flight: The Dynamics of Racial Change in an American Neighborhood*. Ithaca, NY: Cornell University Press, 2011.

Woodly, Deva, Rachel H. Brown, Mara Marin, Shatema Threadcraft, Christopher Paul Harris, Jasmine Syedullah, and Miriam Ticktin. "The Politics of Care." *Contemporary Political Theory* 20, no. 4 (2021): 890–925, www.ncbi.nlm.nih.gov/pmc/articles/PMC8383243/pdf/41296_2021_Article_515.pdf.

Wray, Matt. *Not Quite White: White Trash and the Boundaries of Whiteness*. Durham, NC: Duke University Press, 2006.

Wright, Erik Olin. *Class Counts*. New York: Cambridge University Press, 2000.

Wyndham-Douds, Kiara. "The Diversity Contract: Constructing Racial Harmony in a Diverse American Suburb." *American Journal of Sociology* 126, no. 6 (2021): 1347-1388.

Index

Page numbers in *italic* refer to illustrative matter.

homeownership (cont.)
and, 108–109; through intergenera-
tional transfers, 13, 15, 20, 21, 83–84;
trash talk and, 72–73, 91–92. *See also*
Carthage, Cincinnati; rentership;
Riverside, Cincinnati
Hordge-Freeman, Elizabeth, 162, 163
housing segregation, 10
*How Capitalism Underdeveloped Black
America* (Marable), 57
Howell, Junia, 67
Howell, Pierre, 110
HUD. *See* US Department of Housing
and Urban Development (HUD)
Hügen, Sabine, 74
Hugh, 30, 40, 83, 154
Human Rights Ordinance, Cincinnati
(1992), 20–21

ICE (Immigration and Customs
Enforcement), 110
ideology, defined, 3, 177n11
incarceration, 78, 96, 102, 110–111.
See also policing
income statistics, 4, 178n17. *See also*
poverty
Indian Removal Act (1830), 24
Indigenous peoples, 24, 26, 89, 184n21
industries, 4
infestations of pests, 60, 137, 187n5
intergenerational wealth transfers, 13,
15, 20, 83–84. *See also*
homeownership
interviewee demographics, 171–176.
See also research methods
interview questions, 167–169. *See also*
research methods
Iris, 146–149, 154
isolation, 16–18
Ivory, 22

Jaffey, Rich, 92
Jake, 146–149, 154
Janessa, 122–123
Jefferson, Brian Jordan, 89

Jenny, 134–136, 156
John, 104
Julius, 34–35, 36, 38, 42, 154
Jung, Moon-Kie, 138

Kaba, Mariame, 3, 97, 102, 122, 128,
186n48
Kalisha, 44
Kelley, Robin D. G., 157, 177n7
Kevin, 19, 47–48, 126–127
Kim, 125
Klosterman, John, 91, 184n29
Korver-Glenn, Elizabeth, 67
Koshy, Susan, 89
Kroger, 42

landlord neglect, 59–66. *See also*
rentership
landscaping business, 131–133
Lareau, Annette, 147
Lashonda, 162, 179n20
Latinx, as term, 178n19
Latinx residents: of Carthage, 27–28,
31–32; immigration to Cincinnati of,
26; police responses to, 107–108,
119–120; population statistics of,
26–27, 178n19, 180n34, 181n22;
racism against, 81–82, 91–92,
118–120; respectability politics by,
131–132. *See also* racism; *and names of
specific persons*
Lindsey, 60, 77
Lourdes, 53, 108, 115–117
Lynch, Damon, III, 180n5

Maggie, 38–39, 54–55, 80, 103, 113, 154
manufacturing industry, 4
Marable, Manning, 57
Marcie, 80
Marcos, 28
Margaret, 30
Marie, 106–107
Mark, 67–69
material realities of racial capitalism,
defined, 2, 10, 177n10

social death, as concept, 117

Spears, Tameka, 121

specter metaphor, 2-3, 5, 11-13, 46-47, 102, 129, 153-158. *See also* neglect; racial capitalism; trash talk

Stanley, Eric, 3

state violence, 35, 111. *See also* policing; racial capitalism

St. Boniface Church, Northside, 32

St. Charles Borromeo Parish, Carthage, 32

Stefanie, 44, 123-124

stigma: against Appalachians, 20-21; of poverty, 72-76; against renters, 81-88, 153; of territory, 72. *See also* trash talk

stop and frisk practices, 111

streetcar, 43

student debt, 92, 185n30

subsidized housing, 60-66, 73-77

suburban studies, 41-42

Sue, 105

Sullivan, Maureen, 21

support services, as industry, 4

suspicion, 6, 142-149. *See also* racial capitalism; racism

Tasha, 61-63, 65, 77, 120, 155

tax abatements, 57-58

Taylor, Henry Louis, Jr., 10, 183n45

Taylor, Keeanga-Yamahtta, 57

territorial stigmatization, 72

Thick: And Other Essays (McMillan Cottom), 100-101, 142

"thin blue line" rhetoric, 96, 107

Thomas, Timothy, 35, 180n2

3CDC, 42, 68

Timmy, 29, 146, 154

Tina, 22

Todd, 125-126, 150-151

Tom, 39, 40, 42, 45-46

transportation, 4, 16, 18, 42-44

trash talk: private property and, 70-73, 90-95; against renters, 30, 46, 57, 59, 81-88, 140-141; specter of, 2-3, 5-6, 59, 80-81, 153; against unhoused people, 90. *See also* dehumanization; racism; stigma; white trash, as term

UACC (Urban Appalachian Community Coalition), 9, 20

underdevelopment, 5, 8-9, 34-38, 56-59. *See also* Cincinnati, Ohio; gentrification; neglect; racial capitalism; urban development

unhoused people, discrimination against, 55-56

United Dairy Farmers (UDF), 29

unrest (2001), 35-36, 37, 111, 180n5

Unsettling the City (Blomley), 90

uppity, as term, 81, 184n10

Urban Appalachian Community Coalition (UACC), 9, 20

urban development: gentrification, 1, 35, 36-37, 42-44, 180n4; neglect and, 5, 34-38; racism and, 8-9; white flight and, 47, 181n21, 183n43. *See also* Cincinnati, Ohio; underdevelopment

urban specters, as term, 2-3, 5. *See also* specter metaphor

US Department of Housing and Urban Development (HUD), 60, 73, 76, 182n34

US Department of Justice (DOJ), 1, 36, 112

utilities industry, 4

Valdez, Desmond, 120

Valdez, Nicol, 120

Van Cleve, Nicole Gonzalez, 99

Victor, 22

Vitale, Alex, 109

Wacquant, Loïc, 72

Wall, Tyler, 96, 107

Walnut Hills, Cincinnati, 35, 37, 93

warehousing industry, 4

"War on Drugs" initiative, 79

Warren County, Ohio, 40, 181n8

waste management industry, 4

9 781469 674933